The
NEW
GERMANS

The
NEW
GERMANS

Thirty Years After

John Dornberg

Macmillan Publishing Co., Inc.

NEW YORK

Macmillan Publishing Co., Inc.
866 Third Avenue, New York, N. Y. 10022
Collier Macmillan Canada, Ltd.

Library of Congress Cataloging in Publication Data
Dornberg, John.
    The new Germans.

    Includes index.
    1. Germany (Federal Republic, 1949–   )—
Social life and customs. 2. Germany (Democratic
Republic, 1949–   )—Social life and customs.
3. Germany—Politics and government—1945–
4. National characteristics, German. I. Title.
DD259.2.D59   943.087   75–17953
ISBN 0–02–532170–6

First Printing 1976

Printed in the United States of America

Contents

Is
Schizophrenia
Curable?

Postwar Germany is thirty years old.

Thirty years—that is precisely a generation. And in both West and East Germany a new generation has matured. Indeed, the demographic statistics show that approximately half of all living Germans today—West and East—have been born since World War II came to an end and Adolf Hitler's Third Reich of terror and genocide came crashing down in the shambles of total defeat and unconditional surrender.

For nearly twenty of those years my relationship to those two Germanys has been a special one. I was born in the twilight years of the ill-fated Weimar Republic in what is now East Germany, the only child of Jewish parents with whom I fled the approaching holocaust in 1939. I returned to what is now West Germany, as a U. S. soldier, in 1955.

The Germany I saw on arrival still bore the physical, spiritual, and moral scars of war and tyranny. Its cities were largely in rubble, its people traumatized by the successive shocks of their history. The vaunted "economic miracle" was still in its infancy. So was the weak and delicate child of democracy. Germany in 1955 was huddled and bowed with uncertainty like a huge question mark. Ever since then, except for my tour of military duty and assignments to Eastern Europe and the Soviet Union, I have been covering both West and East Germany as a correspondent for American newspapers and magazines.

Germany has been my beat for nearly two decades—tense, turbulent, and exciting decades during which the Germans tried to come to terms with themselves and the world. They were a nation on trial, a people being tested. I watched them grapple with the great and agonizing issues of the 1950s and 1960s—rearmament, punishment of Nazi criminals, restitution to the victims of nazism, the question of collective guilt versus collective shame and responsibility, democratization, the spectre of neo-nazism and a right-wing revival, reunification, reconciliation with their neighbors, and acceptance of territorial losses as a consequence of the war they had started.

Fifteen years ago—at a time when postwar Germany was in its adolescence—I made my first effort to take stock of the country in a book which I called *Schizophrenic Germany*. In conclusion I wrote:

Germany's repudiation of Hitler was not internal, but an external renunciation forced upon it in defeat. We knew this full well at the time it happened. As a consequence, the Germans were charged with collective guilt for the crimes committed during the Third Reich and collective responsibility for the war which Hitler started. Yet, after only ten years, while many of the war criminals were still in prison, while the physical and spiritual aftermath of war was still everywhere apparent, West Germany was restored to its full sovereignty as a political and military equal in the Western community of nations.

The result, unfortunately, is that Germany is encumbered with an independence granted too fast and a democracy based on too shaky a foundation. Germany must cope with an armed force established too soon after the last war but too late to take advantage of the professional military skill which German soldiers had acquired. Germany is still flailing in the wake of an occupation that was once too harsh and then too lax, an economic catastrophe that was turned into a miracle of economic reconstruction too quickly, and a program of reorientation that failed to reorient. . . .

Is the German democracy solid enough to withstand the test of economic recession or depression? Can it weather a political onslaught from either the left or the right? How will it fare once it has to contend with its first change of top leadership?

These are the real problems . . . and they cannot be answered yet.*

Those words were written in 1960—with a sense of deep concern and under the impact of events and developments that gave ample cause for concern: a series of swastika smearings on synagogues and Jewish cemeteries; signs of overt antisemitism; the dramatic rise of neo-Nazi groups such as the German Reich Party and neo-fascist youth organizations; the shocking disclosure that for the preceding fifteen years

* New York: Macmillan Publishing Co., Inc., 1961.

Germany's young had been taught next to nothing about the causes and effects of the Third Reich because textbooks and teachers alike had skirted the issue; the mysterious and patently abetted escapes of indicted Nazi criminals to South America and North Africa; the discovery of ex-Nazis in high public office; the erosion of the reforms intended to make the Bundeswehr a "democratic" army of "citizens in uniform," and the deliberate isolation and transfer from positions of influence of the reform-minded officers.

Developments during the next six or seven years did little to lessen my concern or allay my fears. There was the 1961 general election, for example, during which Konrad Adenauer gained immense political capital by intimating that his opponent, Willy Brandt, had been "unpatriotic" when escaping the clutches of the Gestapo in 1933 and emigrating to Norway. All may be fair in politics and Adenauer may not have overstepped the bounds of political propriety. But he certainly fanned the flames of German chauvinism by implying that Brandt had betrayed the German cause in fighting nazism "in foreign uniform" from abroad.

Then, in 1962, there was also the celebrated *Spiegel* affair, an ignominious attempt by Adenauer's government to curtail freedom of the press. *Der Spiegel*, West Germany's influential gadfly news magazine, had published an article sharply critical of the Bundeswehr's defense posture and had charged that the army was incapable of defending the Federal Republic against attack. Two weeks later the police moved in. The arrest and months-long incarceration of the magazine's muckraking editors represented an alarming use of naked police and state power in a manner ominously reminiscent of Gestapo tactics. True, there was one heartening note at the time: the massive public protests against those actions. Those protests snowballed into a crescendo of civic concern. But at best they were a silver lining to the far darker cloud of concern about the morals and character of a government that would break and bend the law to protect itself from criticism.

During the ensuing years the West German judiciary certainly displayed a greater readiness to prosecute Nazi criminals still at large, but the lightness of the penalties—sometimes no more than a few minutes in prison for each murder committed—made a mockery of the whole effort at *Vergangenheitsbewaeltigung*, that untranslatable expression for Germany's attempts to come to terms with and to "digest" its own past. The sentences meted out, sometimes by judges whose own records during the

Third Reich required closer scrutiny, were more often than not barefaced travesties of justice.

Nor could I overlook other disturbing signs: the tenaciousness with which Konrad Adenauer clung to power despite the transfer of his office to Ludwig Erhard; the pronounced tendency of the governing Christian Democratic party (CDU) to regard itself as the incarnation of the state itself; the deterioration of those vaunted principles of democracy in the Bundeswehr; the ambivalence of Bonn's policy toward Israel; the growing reluctance to pay restitution to victims of Nazi crimes, and the patent refusal of East Germany to accept responsibility for what had happened in the Third Reich—a refusal that went so far as to imply that not only were there now two Germanys, but there had been two German pasts.

In May 1965, on the twentieth anniversary of Hitler Germany's defeat, I again had occasion to take stock. In the dispatches I sent to the papers which I represented, I found myself asking many of the same questions I had raised in 1960.

"Underneath the veneer of prosperity and abundance," I wrote, "what kind of Germany does one find? Have 20 years wrought essential changes in the German character? Have the Germans come to terms with their own past? Does democracy go more than skin deep? Is there a danger that, under the wrong conditions, the wrong political choice might again be made by millions of Germans?"

The answers I got—from Germans—were equivocal.

There was Erich Mende, for example, then the head of the Free Democratic party (FDP) and West Germany's vice-chancellor. In an interview with him I discussed the ingrained German notion that the state is some sort of special entity, superior to all the people in it, and that most Germans still treat state and government officials with undemocratic deference. Slowly, and with the obvious discomfort of introspection, Mende nodded agreement and almost absentmindedly quoted the German satirical writer Kurt Tucholsky, who once said: "It is the German's fate to stand in front of the counter and the German's ambition to sit behind it." Then Mende paused, and with a sigh added: "We will need a whole new generation before we can achieve complete equality in front of *and* behind the counter."

There was also the Bonn government spokesman who told me: "After the war we donned democracy like a fashionable new suit. I would like to hope that despite the popular adage to the contrary, clothes *can* make the man. It may take a while to grow into them, but eventually we may feel the way we look and, above all, conduct ourselves accordingly."

Two years later, when I left Bonn for assignments in Eastern Europe and Russia, that "new suit of democracy" still didn't fit the Germans very well. On the contrary. In December 1966 an admitted ex-Nazi, Kurt Georg Kiesinger, had just been named chancellor; a man suspected of complicity in the construction of concentration camps, Heinrich Luebke, was its president; and the ultra-rightist National Democratic party (NPD) had won seats in virtually every state legislature.

By the time I returned in 1971 the National Democrats were but a political sect on the fringes of society; Kiesinger and Luebke had disappeared from the stage to be replaced, respectively, by Willy Brandt as chancellor and Gustav Heinemann as president. I discovered a remarkably different Germany—a nation transformed and suddenly mature, a people conscious of their needs and rights, but also acutely aware of their achievements, of their role in the world, even proud of being German again. What had happened in such a short period of time?

Unquestionably there had been a generational change. Those Germans too young to have been contaminated by the Nazi era, and those born after the war, had become a powerful and influential social and political force. In the late 1960s, as students, they had taken to the streets to militate, agitate, and demonstrate—at first against the ossified educational system itself, subsequently against a twenty-year-long, prosperity-oriented policy of political and social sterility embodied in the CDU's popular and effective election slogan: *"Keine Experimente"*—"No Experiments."

One of the leaders of this "youth rebellion" was a West Berlin university student, Rudi Dutschke, who was a master at articulating the wants and aims of his generation. "What holds us together," he said, "is not some abstract theory of history, but revulsion: revulsion at a society which preaches freedom but subtly and brutally suppresses the interests and needs of the individual and of peoples fighting for their social and economic emancipation."

Born in the brief three-year period of the "grand coalition" government of CDU and the Social Democratic party (SPD) when political opposition in parliament had ceased to exist, this youth rebellion had turned into an "extra-parliamentary opposition," the *APO*. By the early 1970s, following the transfer of power from the CDU to the left-liberal coalition government of SPD and FDP, most of this youthful "outside opposition" had been integrated but became the driving force for change within the society. Left wing, to be sure, even radical to a degree, these young Germans rejected not only the values of their parents but their parents' way of doing things. They challenged traditional concepts of the state, government, education, culture, industry, and above all, Germanism.

Instead of more production they are concerned with the quality of life; instead of bigger and better economic miracles they ask what is being done to protect the environment; instead of simply more prosperity for the workers they demand that workers have a larger say in the running of industry; instead of trying to raise their own children to be obedient, diligent, and achieving, they stress anti-authoritarian upbringing and teach them to question and to challenge, to doubt and to reject; instead of dreaming of German unity and pining for restoration of the Reich, they accept with total equanimity the existence of two German states. They sense no burden of guilt for the Germany of the past and reject the suggestion that they should assume one, for they contend, convincingly, that the crimes of the fathers were not committed by the sons. Above all, they have shaken the foundations of the entire German educational system, demanding—and to a degree already achieving—sweeping quantitative and qualitative reforms to make it consonant with the needs of a modern, democratic society.

However, the advent of this generation to maturity and influence does not by itself explain the remarkable transformation of West Germany. Indeed, that generation, or at least its leaders, might still be the "extra-parliamentary opposition" had it not been for the transfer of power from the Christian Democrats to the Social and Free Democrats in parliament. It was that slim victory by Willy Brandt in October 1969 which became the real watershed of postwar German history. As Brandt himself, the first socialist chancellor since 1930, told the *Bundestag* upon his inauguration:

"Two decades after its constitution, our parliamentary democracy has proven its capability for change and has thus stood the test. . . . In the past, many in this country feared that the second German democracy would go the way of the first. I have never believed that. I believe it even less today. No, we are not at the end of our democracy, we are at its beginning."

The significance of the Social Democrats coming to power must be seen in historical context. Ever since the First World War, the 1918 revolution, the kaiser's abdication, and the establishment of the Weimar Republic under Social Democrat Friedrich Ebert, the SPD had labored under the stigma of disloyalty and "treason to the German cause." In the 1920s they became the focus of the infamous *Dolchstoss* legend according to which a "stab in the back" on the "home front" had led to defeat in the war and the "intolerable" terms of the Versailles Treaty. After World War II, Adenauer capitalized on that innate public distrust of the SPD. In the turbulent election campaigns of the 1950s he likened his CDU to Christian good, the SPD to Bolshevik evil. He painted a devil picture of the Social Democrats, portraying them as the "red menace."

In the emotion-charged atmosphere of those cold-war days when the SPD opposed NATO and West German rearmament, Adenauer's tactics may have been smart politics, but they did a grave disservice to Germany's vulnerable, embryonic democracy. Inadvertently, opposition to his policies and administration, either on the floor of parliament or on the campaign trail, became equated with opposition to the state itself and tantamount to treason, for Adenauer and his CDU regarded themselves as the incarnation of the state. Countless had been his dire warnings that a vote for Brandt would be a vote *"fuer den Untergang Deutschlands"*—"for the ruin of Germany."

When Brandt and the SPD finally won in 1969, the traditional roles in Bonn began to change. Opposition, as such, became respectable in the German consciousness, for "the opposition" was suddenly the Christian Democratic party. For the first time in twenty years the ground rules of parliamentary exchange became operable and the Bundestag, instead of being a coliseum where political gladiators fought to the death with verbal vitriol, gradually developed into a forum for meaningful parliamentary debate.

Of course, that transformation did not come overnight, for many Christian Democrats at first refused—and to this day some still refuse—to accept their changed role. Some, such as Franz-Josef Strauss, leader of the Christian Social Union (CSU), the CDU's semi-autonomous Bavarian sister party, continue to stimulate the political glands of their backwoods constituents by alluding to the "red popular-front clique" now ruling in Bonn. Taking advantage of the narrow majority of only twelve seats held by the coalition government of Brandt's SPD and Walter Scheel's FDP, they encouraged, pressured, and even bribed SPD and FDP deputies to defect. Finally the margin in parliament was so narrow that the CDU's leader, Rainer Barzel, egged on by Strauss, attempted to bring Brandt's government down with a vote of no confidence.

That parliamentary ploy in April 1972 failed by just two votes. But in a very remarkable and unexpected way it made West Germany safer for democracy. Millions of people all over the Federal Republic took to the streets and rushed to political rallies to demonstrate and protest against the CDU's tactics which, had they succeeded, would have deprived the majority of the electorate of its legal mandate. Those were the first spontaneous demonstrations in German history on behalf, rather than against, a government in office. And when new elections were finally called in November 1972, the voters reconfirmed the SPD-FDP coalition with a solid majority of forty-six seats in the Bundestag, enough to see it comfortably through until the next scheduled election in the autumn of 1976.

Of the deputies elected to the Bundestag in 1972, three were born after, and another twenty-four were not yet of school age when World War II ended. One of the youngest is the SPD's Dr. Uwe Holtz, a historian, born in 1944, who performed the incredible feat of trouncing Dr. Gerhard Schroeder, the CDU's erstwhile interior, foreign, and defense minister in his home constituency.

"That we won that election—despite the spectre of inflation, despite incipient signs of unemployment, despite the CDU's scare tactics," Holtz told me, "is perhaps the most convincing proof that the citizens and voters of this country have finally been emancipated. They made a clear decision to give this administration, weakened by defections from its ranks, a mandate for another four years."

Two of the key figures who won that mandate are gone, however. Gustav Heinemann has retired and been replaced as West Germany's president by Walter Scheel, a man of no less integrity though perhaps less a living symbol of the *Guter Deutscher*—the "good German." Willy Brandt resigned in May 1974—the victim of intraparty strife, of an East German spy placed strategically at his side in the chancellory, and, perhaps even more, the victim of a certain inborn indecisiveness and a reluctance to come to grips with the domestic economic problems that had taken precedence over foreign affairs.

His successor, Helmut Schmidt, though cut from a different political

mold and not even pretending to the stature and symbolism represented
by Brandt, has thus far proven to be what West Germany needs at this
juncture of its history: a pragmatist, a cool-headed manager of the
business of government, unencumbered by the emotional baggage and
ideological hang-ups of West German leaders in the past.

Although Willy Brandt was Germany's chancellor for less than five
years, his impact is likely to endure. And it was this impact which
changed Germany almost beyond recognition in the 1970s. His daring
new policy toward the Soviet Union, Eastern Europe, and East
Germany—a policy of reconciliation and pragmatism—erased a whole
postwar catalogue of shibboleths and sacrosanctities, of wishful cold war
thinking, and German geopolitical nostalgia.

For that he won the Nobel Peace Prize. And in the eyes of most
Germans, Brandt's prize was Germany's prize. Through it and through
him they were finally able to expiate their sins. The world acknowledged
that. Headlines around the globe proclaimed that at last GERMANY HAS
BEEN ACQUITTED. Brandt himself accepted the prize in this spirit, telling
the Nobel committee in Oslo: "It means much to me to accept the prize
in the name of the German people. . . . It means so much to me, after the
inexpatiable horror of the past, that the name of my country and the
desire for peace have become symbiotic."

And in 1970, after he had spontaneously dropped to his knees before a
memorial plaque on the site of Warsaw's former ghetto, he said: "It was
something I felt I had to do—on behalf of my people."

"It was something," says the SPD's Dr. Holtz, "which many of our
politicians should have done before him."

Perhaps. But could a Konrad Adenauer have knelt in a symbolic
gesture of German atonement? An Adenauer who once defended the
large number of erstwhile Nazis serving in West Germany's foreign
service with the laconic remark: "You can't create a diplomatic corps with
amateurs"? An Adenauer who once suggested that "it's about time to end
the witch-hunt for Nazis" after he had been challenged to dismiss a
number of ex-storm troopers in his cabinet?

"Brandt really did kneel on my behalf," a twenty-five-year-old
German once told me. "Because of that I can now go to Warsaw, or
anywhere else, without feeling ashamed or embarrassed."

Brandt's approach was not to simply forget the past, as other German
politicians had tried to do, but, on the other hand, not to wallow in it

either. As a result only Brandt could have conducted an election campaign, like the one in 1972, with the slogan: "Germans, we can be proud of our country." He had given them cause to be proud.

"Ours is not the old Hitlerite pride of being a super race," said one German official when posters with that slogan began appearing during the 1972 campaign. "It's a new pride. A pride of rebuilding Germany, for working together with our European partners, for recognizing new trends in the world. Brandt does make us feel proud again."

"And when I say I'm proud to be German," said one young man, "I'm saying that being German is no better than anyone else, but no worse either."

The Brandt era, however, imbued the Germans with more than pride. It instilled in them a sense of confidence in their democratic institutions. In the early 1950s, for example, most Germans considered the infant Federal Republic somewhat of a joke. And when buses and excursion boats took them past the ugly, concrete college building on Bonn's Rhine River embankment in which the new parliament was housed, they would taunt the men in it with a popular carnival drinking song:

> Who is going to pay for this,
> Who ordered this for us?
> Who has enough moola,
> Who's got so much dough?

Parliament is still in that building. But today the Rhine boats and the buses disgorge their passengers who filter into the *Bundeshaus* to sit attentively in the galleries and listen to the debates. The song is no longer heard and Germans take their parliament seriously.

As Dr. Hildegard Hamm-Bruecher, one of the foremost women politicians and deputy-national leader of the Free Democratic party, once put it: "To build a democracy out of the materials left over from a destroyed dictatorship is no easy task. It cannot be done until each brick and block of stone has been baked and hewn anew. And that takes strength, effort and time."

By the late 1960s West Germany had undoubtedly emerged as an economic Goliath, but it was still a political and diplomatic dwarf. I recall asking one Bundestag deputy in those days what role he thought the Federal Republic should or would play in the world and the Europe of the future. He threw up his hands in despair and replied: "No role. Spare us the playing of roles. Too long and too often we have tried to make our mark upon the world. If anything, we should try to become a larger Switzerland."

Today Germany is assuming its rightful role as a central European power and its people have achieved a new political maturity, not only at home but abroad. As one American diplomat explained in 1972: "I've been dealing with German officials for many years and it is apparent to me they are now awakening to their own interests. They know their own position and they're determined to press it. Germany is speaking up and the Germans are being listened to."

The spectre of a neo-Nazi revival, so frightening in the late 1960s when Adolf von Thadden's National Democrats captured seats in one state legislature after the other, has vanished. Von Thadden, once feared as the putative *fuehrer* of the 1970s, was discredited by his own party because of his extremism and did not even stand for reelection as its chairman at the NPD's last national convention. In 1969 the NPD had come within a hair of entering the Bundestag, polling only $7/10$ percent short of the necessary 5 percent which a party must have under West Germany's proportional representation system. Three years later, however, it had not only disappeared from all the state legislatures in which it was once represented, but it polled only slightly more than a half percent of the total vote cast.

To most Germans the sudden and spectacular rise of the NPD between 1966 and 1969 is still somewhat of a mystery and a cause for deep concern. Was it the economic recession of the waning months of the Erhard administration that strengthened the NPD? And if so, what does this forebode for the future should the economy dip further or perhaps even nosedive? Or was the vote for the NPD a sort of protest vote against the formation of the CDU–SPD "grand coalition" government which deprived the electorate of real alternatives? And what has happened to the 1.2 million people who voted for the NPD in 1969 but didn't in 1972? For whom *did* they vote and for whom *will* they vote in the future?

"The NPD did pose a threat and the large number of supporters it attracted was alarming," says Juergen Moellemann, a teacher by profession, a Free Democrat by political affiliation and, at age twenty-nine, one of the three Bundestag deputies born after the war. "Its appeal, based on simplistic slogans and a plucking of chauvinistic heartstrings, was to a generation older than mine. That generation is a diminishing minority and even it did not take very long to realize the dangers inherent in the NPD. While no one can offer guarantees against voters gravitating to pseudodemocratic parties which offer panaceas in a period of economic slowdown or recession, I do believe the threat diminishes with each passing day that democratic thinking and democratic concepts become more deeply ingrained and democratic institutions become firmer."

Today, if there is any threat from extremist forces to German democracy, it comes not from the extreme right but from militant, bomb-planting anarchists, from young Maoist radicals, and from the militant intellectuals of the far left who believe that the road to salvation leads through the shambles of the institutions they seek to destroy. To some Germans they are already a massive and imminent danger. But the danger is in part a phantom created by the conservative press and those opportunistic politicians of the right who exploit fear as a powerful political weapon against the left-liberal coalition. To the extent that the danger is real, it is vastly overstated. A far greater danger is that the overstatement might rekindle the police-state and "law-and-order" streak still latent in the German populace, especially among members of the older generation and the less educated.

It is true, of course, that there are Marxist grade school and high school teachers, that there are Maoist cadres in all the universities and that some of them have gained control of student councils and even university governing boards. It is also true that radical youth groups, using filibustering techniques, have gained control of some of the local and district organizations of the SPD. But the trend among the next generation of West German students—those now in high school— appears to be toward more conservatism. Practice has shown that even the most radical Young Socialists, or *Jusos* as they are called, become progressively less fiery and revolutionary as they rise in the SPD's ranks and assume positions of political and governmental responsibility, be it on the local, state, or national level. And the Moscow-oriented German Communist party—hardly the epitome of radicalism—polled the grand total of $3/10$ of 1 percent of the vote in the last election.

In the 1950s and 1960s, too, concerned Germans and a worried world observed the growth of a new West German army with alarm, fearful that it bore the seeds of a new militarism. But by the early 1970s the long-maned and bearded appearance of its officers and men, their patent lack of anything reminiscent of Prussian discipline had won the

Bundeswehr the nickname "German Hair Force." While serving as defense minister, Chancellor Helmut Schmidt did order the tresses cut to a reasonable length, consonant with what he considered safety require- ments, while allowing the beards to stand more or less unclipped. But even with shorter hair the Bundeswehr appears totally integrated into the democratic system and young Germans are wholly unmilitaristic. Indeed, nearly 70 percent of draft-eligible German high school graduates and university students now register as conscientious objectors, and the draft evasion and conscientious objection rate in the Federal Republic is higher than in any Western country. During 1973 more than 37,000 young West Germans applied for objector status—more than three times as many as in 1968, and half the total number called up for induction and expected to report at basic training camps. By 1980, according to a Munich-based sociopolitical think tank, draft rejection and conscientious objection may well be "the dominant attitude" among eligible youth.

By far the greatest impact of the Brandt era, however, was on West German attitudes toward reunification, East Germany, and what had previously been regarded as the primary national goal. That goal and the general public attitude toward reunification had been largely misrepre- sented and misinterpreted over the years by all manner of politicians who either sought to gain political capital by beating the nationalist and reunification drum or feared they might lose votes if they didn't. A look at opinion surveys reveals that it was never as important an issue to the average West German as it had been made out to be.

In 1967, for example, only 18 percent considered reunification the most important sociopolitical problem that should be solved, and only 50 percent considered the division of Germany an "intolerable state of affairs." But at the same time it bordered on sedition to refer to East Germany as the GDR, or German Democratic Republic. Parliamentary and journalistic vernacular demanded the expressions "Soviet zone," "East zone," or euphemisms such as "over there." The daring might venture to say: "the so-called GDR." For a politician even to suggest that there was no hope of reunification took courage; to imply that it was not even a desirable national goal was close to committing political suicide. To suggest any kind of formal contacts with East Germany was tantamount to treason.

But then, in 1970, Brandt went to Erfurt for his historic meeting with Willi Stoph, East Germany's premier at the time, and Stoph came to

Kassel. A whole series of East and West German exchanges and negotiations got underway, leading eventually to the admission of both Germanys into the United Nations and the basic treaty of de facto recognition between the two. Relations between the two Germanys are often strained, but as Egon Bahr, Brandt's chief advisor and the architect of Brandt's German policy, once put it: "Before this we had no relations at all. Now at least we have bad relations and that is a start, for they can at least be improved."

While Brandt's policy, despite its intents and promises, has not brought German reunification closer, reunification is at least no longer the alpha and omega of all German foreign policy. As an issue it has been largely deflated and, as such, will enable the West Germans to enter the fourth decade of their post-Hitler history without the emotional, ideological, nostalgic, and chauvinistic ballast that weighted them down during the better part of the first three. At age thirty, Germany is a completely different ball game.

"To speak of Germany's good features," says Sebastian Haffner, a Berlin-born British journalist who writes a weekly column for the German illustrated weekly *Stern*, "is unusual, almost a bit odd, even somewhat embarrassing."

But Haffner does. "For the German consciousness today," he says, "the Third Reich and its intellectual history are worlds away. The entire intellectual and emotional world in which three generations lived and moved is dead as a doornail. For the younger generation it's no longer even worth arguing about. Even the ridicule has grown stale."

Biographies about Hitler and books about the Third Reich can now be published, and some of them even become best sellers—though not to the extent that similar books have in the United States. The "Hitler wave" of the early 1970s was largely an Anglo-American phenomenon. By comparison, in Germany itself, it was a ripple, and any journalistic attempt to make it out to be something else borders on cheap sensationalism. Yes, the Germans read the books—but with almost the same detachment that they read biographies about Napoleon. And when they go beyond that, as many of the young generation do, they seek to find out what made Hitler tick, how he succeeded in mesmerizing an entire people—their parents and their grandparents: in other words, how it had all been possible, how the horror of the Third Reich had come about.

The nicest thing about Germany today," says Haffner, "is that it is a country like every other one." That it is so commonplace and not unusual at all. To this Max Frisch, the Swiss playwright and novelist, adds: "In many ways contemporary Germany is more democratic than modern-day France or Switzerland, both of which are so boastful of their democratic traditions. All that talk about *the* Germans being unable to come to grips with the rules of the democratic game is something we simply need no longer buy."

Shortly after the publication of my book *Schizophrenic Germany* in 1961, I was maliciously attacked and accused of being either a Communist or a stooge of Moscow by a number of neo-Nazi and ultrarightist newspapers and magazines in the Federal Republic. I demanded retractions and apologies, and failing to get either from one paper, sued its editors in court. The presiding judge, Hans Hofmeyer, a former Wehrmacht judiciary officer, was hardly sympathetic to my cause and at one point during the hearing picked up a copy of the book, leafed through it, and then said accusingly: "It is not so much what you wrote that disturbs me. That may be all right. But it's the dust jacket, with all those blots in our national colors, and the title. Yes, the title—"Schizophrenic." That's a defamation and an insult to my country to call us schizophrenic."

With equal curtness and in a manner in which probably no one had ever spoken to a German judge, I shot back: "Where I come from schizophrenia is an illness. A curable illness—provided the patient is *willing* to be cured."

That obviously didn't help my case and I had to appeal all the way to the German supreme court in Karlsruhe before I got that retraction and apology.

Judge Hofmeyer went on to preside over the twenty-month-long Auschwitz trial in 1964 and 1965. His conduct of that case was admirable. I know. I covered much of it. And as I sat in the press gallery day in, day out, and along with Hofmeyer heard the horror of those crimes committed by Germans unfold, I often wondered what the judge thought about Germany's schizophrenia then. But, I must also confess, I didn't ask.

And the patient? The schizophrenia? Is it cured? Yes, I believe so, though I will leave it to the reader to judge from the succeeding chapters. No doubt, the patient requires periodic observation to prevent relapse. And close scrutiny will still disclose residues of supernationalism, some racial arrogance, hyperlegalism, an inclination toward deference in the face of authority as well as an excessive tendency to exercise authority, a certain nostalgia for lost greatness and power, not to mention a slightly pathological mixture of guilt and paranoia.

But on balance, Germany at thirty has come of age. And it is healthy.

1

The Wounds of History

HIS name was almost a German cliché—Hans. So was his appearance—fair skin, blue eyes, and straw-blond hair which had been cut and combed in the Caesar style that was the rage among young German intellectuals at the time. And the time was January 9, 1964, the fourth day of the marathon Auschwitz trial.

Hans, who had just turned twenty, was one of approximately sixty university students in the press and spectators' gallery of the city council chamber in the Roemer, Frankfurt's medieval town hall, which had been converted into a courtroom. The defendants—twenty-one former SS officers and guards and one prisoner-trustee—were standing trial for the murders they had committed at the largest and most notorious of the Nazi death camps.

The atmosphere was one of benign dignity. The defendants, apparently relaxed, sat with their lawyers in the comfortable foam-padded leather armchairs of Frankfurt's city council members. The court—three black-robed judges, two alternates, six lay jurors, five alternate jury members, and four prosecutors—were on the slightly raised city-government bench facing the defendants, the press, and the spectators.

The tone struck by the presiding judge, Hans Hofmeyer, was one of subdued politeness. It was "*Bitte schoen Herr Kaduk* [or Herr Boger or Herr Mulka], won't you take the witness chair over there, pull the microphone up closer and tell us about yourself: where you were born, where you went to school, when you joined the party."

Periodically, as the defendants told the self-pitying stories about their lives, I could see Hans lean forward to grip the rail of the spectators' balcony and shake his head vehemently. During recesses I observed him ambling along the corridors trying to catch a closer glimpse of some of the men on trial. It seemed as if he were trying to etch their faces in his memory.

It was during one long recess, which he and I had both used to go across the street to St. Paul's Church to look at an exhibition of photos and documents from the Warsaw ghetto, that we started a conversation. He was staring at the life-sized portrait of two undernourished ghetto children and I was studying him.

"The whole thing seems unreal," he said, turning toward me. "It's hard to put your finger on it, but it's just unreal. The whole atmosphere, the things they're saying, the way they behave in court and in the hallways, the formal cordiality between the defense and prosecution, between the judge and the defendants. It's Kafkaesque.

"I look at those men down there and listen to them talk, and they seem no different from anyone else. They're just like my neighbors or relatives. They speak softly and some even articulately. They seem gentle and kind—good fathers, good citizens, hardworking. But then I glance at the indictments and read what they did. It just doesn't seem possible. These are not even Eichmanns who murdered by administrative decree, but men who killed with their bare hands, with injection needles, clubs, spade handles, their pistols, or their boot heels.

"Perhaps I am naive, or maybe I've just seen too many movies. But they don't look like SS guards. I mean, I have visions of men in stiff black uniforms, high riding boots, clubs or whips in their hands, and mean faces. But there they are, sitting down there, no different from anyone else, and just look at what they did. It's incongruous."

As incongruous, in one sense, as the thirty-year-long effort on the part of the Germans to "come to terms" with the Nazi past because that effort has also meant that they had to come to terms with themselves. Nothing would have been easier—and millions of Germans have attempted it—than to write off the Third Reich and its crimes against humanity as aberrations of history, as phenomena apart from the mainstream of German society. But they weren't.

"Prosecution of Nazi criminals is like looking into a mirror," Fritz Bauer, the solicitor general of Hesse and one of the most relentless prosecutors of Nazis, told me shortly before his death in 1968. "No one really wants to do that and especially not when he knows the reflection will be an ugly one."

But the Germans have been compelled to look at themselves for three decades. The history of that self-evaluation is one of the most dramatic chapters of postwar Germany's development. Its impact on the German psyche must be understood in order to understand the Germans today.

In the early postwar years punishment and atonement for the crimes of nazism were imposed upon the Germans from outside—by the victorious powers. War crimes tribunals, such as the one in Nürnberg, and courts in France, the Netherlands, Belgium, Denmark, Norway, Poland, the Soviet Union, and Yugoslavia prosecuted thousands of Germans for crimes against humanity and crimes against peace. Though precise figures are not available, West German judiciary authorities estimate that between 50,000–60,000 were tried and convicted. In the three Western occupation zones 806 death sentences were passed and 486 persons were executed.

It was the avowed policy of the occupation powers that they would punish the Germans. Except for the highly unpopular and ineffective German-run "de-Nazification tribunals" that had been instituted by order of the military governments, German jurisdiction was virtually nonexistent. Insofar as it did exist, it extended only to Germans who had committed crimes against other Germans.

But the advent of the cold war, and the changing relationship between the Western powers and their zones of occupation, led not only to the creation of an independent West Germany but to a new Allied policy regarding prosecution. Gradually, jurisdiction passed to the West German authorities. The first trial of a German by a German court for crimes committed against non-Germans outside Germany took place in Munich in May 1949. The defendant, Max Raettig, was convicted of the murder of forty-two Jews in a Polish ghetto.

Full jurisdiction was transferred to the West German authorities in May 1952 upon the signing of the Bonn Conventions that ended the postwar occupation. Thus began the unique and agonizing attempts of the Germans to judge themselves.

From the outset it was viewed with skepticism and fraught with all manner of legal, political, moral, and technical obstacles that continue to the present day. First of all, there was the law itself. Although the new West German constitution, and legislation passed since 1949, provided for punishment of "crimes against humanity" and genocide, these laws could obviously not be applied retroactively to crimes committed before they had been passed. The only legal basis on which to prosecute Nazi criminals was the traditional penal code's sections on homicide and assault. This required following the normal rules of evidence, the examination and cross-examination of witnesses, and perhaps even visits to the scene of the crime—no easy procedure in the case of defendants charged with the murder of thousands, tens of thousands, and sometimes even hundreds of thousands.

Moreover, West German prosecutors and judges, suddenly confronted with this task, did not and could not know the immensity of it. The vast numbers of Nazi officials already prosecuted by international tribunals and military government courts had created the impression that very few war criminals were left to judge and punish. The few judiciary officials who may have doubted this had virtually no evidence with which to support their theses. Virtually all the Gestapo, police, Wehrmacht, and SS records had ended up in foreign archives and were not available to West German prosecutors and courts. Indeed, much of this material remains inaccessible today. Polish authorities, for example, are still investigating Nazi crimes in which an estimated fifteen thousand West and East German citizens are implicated. The documentary evidence in the archives in Warsaw is being made available to West German judiciary authorities haphazardly, sporadically, and incompletely.

Then, too, there was a noticeable reluctance on the part of a large number of judges and prosecutors to get the legal machinery moving. The wheels of German justice have always tended to move rather slowly. They were bound to move even slower when many of the judiciary officials were themselves implicated in the crimes of the Hitler regime. Hundreds of German judges and prosecutors had aided and abetted the adulteration and rape of justice during the twelve years of the Third Reich. They brought the Nazi concept of a "new law and order" to the countries and territories under Hitler's yoke. They served on special tribunals that meted out death sentences en masse to Poles, Russians, Yugoslavs, Greeks, Norwegians, Frenchmen, and Dutchmen for the slightest acts of "resistance" to Nazi might. They participated in courts-martial that ordered the execution of hundreds if not thousands of German soldiers for infractions that in other armies would have been punished with a brief term in the stockade.

At home they presided over "people's tribunals" that were but kangaroo courts and naked travesties of due process. And when the war was over, being civil servants entitled to lifetime tenure, the vast majority of these Nazi judges and prosecutors were promptly co-opted in the new judiciary. Suddenly they were supposed to prosecute and pass judgment on Nazi criminals? They did nothing of the kind. They used all the tools of the law to delay proceedings and to obstruct justice. And failing at that, they passed sentences on mass murderers that were tantamount to sheer mockery of the victims. It was not until 1963 that 150 of the worst of these judges and prosecutors—those implicated in "irresponsible and inhuman death sentences" during the Third Reich—were forced into "voluntary" early retirement. And it took until the late 1960s before an additional 400 judges with "unacceptable" Nazi records were finally eased out of the West German judiciary.

Finally, there was also the humanly understandable desire of the German people to be done with the past, to no longer be reminded, to end what Adenauer had called "the witch-hunt for Nazis," to stop what the majority of West Germans regarded as "defiling our own nest."

Thus, German prosecution of Germans, or what might also be considered the first real effort to "come to terms with the past," got off to a slow, hesitant, and desultory start. Investigations were opened and cases came to trial largely through chance. A former concentration camp inmate would spot one of his guards on a street corner. Some drunken SS veteran would boast of his "exploits" and be overheard in a corner tavern. A death camp doctor's name would crop up accidentally during another SS officer's trial. A chain reaction set in, gaining momentum in 1955 when the Soviet Union released some ten thousand German prisoners of war it had been holding. Among them were many men who had been concentration camp guards or members of special execution squads that had murdered people by the thousands in Poland, the Baltic republics, and the Ukraine.

By the summer of 1958 West Germany faced a growing mountain of evidence pointing to the likelihood of thousands of war criminals as yet unidentified and not indicted, and the prospect that they might all get off without punishment when the statute of limitations would protect them in 1965. The demands for coordinating, organizing, and accelerating the judiciary process could no longer be overheard or ignored.

The result was the Center for the Investigation of National Socialist

Crimes, established in December 1958. Located in Ludwigsburg, near Stuttgart, it is jointly sponsored and operated by the ministries of justice of the ten West German states. Its business—to hunt for, investigate, and indict the Nazi murderers—is still unfinished.

Since 1952 West German courts have tried and convicted more than six thousand Nazi criminals, the majority of them since the Ludwigsburg Center began operating. The list of those indicted or now in prison covers a broad spectrum of accomplices in the vast machinery of Nazi genocide: bestial prisoner-trustees, such as Emil Bednarek, who, in exchange for better treatment, killed countless numbers of their fellow concentration camp inmates; high-ranking SS officers, such as Hermann Krumey, Adolf Eichmann's deputy; German railway officials, such as Albert Ganzenmueller, who was indicted of planning and organizing the deportation in freight cars of millions of Jews to the extermination camps; senior police officers, such as Ludwig Hahn, the dreaded Gestapo chief of Warsaw; ex-diplomats, such as Horst Wagner, indicted for his role in organizing the extermination of European Jewry; and a seemingly endless roster of SS men, camp guards, executioners, Gestapo officers, and security agents collectively responsible for the murder of millions.

But the end of the manhunt is not in sight. Nor can it be when one stops to consider that only a few hundred Auschwitz guards have been indicted or tried by German and Polish courts, though the records indicate that, in the five years during which that death camp was in operation, some six thousand SS officers and men were assigned there. Who were they and where are they now? Could their names and identities be hidden in the mountains of documents still jealously guarded in the archives of the Soviet Union and other East European countries?

Then, too, scores of cases remain pending before West German courts—stuck somewhere in the labyrinth of the Federal Republic's legal machinery. And at the Ludwigsburg Center a team of fifty prosecutors is still investigating an additional five hundred cases of mass murder in many of which two or more suspects may eventually be implicated.

Twice in the past decade the West Germans have extended the statute of limitations on crimes of homicide so as to make sure that no Nazi criminal could slip through the dragnet or come out of hiding and go free. The first time was in 1965 following months of protracted and emotional debate and in clear contradiction of public opinion, polls of which showed that 60 percent of West German adults favored an end to further prosecution. Four years later, when the deadline approached once more and it was thought that as many as sixteen thousand Nazi criminals might not have been identified or indicted, the statute was extended again, this time to December 1979.

And what will happen then? Will the statute of limitations be extended a third time to cover those Nazis still undiscovered or still in hiding? Probably. Though it seems doubtful that it will then still be possible to prosecute them and unlikely that any legitimate cause of justice, expiation, atonement, or righting the wrongs of history would be served.

Frankly, those causes are barely being served today, and it is already difficult to obtain convictions thirty years after the fact. As time passes, it will become even more difficult. The witnesses are either dying or losing their credibility because of advancing age and fading memories. Yet due process demands that there be witnesses. And even when convictions are possible, the imposed punishments stand in no relationship to the immensity of the crimes. Countless defendants are now getting off on technicalities or for medical reasons. Once-arrogant young "supermen," the majority of them are now sexagenarians and septuagenarians who find refuge from imprisonment behind doctors' certificates attesting to their frail health. If it isn't their cardiovascular condition, then it's their arthritis, their failing eyesight, or, in the case of some, just plain senility.

But the acquittals, the light sentences, and the decrees of medical immunity from imprisonment raise the worrisome question of whether it may not be better to have undiscovered and unindicted murderers than acquitted ones. One young German who answers that question with a categorical "no" is Beate Klarsfeld. At a time when many people in West Germany and other Western countries have been trying to get Rudolf Hess, the last of the top-ranking Nazis, out of the Spandau war-crimes prison in Berlin, she is trying to put more of the murderers in jail. While many think that the wounds of history can best be healed by silently allowing old Nazis to retire to their graves, she is arguing that the wounds will never heal so long as one criminal remains free and one ex-Nazi holds high public office.

An attractive, petite mother of two, herself too young to have consciously experienced the Third Reich, Beate Klarsfeld, at first glance, is typical of the generation of Germans in their thirties. The daughter of middle-class Berlin parents, whom she has described as "fellow-travellers of the Third Reich," she was not yet of school age when the war ended.

Her education began amidst the rubble of an occupied, bombed-out Berlin and lasted through the great political events of the 1940s and 1950s: the blockade, the airlift, the workers' uprising in East Germany, rearmament, West Germany's admission to NATO, growing prosperity, and Franco-German reconciliation. She took history courses in school at a time when some textbooks were passing off the crimes of the Nazi regime in a single paragraph, and teachers, many of them ex-Nazis themselves, skillfully avoided ever mentioning the subject in class. And like many young German women at the time, she dreamed of going to Paris to learn French, and eventually did: as an *au pair* girl.

But there the similarities end, for when she went to Paris in 1960 she met her husband, Serge Klarsfeld, a history major at the Sorbonne, a Jew whose father had been killed at Auschwitz. From him, his surviving relatives, and his friends she got belated but intensified instruction on the real recent history of her people.

"One day," she has explained, "I got the feeling that I had to do something to save the good name of Germany. . . . I seized the torch of resistance. . . . I felt myself the daughter of Goethe, Schiller, and Beethoven, to be sure, but also of Hitler, Himmler, and Eichmann."

A bit high-flown, self-righteous, and superpenitent? So her critics have charged. Be that as it may. Whatever her real inner motivations may have been, Beate Klarsfeld became a sort of avenging angel, an apostle of repentance with a touch of St. Joan, who launched a one-woman crusade to right the wrongs. She first made news in 1968 in her native Berlin by stepping up to Chancellor Kurt Georg Kiesinger at a CDU party convention and slapping him in the face. Her pithy comment at the time: "He's got a *big* face and I thought to myself how much I'd like to smack it." In doing so, she expressed the revulsion and frustration felt by many Germans at the thought that a man who had been a member of the Nazi party for twelve years could have become West Germany's chancellor.

In April 1970 she staged a demonstration in Brussels against Ernst Achenbach, an FDP Bundestag deputy and erstwhile political counsellor of the German embassy in Paris during the Nazi occupation. Achenbach had been nominated by Bonn to become one of the commissioners of the European Common Market. Beate Klarsfeld helped drag out his shady past and triggered the withdrawal of his nomination. She went to La Paz to demand the extradition of the former chief of the Gestapo in Lyons,

Klaus Barbie, who had been living in Bolivia since the end of the war under an assumed name.

Her protests and demonstrations soon won her accolades from the Communist countries, which never pass up an opportunity to point an accusing finger at West Germany for harboring and promoting ex-Nazis. But she soon demonstrated that her crusade for justice cuts both ways. In Warsaw she chained herself to a tree in the Marszalkowska, the main shopping street, and distributed pamphlets condemning antisemitism in Poland. In Prague she staged a protest demonstration against Czechoslovakia's re-Stalinization. In Damascus she stood in front of President Assad's residence demanding freedom for Syrian Jews. And as a result of all that, she is now persona non grata in all the East European countries, including East Germany.

But the coup that won her international attention was her attempt in March 1971 to kidnap Kurt Lischka, the former Gestapo chief of Paris, on a Cologne street corner and to spirit him in the trunk of a car to France to stand trial.

The case of Lischka, a former SS lieutenant colonel and Adolf Eichmann's deputy in France, was one of the anomalies of postwar justice. One of the key figures in the far-flung SS and Gestapo murder mechanism, Lischka managed to escape the clutches of the Allies after the war by going into hiding like so many other high-ranking officials. Unable to find and apprehend him, the French tried and convicted him in absentia in 1950 for organizing the deportation of at least a hundred thousand Jews to the extermination camps. The sentence, provided Lischka could ever be found, was life imprisonment.

In May 1952 the occupation of West Germany was ended formally with the signing of the Bonn Conventions. Although the treaty gave the West German judiciary full authority to try Nazi criminals, one of its clauses, to prevent double jeopardy, excluded prosecution, for the same crimes, of those who had already been tried either by the Allied military government courts or the domestic courts of France, Great Britain, and the United States. And since West German law also prohibited the extradition of a German citizen to stand trial in a foreign country or to serve sentences imposed by foreign courts, Kurt Lischka was, thanks to those two legal technicalities, a free man—as were some thousand other Nazi criminals who enjoyed the same legal protection. He emerged from underground and as a businessman in Cologne had to be careful of only one thing: not to travel to countries from where he might be extradited to France.

In February 1971 France and West Germany signed a treaty nullifying that section of the Bonn Conventions which protects men like Lischka from double jeopardy and from being tried by West German courts. But Beate Klarsfeld feared that the treaty might never be ratified by the West German Bundestag. Until it was, Lischka and others like him could not be indicted. Her fears were well founded, for the ratification bill was pigeonholed in the Bundestag's foreign affairs committee by one of its senior and most powerful members: Ernst Achenbach. The same Ernst Achenbach who had served as a top Nazi diplomat in France while Lischka was Gestapo chief of Paris; the same Achenbach who in his private law practice represented a number of Nazi criminals, including the former Gestapo chief of Bordeaux who had also been tried in absentia; the same Achenbach whose appointment to the Common Market Commission Beate Klarsfeld had helped to block; the same Achenbach who as recently as July 1974 called for a general amnesty for all Nazi criminals and announced blatantly that the ratification bill for the treaty with France would not be read out of the foreign affairs committee so long as he was a member of it.

A month after the treaty had been signed, Beate Klarsfeld, accompanied by her husband and three friends, attempted to grab Lischka in broad daylight on a street in Cologne, force him into the trunk of a rented Mercedes, and abduct him. As the four men pounced on him, Lischka, a huge man weighing two hundred pounds, struggled, shouted for help, and caught the attention of an off-duty policeman who came to his aid. The would-be kidnappers fled across the border to France.

A warrant was issued for Beate Klarsfeld's arrest. In April 1974, three years after the abortive abduction, after first calling the authorities, newspapers, and television studios to say where she would be, she "surrendered" to the police on the grounds of the Dachau concentration camp, now a museum. At her subsequent trial in Cologne, at which she received a two-months' jail sentence for assault and attempted kidnapping, and against which an appeal is pending, hundreds of former French Resistance fighters and concentration camp inmates demonstrated on her behalf. The trial was one of those typical manifestations of German judicial insensitivity to the mood of world public opinion and the political realities of life. It left most observers wondering whether justice is really well served by being blindfolded. Above all, it served Beate Klarsfeld's avowed intentions: to remind her fellow Germans of the "undigested past."

In that endeavor she wages a lonely battle, for the majority of her countrymen would like nothing more than to forget that past. To them, the trials, on which the West German government has spent an estimated $300 million, have been anathema for decades—a form of self-flagellation in which they did not want to indulge. Despite the extensive publicity accorded these proceedings, most West Germans paid little attention. An opinion survey conducted midway through the twenty-month-long Auschwitz trial revealed that 40 percent of the people were not even aware that it was taking place. And of those who knew of it, nearly half objected to its being conducted, and voiced the opinion that twenty years after the war it was time to end prosecution.

Today, thirty years after the war, that view is even more prevalent, especially among the young, among those too young to be in any way implicated or held responsible. With every right they ask: "Why blame us for the crimes of our parents and grandparents?" And with every right a thirty-four-year-old aircraft technician said several years ago: "Wherever I go on vacation—to France, Switzerland, England, or Holland—people criticize the Germans. They keep saying: 'Look at the terrible things you did.' *We?* All I did was go to kindergarten."

The backlash among Germany's young has been apparent to observers of the scene for many years and it has become stronger, especially as the knowledge has deepened that the Germans as a people do not hold an exclusive patent on national criminality. What, in good conscience, does one say to a young West German like the student who once asked me: "Was Hitler really worse than Stalin? And how do you Americans account for the My Lais of Vietnam? Every nation has committed its crimes in history—some worse than others, that is true. But what makes our crimes so special?"

To answer questions like that with the standard numerical tabulation of those killed or the worn-out retort that two wrongs do not make a right will hardly do. In such an atmosphere it is hardly surprising that the opposition Christian Democrats found widespread resonance in the summer of 1974 when their Bundestag whip, Heinrich Windelen, demanded that the government make public a secret study about crimes committed against the *Germans* during and shortly after the war.

The view of most young Germans today was expressed to me once by a woman journalist born just shortly before Hitler committed suicide in the Fuehrer Bunker: "Of course the guilty should be punished. But what good does that really do? Will it right the wrongs? What more must we do to atone? Pay for the damage and the pain? We already have—more than twenty billion dollars in restitution and reparations to individual victims of nazism and to Israel thus far. And we shall continue to pay—most likely another ten billion dollars before the end of this decade. The world should at least leave us alone to look toward a better future, not always the grim and ugly past."

Such views, legitimate and understandable as they may be, raise the question of whether all the trials of Nazi criminals, whether the twenty-year-long effort to prosecute, didn't perhaps fail in what should have been the quintessential aim: to imbue in Germans the innate feeling that they cannot bear to live with murderers in their midst. Ask almost any German the purpose of all the trials and why prosecution should continue, and you will get a variety or combination of trenchant, certainly valid, but to me still inadequate answers: to atone for Germany's crimes; to right the wrongs; to punish the guilty; to educate; to palliate world opinion; to clear our conscience.

You will get these answers even from the most concerned, well-intentioned, and sincere young Germans. For example, Dr. Uwe Holtz, the youngest SPD deputy in the Bundestag, told me: "We cannot absolve ourselves of the debts of history. They simply have to be paid. Moreover, these trials are instructional for the young generation. They fill the gaps left by their teachers and in their textbooks."

To this Anke Riedel-Martiny, thirty-five, a mother of three and also an SPD Bundestag deputy, added: "I see prosecution as having a cathartic effect on our society, as a means of cleansing it of the guilt it shares."

But only once in all the years of covering German affairs did I hear a responsible public official touch on what seems to me the fundamental issue. That was Dr. Ernst Benda, now chief justice of the West German supreme court, who as a CDU Bundestag deputy in 1965 initiated the bill to extend the statute of limitations. "One unpunished murderer among us," he said at the time, "is one too many. And if we abandon the hunt for them we may as well abandon the republic and return to living in caves."

Looking back, in that context, over all the years of West Germany's painful and agonizing attempts to come to terms with the German past, to digest it, so to speak, I can only conclude that it has been merely half successful. And the responsibility for its half failure by no means lies only with the Germans, but with the peoples who were their victims, their conquerors, their occupiers, and their often-vengeful neighbors. No one could have or even should have suggested that they forget Germany's crimes. But neither did they forgive. And in their ceaseless demands for German self-flagellation, in the incessant calls upon the Germans to atone and expiate, and in the interminable challenges to the Germans to prove themselves again and again, the quintessential purpose of *Vergangenheits-bewaeltigung* has been defeated. The crucial question to pose at this point is, of course: What then *should* have been done? I really have no answer to that except to say: certainly not what the East Germans did.

Arnold Zweig, the left-wing German-Jewish novelist who had reset-tled in East Germany after the war, once told Amos Elon, a well-known Israeli journalist: "We did not master or digest the past. We vomited it out." What Zweig was trying to say was, in essence, what East Germany's rulers, or their propagandists, maintain. Nazism, they claim, was the ineluctable consequence of monopoly capitalism, and wherever capitalism has been uprooted and replaced, such as in the German Democratic Republic (GDR), nazism and its seed are dead. But wherever capitalism still flourishes, such as in the Federal Republic (FRG), nazism remains alive and, ergo, the past has not been digested. Were it only so simple.

But Zweig's pithy remark had a double entendre which he probably didn't realize himself.

For in "vomiting out the past," as Zweig indelicately phrased it, East Germany has also conveniently divorced itself from it by washing the common stain of the past down West Germany's drain. To the incontestable fact that there are now two German states, the GDR's rulers have tried to add the spurious thesis of two German histories. Thanks to the propaganda with which they have been inundated, to hear East Germans talk you would think that the GDR had been a victim, not the integral part of an aggressor nation. At no time is this attitude fostered more blatantly than on each May 8, the anniversary of V-E Day, which, in contrast to the FRG where it is ignored, has become a public holiday in East Germany and is celebrated as "liberation day."

Questions about how the past weighs on the conscience of East German society are better not posed by foreigners with long memories or strong sensitivities. It doesn't. A known Nazi in someone's circle of friends or family tree is generally dismissed as an unsuspecting former dupe of powerful Fascist propaganda. I do not mean to imply that the GDR has done no grappling with its own past. After all, some 13,000 Nazi criminals have been tried and convicted before East German tribunals—twice as many as in West Germany, which has three times the population. And while prosecution in the East has passed without much fanfare or publicity, the penalties meted out were usually the maximum—death or life imprisonment. West Germany, which has no death penalty, has sentenced but 126 of the 6,300 it has tried to the maximum term of life.

It is also true that when important ex-Nazis *are* discovered in influential public positions in East Germany, they are usually disposed of quickly and generally under the cloak of secrecy—easy enough to do in a more or less totalitarian society. Thus, in 1959, little time was wasted in expelling Ernst Grossmann from the Socialist Unity Party's central committee when it was revealed that not only had he been a Nazi but an SS guard at Sachsenhausen concentration camp. And four years later the party moved with equal speed when Karlheinz Bartsch, the minister of agriculture and a candidate member of the politburo, was exposed as a former SS man. Bartsch, an agronomist, is now director of a state farm near Neubrandenburg.

In West Germany, even today, exposed officials invariably spend agonizing and embarrassing months clinging to the emoluments of office—to the delight of East Germany's ever-ready propaganda machinery, which can point an accusing finger and pillory the Bonn government in front of "incensed world public opinion." And when the West German official finally does resign, it is inevitably under massive public and media pressure.

Hunting Nazi skeletons in the other fellow's closet has been a form of *Vergangenheitsbewaeltigung* at which both Germanys have tried their hands periodically over the years. Thanks to the effectiveness of East German propaganda, however, the misleading impression has been created that while the West German government is laced with ex-Nazis (which is no longer true), the GDR's is pure and clean (which is also not true). In fact, despite its claims to the contrary, there are quite a few. Three members of the East German State Council, the country's "collective presidency," are former Nazi party members. So are five of the ministers in Premier Horst Sindermann's cabinet and twelve members of the ruling Socialist Unity party's central committee. A score of other top-ranking government and party officials are also former Nazis. Admittedly, most of them joined the Nazi party at a very late date—the majority in the 1940s—and at an age when most of them could not have been expected to have acquired prodigious amounts of political wisdom or courage. And in some instances, as was the case with many Germans during the Third Reich, they may have joined under duress. But the same excuses could be offered in defense of numerous West German officials who turned out to be ex-Nazis, and it certainly cannot be applied in the cases of Dr. Heinrich Homann and Dr. Guenter Kertzscher.

Homann, sixty-four, is one of the five deputy chairmen of the state council, that is, one of the GDR's five "vice presidents." He joined the Nazi party in 1933, and in 1934 became a professional army officer. A major by the time he was captured by the Russians at Stalingrad, he joined the Soviet-sponsored National Committee for a Free Germany in a prisoner-of-war camp and "recanted" his Nazi views. Kertzscher, sixty-two, is deputy editor-in-chief of *Neues Deutschland*, the official Socialist Unity party daily, and author of some of its most vitriolic articles about Nazis in West Germany. He himself became an SA storm trooper in 1937, joined the Nazi party the same year and "switched" beliefs while a POW in Russia.

For many years, too, East Germany boasted that antisemitism had been completely uprooted in the GDR, while claiming that its seed continues to ferment in the Federal Republic. And whenever a swastika is daubed on a Jewish headstone in a West German cemetery—something that has happened rarely in the past ten years—East Germany's propaganda machinery runs at full speed and top volume. But there must be some reason why the miniscule community of Jews who lived in East Germany thirty years ago—some 3,200—has dwindled to less than 1,000, while the Jewish population of West Germany—approximately 32,000—has grown and in recent years has even enjoyed a mild renaissance.

The fact of the matter is that antisemitism has been fostered by the East

German regime for quite some time, first in Stalinist garb, then under the guise of anti-Zionism and as an anti-Israeli policy. The tremors of Stalinist-inspired "anti-Zionism" in the early 1950s were felt strongly all over Eastern Europe, of course, but reverberated with especially vicious impact and purges in both Czechoslovakia and the GDR. Though anti-Zionism was a mute ideological issue in the other Communist countries in the early and middle 1960s, it became an instrument of foreign policy for East Germany. It was by beating the Israeli horse, then secretly getting military aid from West Germany, and by palliating the Arabs, that Walter Ulbricht succeeded in breaking the ring of diplomatic isolation which Bonn's Hallstein Doctrine had forged around the GDR. In February 1965 he went to Egypt on an official visit, thus starting on the long, hard road to international diplomatic recognition that led, first and foremost, through the Arab countries. By the start of the six-day Middle East war in 1967, East Germany, more than any other Communist country, including the USSR, was already solidly locked into an irreversible anti-Israeli stance. Since that war, not to even mention the Yom Kippur war of 1973, East Berlin has been outdone only by Moscow itself in the militancy of its anti-Israeli and anti-Zionist policy.

Actually, the "past" in East Germany has been neither digested nor vomited. It has been simply and conveniently forgotten. And on those rare occasions when it is conjured up or resuscitated, it is not regarded as the *German*, but the *West* German, past. As blatant a falsification of history as this may be, it is a situation to which the West Germans themselves contributed immeasurably by contending for decades that the Federal Republic was the only legal German state and the legitimate successor to the German Reich. Besides making West Germany's diplomatic position untenable in the increasingly complicated game of international power politics, that doctrine made it easy for East Germany to absolve itself of moral and material obligations deriving from the Third Reich.

"Look," an East German official once told me, "the West Germans, not we, have claimed that there can be but one Germany and that the Bonn government is its sole legitimate representative. They deny us the right of diplomatic recognition abroad and arrogate to themselves the right to succeed the old Reich. Under the circumstances they can damn well assume the responsibility that comes with it. Why, for example, should we pay reparations to Israel when Bonn insists on doing so in the name of all Germany?"

This argument lost its validity quite suddenly in September 1973 when both Germanys were admitted to membership in the United Nations as separate states, and the GDR gained the diplomatic recognition of nearly all countries in the world, including, for all practical purposes, West Germany itself. Since then, East Germany has been under considerable pressure to pay. The potential bill that has been, and is being presented is enormous. For example, according to the Luxembourg Agreement of 1952, West Germany agreed to pay two-thirds of what it had cost Israel to absorb the victims of Nazism, while one-third remains for East Germany to pay—an amount totalling nearly $400 million. Material claims for property confiscated and expropriated by the Nazis, though difficult to estimate, could come to as high as $4 billion. Finally, there are claims for damages to life and health. These may turn out to be small, for West Germany, as a result of its now outdated diplomatic policy of attempting to speak for Germany as a whole, took over most of them, agreeing to pay out some $18 billion.

Thus far the GDR has vacillated about paying and recognizing the validity of any claims. It contends that under the Potsdam Agreement of 1945 it was responsible for making all reparation payments to Russia and Poland, and did so, whereas the Western occupation zones were to pay war damages in the West. Since Israel did not become a state until 1948, that is, after the Potsdam Agreement, it can base no claims on it. Nor, says the GDR, was East Germany even a party to the 1952 Luxembourg Agreement and, as a result, has no obligations to it. Moreover, the GDR says it does not maintain diplomatic relations with Israel and has no interest in establishing them. The East Germans also contend that surviving victims of Nazism still living in the GDR receive pensions and other compensation, which is true. Another East German argument is that the GDR owes no compensation for expropriated property because this was capitalist property, whether Jewish or non-Jewish, all of which is now owned by the East German people. Finally, the East German regime contends that in abolishing capitalism, "the soil of Nazism," and in "completely expunging Nazism and racism," it has already paid the "greatest reparation and made the greatest restitution" for the crimes committed.

This last argument, in particular, plays a predominant role in the treatment of the past in East German education. Whatever may have been wrong about the teaching of history and textbooks in West German schools for many years after the war—and there was plenty wrong—it was mild compared to the distorted and erroneous picture of recent German history still being presented to youth in the GDR. In East German textbooks and lesson plans, the history of Hitler's rise to power and the Third Reich is presented largely through the ideological filter of the international class struggle. Thus, the most widely used modern history book for tenth-graders says:

German monopoly capitalism was looking for ways with which to transfer the burdens of the international economic and financial crisis onto the shoulders of the working masses, and for means with which to break the resistance of the working class against a policy of repression. To accomplish this, and to realize their ambitions of aggression, the most reactionary forces of German monopoly capitalism planned the total abolition of bourgeois democracy and the establishment of a brutal reign of terror.

To establish this brutal regime of terror, they needed a tool—a political party—that would divide and confuse the working masses. For this purpose the most reactionary forces of monopoly capitalism furthered the fascist party led by Hitler. . . . The vast amounts of money they contributed to the Hitler party enabled the German fascists to build up a large organization, publish newspapers, create and arm terrorist bands such as the SA and SS, and stage mass rallies and demonstrations.

The principal political and propagandistic instrument of the fascistic party was demagoguery, that is, to confuse the masses with false promises which it had no intention of fulfilling.

Resistance to the Hitler regime, according to this book, was organized and waged exclusively by the German Communist party. The crimes of nazism—except for those committed against the Soviet people—are treated almost as superficially as they used to be in the West German schoolbooks of the 1950s. And what may seem strangest of all, those crimes were committed and the war of aggression was waged, not by Germans, but by nationally anonymous people persistently referred to merely as "the Fascists." It was not the German Wehrmacht that occupied Western Europe and invaded Poland and Russia, but "the fascistic army." The caption under one picture showing the mass execution of Jews by an SS firing squad reads: "Fascist soldiers carried out mass killings." The text under another photo of weeping Russian women reads: "Soviet women were forced to watch the murder of their relatives by the Fascist soldiers." The British and American forces landed in Normandy, according to the book, because "the governments of the U.S.A. and Great Britain realized that the USSR might liberate all of West Europe and that under those circumstances the masses in those countries would surely rise against the rule of imperialism." And the end of the Third Reich, of course, is described as "the liberation of Germany from the Fascist yoke."

"Peoples and governments," the German philosopher Georg Wilhelm Friedrich Hegel once said, "never have learned anything from history or acted on principles deduced from it."

That is one Hegelian thesis, I fear, which Communist East Germany's educators seem to have overlooked. One can only hope that their approach to the recent past will not come to haunt them one day.

And what about West Germany? One of the first missions of the Allied military government was to clean out the Augean stable of German education: to sift and screen the teachers for their past records and for their political leanings; to throw out the Nazi schoolbooks filled with propaganda and racist and chauvinistic lies. And for more than a dozen years after the end of the war it was generally assumed that this had been done, that everything in West German education was in order, that the teachers were democratically oriented, that the textbooks were properly written. The new generation, the generation that had not been poisoned by Nazi indoctrination, was expected to emerge as the hope of the future.

Then, in the late 1950s, a succession of shocking incidents and disclosures challenged all those comfortable assumptions. There was, first of all, the case of Ludwig Zind, a high school mathematics teacher in the Black Forest town of Offenburg, who had been a Nazi party member and SA storm trooper and who made headlines by escaping to Egypt after a local court had convicted him of uttering antisemitic remarks and defamatory racist statements during a restaurant argument with a half-Jewish textile wholesaler. Then Edgar Fernau, a grade school teacher in Hanover, was accused of having said in public: "It's too bad about the Jews, I mean that they weren't all gassed to death." A few weeks later there was the case of Lothar Stielau, a Luebeck high school teacher, who had claimed in an article in the school paper that the diary of

Anne Frank was a forgery. Then, too, there were reports of several teachers belonging to and campaigning for neo-Nazi and radical right-wing parties.

The shock waves from those incidents were still reverberating in April 1959 when Juergen Neven-duMont, a muckraking television journalist, touched off an even bigger one. In a forty-five-minute documentary film, telecast nationwide and based on interviews with pupils and teachers in twelve elementary and secondary schools in four West German states, he demonstrated that the postwar young had been taught virtually nothing about the Third Reich or Hitler's rise to power. Textbooks passed over the period in brief, sweeping, and often distorting generalities. Teachers were skillfully eschewing it. They gave as an excuse that lesson plans left no time for instruction on "more recent history," that is, the era beginning after the *First* World War. A few frankly conceded they were too embarrassed to admit to students that they, too, had supported the Nazi regime. For years, apparently, Germany's youth had been the victims of a conspiracy of silence which left them almost wholly ignorant of the most recent, in a sense most important, epoch of German history.

"Who was Adolf Hitler and what did he do?" Neven-duMont asked a class of *Volksschule* seniors, that is, fourteen-year-olds who, like 85 percent of all German youngsters at that time, would be leaving school at the end of the semester to enter apprenticeships and would have virtually no further formal education. Up went several hands. "Hitler sold badges in order to take over the government," one boy replied. "He had a mustache, gave work to the unemployed, and built the *Autobahn,*" explained another. "He did a lot for the workers by sending them out on pleasure ships at low rates," answered a third. "It was pretty good under Hitler in one respect," said a fourth youngster, "because there were no murderers of taxi drivers and women like we have today. They were done away with right away. Also, young people were able to join organizations like the Hitler youth."

Asked to identify some of the other top leaders of the Nazi party besides Hitler, the pupils rattled off such names as Hindenburg, Tito, and Khrushchev. Queried about the crimes of the Nazi regime, one girl replied: "Poles, Jews, and enemies of the state were killed by the thousands, the tens of thousands, in concentration camps." And when Neven-duMont asked the youngsters to state how many had been killed, he got a shocking reply of guesswork, obviously based on total ignorance.

"I think about fifty thousand," said one boy. "Forty to fifty thousand," said another. "Thirty-five thousand." "Maybe twenty thousand." "About eighty thousand?" one girl asked uncertainly. "About eleven million." "I think it was around two million."

Out of ninety-five *Gymnasium*, that is, high school, students only two were able to give reasonably intelligent and accurate answers about the Nazi regime, the principles for which it had stood, and how it had been able to come to power. And both those pupils had acquired their knowledge on their own initiative outside of school. Answers to questions about contemporary West Germany, its political structure, and organization were equally vague.

A few months after Neven-duMont's television program, West Germany was ravaged by a series of antisemitic incidents and swastika smearings, the majority of which involved teenagers and youths in their early twenties.

Under the impact of these disclosures and events, and under pressure of criticism from abroad, a painful reappraisal of history and civics instruction in West Germany's decentralized, state-administered school system began. Lesson plans were reshaped. Precise instructions were issued to teachers and school administrators, telling them not only what should be taught, and how, about the Hitler era, but how many hours a week should be devoted to it. Textbooks were scrutinized for omissions or possible pro-Nazi views. Those which did not meet the new standards were ordered rewritten. Publishers were warned that failure to comply would mean automatic exclusion of the books from the annual catalogues of those approved for use in the school systems. Schools were supplied with countless teaching aides and supplementary books. To prepare future teachers for the new task of "teaching democracy," special "social studies" departments were established at universities and teachers' colleges. Refresher courses and seminars were organized for older teachers. The regulations governing the final school-leaving exams for high school students were changed so that in order to receive their diplomas they would have to demonstrate not only their knowledge of Homer, Euclid, and Goethe but their knowledge of Hitler and Adenauer as well.

The results, after a few years of doing what should have been done immediately after the war, were encouraging. In 1965 I retraced some of Juergen Neven-duMont's steps, visiting the same schools to which he had gone in 1959 and asking the same questions. Where less than 2 percent had been able to give him satisfactory answers about the Third Reich, 70–80 percent of those pupils I interviewed and tested were well informed and replied with spontaneity and in great detail.

At Bonn's grim-looking, gray-walled Beethoven Gymnasium, for example, only 10 percent of the seniors Neven-duMont had interviewed could name and describe the political parts into which postwar Germany had been divided. Only a quarter of the students gave him a reasonably accurate estimate of the number of Jews killed in concentration camps. Not a single student had been able to name the date—July 20, 1944—of the assassination attempt on Hitler, and less than 5 percent had been able to give a reasonably intelligent explanation of how the Nazis had come to power. But in 1965, when I confronted a class of seniors with the same eight questions Neven-duMont had asked, plus thirteen others, I found the students fully informed. As soon as any question was posed a forest of hands went up and the answers revealed a thorough knowledge of the Hitler era and a basic understanding of the mechanics and principles of West German democracy, albeit, with one serious lapse. When I asked who could recite the first article of West Germany's constitution, only one of the twenty students raised his hand and replied correctly: "The dignity of man is inviolable. To respect and protect it shall be the duty of all state authority."

I also evaluated revised editions of those history books I had first examined and analyzed for a chapter in *Schizophrenic Germany* in 1960, as well as new textbooks that had been issued to replace those which had been dropped from ministerial lists because they had failed to meet the new standards. Those in use in 1960 had all been characterized by their brief and superficial treatment of the Weimar Republic and the Third Reich; by the way they glossed over the crimes, injustices, and atrocities of the Nazis; by their far more detailed discussion of Germany's suffering during and after World War II; by strong nationalistic terminology that bordered on chauvinism; and by the sympathetic tone used to describe the plight of war criminals, a term occasionally printed in quotation marks. Not one of those books had really attempted to explain how Hitler came to power, much less give their young readers any meaningful guidelines to protect themselves and their society against the rise of some new demagogue in the future. None had drawn clear connecting lines between the illegality and injustice of the Nazi regime, the blindness of the German people in following Hitler, and the subsequent German fate during and after the war. They tended to glorify the victorious actions of the Wehrmacht and to suppress or belittle the innate injustice of Hitler's conquests. They had been totally devoid of a "cause and effect" interpretation of recent history. Some had struck me as blatantly neo-Nazi in outlook and tone.

One that I had found especially objectionable was Ernst Klett Publishing Co.'s *Lebendige Vergangenheit* (The Living Past) for use at what would be the American equivalent of high school freshman and sophomore level. Aside from the fact that it had devoted a total of only thirteen lines to the atrocities and crimes committed by the Hitler regime, it contained such obviously anti-American and anti-British passages as the following:

The victorious powers adopted the same methods [in Germany] which Hitler's emissaries had employed in the occupied countries; and again the innocent were the real victims of ruthless power politics.

In Nürnberg the occupation powers, in cooperation with the Soviets, conducted trials, not only of leading National Socialists, but senior officials, officers, scientists and industrialists. Numerous death sentences were passed and long terms of imprisonment imposed.

[After World War II] cartels and trusts were supposed to be "decentralized." But in many of the laws [of the Allied military government] the desire to destroy German competition on world markets was all too apparent.

German industry lay paralyzed and was hindered by the occupation powers more than it was helped.

The remnants of the German fleet were divided among the [Americans, British and Russians]. It was decided that in the future Germany was not to have a high seas fleet or airplanes.

In the revised, 1962 edition of the same book, some, though not all, such passages had been deleted or subtly changed, and the section dealing with the crimes of the Nazi regime had been magnanimously expanded from thirteen to thirty-nine lines of text. On the whole, however, even this newer version, once used widely in German schools, remained tendentious, and the book was subsequently removed from the catalogues and has gone out of print.

With the exception of this particular volume, however, most of the books I examined in 1965 had a completely new approach. Books that had devoted only a sentence or two to the persecution of the Jews, dwelled on the subject for several pages. Photographs had been exchanged to give an entirely new slant on history. Whereas in the earlier editions there had been pictures only, or primarily, of bombed out *German* cities, hungry and ragged *German* children, and German refugees fleeing from Silesia and Pomerania, the new editions had photographs of bombed-out Rotterdam and Londoners cowering in air raid shelters, massacred Russian soldiers, innocent civilians being executed by German troops, and Jews being marched at gunpoint from the Warsaw ghetto toward death in concentration camps.

I detected an entirely new tone:

"It is terrible for us Germans to recall the murder of millions in the concentration and extermination camps," said one textbook used primarily in Bavarian schools. "But we must do so, for the war with all its horrors has been largely forgotten and because we must do everything possible to prevent such crimes from being committed again."

Altered, too, was the approach to the question of collective German responsibility and the widely propagated view that no one in Germany had really known about the concentration camps until the war was over and the truth came out. One book, Westermann Publishing Co.'s *Reise in die Vergangenheit* (Journey into the Past), initially published in 1964 and still in wide use, has an especially interesting approach to this problem. Following a very lengthy and detailed section on Nazi crimes, it says:

You probably cannot comprehend how all this was possible, for Hitler obviously needed thousands of accomplices to commit such crimes. Conversely, one could ask: Was there no one who protested against these crimes, for on records and films from that period you will see German citizens cheering and pictures show them enthusiastically raising their right arm in salute.

The majority of German citizens had heard, here and there, of the existence of concentration camps and about other things. But very few could conceive or know of what was taking place in those camps, for anyone released from one, as well as the guards, were compelled to keep silent. Only a small minority of Germans had any idea of the extent of mass extermination. The crimes, in the totality of their horror, were not divulged until after the war had been lost. And then, people abroad could not believe that the Germans had known nothing.

To this day there are many who do not want to hear and know about these crimes. But it is a folly and cowardly to shun the truth.

Perhaps there are reminders of this aspect of National Socialist rule in your town: street names, for example, of some of Hitler's victims; cemeteries; monuments, or buildings behind whose walls these terrible things happened. Find out about them and keep the memories alive. Perhaps there is a former concentration camp nearby. You should visit such sites to envision for yourselves what transpired there.

In 1974, I again examined those history and civics books most widely used in West German schools and found them even more frank and detailed in their treatment of the Weimar period and the Nazi regime than a decade ago. In particular, I noted a pronounced improvement in the questions and work assignments at the ends of sections and chapters, for they encouraged pupils to think about the causal relationships and to think critically.

The following examples were chosen at random from a number of textbooks.

Explain how Hitler won so many votes in elections.

What interest groups helped him come to power and why?

Hitler declared unequivocally that the goal of his party was the abolition of democracy. Under those circumstances, what should have been the obligation and responsibility of the Weimar Republic governments and why do we say they failed?

What is the basic difference between democracy and dictatorship?

Why is the Reichstag fire considered symbolic for the beginning of National Socialist dictatorship? What effect did the Enabling Act of 1933 have on democracy? Could a similar act be enforced in the Federal Republic today?

Which basic civil rights did Hitler violate and abolish? Read the Constitution of the Federal Republic—especially Articles 1–19.

Democracy is based on the principle of checks and balances and on the division of powers. Which powers did Hitler unite and take into his own hands?

Explain how Hitler misused the country's youth for his purposes. Can we condemn the youth of the Third Reich for having believed in Hitler?

Explain Hitler's hatred of the Jews. Why did anti-Semitism take roots among a portion of the German people? Why is Hitler's theory on the inferiority of the Jewish race erroneous? Think about the achievements of the new Jewish state of Israel. What impact did the emigration of countless Jewish intellectuals have on the cultural life of Germany?

After the war the Allies spoke of "collective guilt," that is, they charged the entire German people with guilt for Hitler's dictatorship and its crimes. What is your view on this?

The swastika smearings in the spring of 1960 did great harm to our reputation abroad. What could have been done about them? To this day there are still trials of leading Nazis and concentration camp guards. You should read about them in the newspapers.

To this day, too, textbooks are still being rewritten. And not just those sections pertaining to the history of the Third Reich. In 1972, for example, a commission of Polish and West German historians, educators, authors, and publishers began a series of meetings, first in Warsaw, then in Braunschweig, to draft guidelines for the treatment of Polish-German relations in the two countries' history books. No two peoples in history have warred against each other as long and as frequently as the Germans and the Western Slavs, and nowhere, perhaps, is the schoolbook picture of each other more distorted than in West Germany and Poland. The guidelines, when implemented by German authors and publishers, will give an entirely new slant to the aggressive, colonizing role of the Teutonic Knights in the Middle Ages, to the strong Polish-German cultural ties in the sixteenth and seventeenth centuries, to Prussia's role in the partitions of Poland, to relations between Poland and Germany in the twentieth century, and to the territorial and border disputes between the two countries. Future German schoolbooks are expected to underscore the historical Polish claims to Silesia and Pomerania. They should provide German schoolchildren with a completely different impression of Polish and Slavic culture from the "inferior race" notion cultivated in the 1930s (and earlier) and still lingering in German history books.

Efforts are also being made to devote more attention in schoolbooks to the great democratic episodes in German history, such as the peasant uprisings and wars of the Middle Ages, the revolution of 1848–49, and the revolution of 1918, which led to the creation of the Weimar Republic.

The Germans are a people in search of their own history and German youth wants ideals. Those ideals are there. They were merely suppressed in the historiography of the Kaiser Reich and the Third Reich, with their twisted values and ambitions. The impetus to look toward those ideals and to emphasize them in schoolbooks and curricula was given by former President Gustav Heinemann. In 1974, with the cooperation of the privately endowed Koerber Foundation of Hamburg, he initiated a nationwide essay contest on the significance of the revolutionary movement of 1848–49. Hundreds of thousands of pupils participated and prizes totalling $100,000 were awarded. The tentative essay theme for 1975 is the revolution of 1918. Meanwhile, at the International School Book Institute in Braunschweig, studies are being conducted for ways to revise and expand the treatment of such historical events in the textbooks.

Textbook treatment of East Germany and relations between the two German states, influenced for nearly three decades by the exigencies of the Cold War and East-West confrontation, is also under scrutiny, and revisions are being written.

Ultimately, of course, what Germany's young people learn about the past and the Third Reich depends less on the content of their schoolbooks than on their teachers and what the teachers do with the materials available. That varies greatly. Two of the young Bundestag members, both in school in the late 1950s and early 1960s when textbooks taught them nothing, had strikingly different experiences in this regard.

"There was nothing in the books," says Anke Riedel-Martiny, "but I learned everything I needed to know. I wasn't spared a single atrocity or a single causal relationship. But that was entirely due to the teacher—a very special person, very involved and *engagé,* who went out of her way to tell us precisely what happened, why and what impact it has had on the German image in the world. As a result, perhaps, my relationship to Jews, as well as that of my husband, who, by the way, had a similar school experience, can never be 'normal.' The crimes of the Third Reich, the burden of the past which I was taught to sense so deeply, stands between us."

"The Third Reich? In school?" asked Uwe Holtz, himself a historian. "Nothing. We followed the textbooks, and they had little, a few pages each day, reading and copying. There were hardly any outside materials. We never went into depth or discussed how to prevent something like the rise of nazism from happening again. But it wasn't just recent history about which we learned so little. Ancient history and medieval history too. We are in the process of becoming an ahistoric nation and I see a disturbing trend toward treating history as a secondary subject in the schools. And that is dangerous, for the absence of causal knowledge of history is the soil in which the seeds of biases and false notions grow today. Yes, I had a history teacher who told us that a dictatorship must never happen again. She was also our home-room teacher and one day, when we elected a class president, she disapproved of him. 'I'll go outside again for 15 minutes,' she told us, 'and when I return I will expect you to have elected someone else.' "

Yet, West German youth wants to know. A number of years ago, during International Brotherhood Week, one of the television networks broadcast a series of programs about three individuals who had resisted the Nazi dictatorship in a modest but very personal and courageous way. Bonn's *General Anzeiger*, the capital's largest daily, subsequently conducted a survey among younger readers, asking their impressions of the programs and their views on whether more should be taught about the past. The overwhelming majority said yes.

"My parents, however, don't want to hear about it anymore," said a twenty-year-old Gymnasium graduate working as a secretary in a government office. "What's more, they don't want me to hear about it, either. My father forbade me to see those programs and I had to go to a friend's house to watch. He said they would be tendentious, that too much was being written, said, and shown about the Third Reich and that most of it was exaggerated propaganda. He's my father and I have to do what he says, but I think he was a very active Nazi. He doesn't talk about it and my mother told me never to ask him. But I want to know."

"We should be told the truth—without exaggeration and without leaving things out," said a nineteen-year-old university freshman. "And did my teachers ever leave things out. What I learned, I learned outside of school from a great deal of reading. But to obtain a complete picture, one has to piece it together like a puzzle."

Perhaps it is this search for the pieces that spurred the sudden interest in Hitler and the Third Reich in 1973 and 1974. The scope and intensity of that "Hitler wave," I reiterate, was grossly exaggerated in reporting outside Germany. Compared to a similar wave that had engulfed Great Britain and the United States at about the same time, it was a ripple, and many of the books sold and films shown in Germany were imports from abroad. And many of them did not do too well. The British film *Hitler—the Last Ten Days*, premiered in Munich on the Fuehrer's birthday, played to near-empty houses. Moreover, a lot of the "wave" was nothing more than clever marketing and not overly successful at that. Although two national magazines, *Der Spiegel* and *Stern*, serialized the two most important German books about Hitler, neither recorded a perceptible increase in circulation as a result. Although Joachim Fest's excellent biography of Hitler was on the best-seller list for ten months, it sold less than 350,000 copies in a country of sixty million people who buy their books rather than go to a library to borrow them. And no other Hitler tome came even close to that sales figure.

Nor has the significance of the wave been fully understood. Fest himself ascribed the commercial success of his book to the advent of the younger generation which did not experience the Hitler years and now are curious about a past which does not embarrass them. That may be so, but as one reviewer of the various Hitler books, Wilfried von Bredow, pointed out: "As yet we do not have the data that would permit an exact sociological analysis of the Hitler wave. We do not know who reads the Hitler books. Is it the older generation, now pensioned and hungry to catch up on what they missed—a gap of which their own children frequently remind them? Or is it the young? Nor can we assess their impact." Only one movie played to packed houses: Charlie Chaplin's *The Great Dictator*, never before shown in Germany. The audiences roared with laughter. So did those who attended or watched on television Austrian actor Helmut Qualtinger's imitations of Hitler while reading lengthy passages from *Mein Kampf*.

Those who condemned the sudden German interest in Hitler criticized the books for "minimizing his crimes." Alfred Wolfmann, a German-Jewish journalist reporting for Israeli papers from Bonn, said sharply: "These books and articles show the human side of Hitler. That's scandalous. Hitler is being reduced to the status of an ordinary man, and that shames us all."

But should it?

In his *History of Germany*, Michael Freund said "Hitler cannot be measured in human terms." Golo Mann considered him so repulsive that he refused to spell out his name, using only the initial "H" when referring to Hitler in his *German History in the 19th and 20th Centuries*.

But Hitler *was* a man. Men twisted his psyche, fired his ambitions, brought him to power, hailed him, fought his wars, and committed monstrous crimes in his name and at his command. Hitler *was* human—a product and a part of humanity—and only when his humanness has been fully understood by the German people will they be able to come to terms with the phenomenon of Hitler. Josef Goebbels used to call him endearingly "our Hitler." The Germans seem at last to be realizing that this, precisely, is what he was. And only in that realization can they fully digest the past and heal the wounds of history.

2

Democracy Ueber Alles

A DECADE or so ago a Munich newspaper reporter donned a make-believe uniform replete with enough insignia and gold braid to look like a cross between the police chief, a hotel doorman, and an operetta hero. Then he tested the legendary German respect for authority. Posting himself outside a row of public phone booths, he haughtily and officiously asked each caller to identify whom he had telephoned, what had been discussed, and for good measure, even demanded to search their briefcases or purses.

With the exception of a number of young people, all under twenty-five years of age, no one refused to answer his questions or seriously objected to his search. Some even stammered out more information than he had asked for. An elderly civil servant, for example, whipped out his official identity card and apologized: "I'm sorry, officer, but I just had to take a few minutes off to call a repairman for my furnace."

The reporter's test seemed to confirm a widely held and rarely challenged notion about *the* Germans: their proclivity to subordinate themselves to authority, especially when it appears in uniform. *Disziplin, Ordnung und Gehorsamkeit*—discipline, order and obedience—it is assumed, are virtues they place above all others.

"The German," Heinrich Heine, the great nineteenth-century poet and critic once said of his own people, "is like the slave who, without chains, without whip, obeys his master's merest word, his every glance. The condition of servitude is inherent in him, in his very soul; and worse than the physical is the spiritual slavery."

Erich von Kahler, in his posthumously published book *The Germans*, a collection of the lectures he delivered at Cornell University and the University of Manchester in the 1950s, spoke of the German longing "to escape from the complexity and loneliness of freedom."

Dr. Wolfgang Mueller, a Bonn University social psychologist, told me many years ago: "The difference between us and the Latins or Anglo-Saxons, for example, is that we are disciplined while they are *self*-disciplined. We Germans do not understand the difference between *unterordnen* and *einordnen*, that is, between subordinating ourselves to authority and fitting into society.

"Partly, this is a consequence of historical developments. The British, French, and Americans have all had their revolutions and accept government authority only as an agent acting on their behalf. But for Germans it is always *'die da oben,'* that is, those up there on the top, because the Germans view government and the state as an authority above and apart from them. It is our feudal legacy and the belief that the king or kaiser or whoever was in charge reigned by mandate of God."

These "traits of German character," so numerous historians, political scientists, philosophers, and social critics have maintained, paved the way for the totalitarian Nazi state. They were why Germans were capable of committing the most horrendous crimes only to claim afterwards they were merely "obeying orders." They are the root of that "most German" of all attitudes: *"Ruhe ist des Buergers erste Pflicht,"* which in effect means that "keeping quiet and obedient is the citizen's first duty to the state."

But are these still the Germans of the 1970s? How does one explain the tens of thousands of young German students who took to the streets to demonstrate for better educational opportunities, abolition of hierarchical structures in the schools, and more civil rights? Or consider the hundreds of thousands who belong to "citizens' action groups" militating and lobbying for every conceivable cause—from more playgrounds for their children to less air pollution, for abortion-on-demand to better garbage collection. And what about the fact that thirty-seven thousand young German men registered as conscientious objectors last year and that nearly half the adult population believes that *Beamten*—civil servants— have the inherent right to strike?

Nothing is more comfortable than a well-worn cliché, nothing more reassuring than a preconceived notion reconfirmed. But the simple fact is that in the Germany of the 1970s obedience and quiescence are no longer considered marks of good citizenship. On the contrary. In 1968 one of the annual Theodor Heuss awards, founded by the widow and political friends of West Germany's first president, was given to nineteen-year-old Karin Storch, a high school graduate, for her valedictory address which she had entitled: "Education toward Disobedience: The Task of Democratic Schools." Portions of her speech, in a sense so representative of the mood of her generation, deserve repetition.

"In civics classes," she said, "we discussed the fall of the Weimar Republic, one of whose principal failings had been its inability to raise and educate a sufficient number of crisis-proof democrats. Though critical and disobedient, they were not prepared to accept the state as their state. In those days, whenever Germans expressed criticism they directed it at the roots of the state, thus destroying rather than improving it. This basic failing of the Weimar Republic must be avoided in the Federal Republic and the task falls primarily on our civics and social science teachers. It is their responsibility to raise and educate democrats capable of withstanding crises by teaching them disobedience—but a form of disobedience that is democratically oriented. . . ."

Five years later, in 1973, the Theodor Heuss prize was awarded to an anonymous recipient—"the mature citizen." The criteria for "maturity of citizenship" were spelled out at the award ceremony in Munich in a speech by former President Gustav Heinemann, himself a shining example of such a citizen. (Heinemann, among other things, had resigned as interior minister of Konrad Adenauer's first cabinet over the West German rearmament issue and later, as president of the Federal Republic, was, to my knowledge, the world's only head of state who was also a dues-paying member of Amnesty International.)

"A mature citizen," Heinemann said, "is first and foremost an alert citizen who, instead of merely being administered and represented by others, wants to have a say and to participate. . . . Maturity of citizenship demands a specific attitude toward the state and society. You either have it, or you don't have it, or you develop it. . . . We waited for its development a long time."

But that development, as consistent observation of the scene can attest, is no longer to be denied, and surprisingly, this is true in *both* Germanys. Increasingly, people in both West and East Germany are disinclined to accept authority blindly, to think of the government and state as something above and apart from them. Concomitantly they are also accepting responsibilities and duties which heretofore had been regarded as the exclusive preserve of government.

One of the most striking examples in the Federal Republic of both "constructive civil disobedience" and "maturity of citizenship" is the rise in the 1970s of *Buergerinitiativen*, or what one could call citizens' action groups. Entirely spontaneous, comprised primarily of younger people, their number is impossible to estimate accurately and fluctuates steadily, for as soon as a group's goals have been achieved it is likely to disband. But there must be thousands of them, and membership in them must be in the hundreds of thousands. According to several haphazard surveys conducted in late 1972 and early 1973, there were at least 1,000 groups calling for, and in many cases already operating, progressive preschools and day nurseries; some 200 working for the establishment of teenage recreation centers; 350 fighting pollution.

Most of them function on the local level and address themselves almost exclusively to what are largely local, sometimes merely neighborhood, problems. They agitate and militate on a grab bag of current issues: for playgrounds and play streets; for ecological balance and environmental improvement; against slum landlords and real estate speculators who tear down apartment houses and historic areas of cities and towns in order to build more profitable office blocks; against airport noise and overcrowded classrooms; for education reform and legalized abortion; for telecasting "Sesame Street" and against violence on TV.

In Neubiberg, a Munich suburb in which I lived for a number of years, a group of housewives banded together to fight what they considered profiteering on the part of several local supermarkets. They went out in teams to do comparison shopping, printed up the results on handbills, and placed them in mailboxes all over town. In the city of Munich one of the most controversial issues has been whether it is legal or illegal for people to warn motorists of police speed traps ahead. The practice has been that on streets where the police have set up temporary radar traps, residents and other drivers will set out signs—usually hastily painted on a cardboard box or board—warning others to slow down.

The groups are usually small, rarely comprising more than a hundred members, sometimes as few as a dozen. The methods are often amateurish: hand-drawn posters and mimeographed leaflets. Meetings are usually held in someone's living room. The telephone is their most sophisticated means of communication. And funding is limited to whatever can be scrounged from the household budget.

To Americans, such citizen action and participation may not seem unusual at all. In Germany it is an unprecedented phenomenon. It is a reflection of the German's growing awareness of his rights, not to mention a spreading inclination to bend and break the laws in order to get better ones. For that, in effect, is what an action group is doing when it posts bills where none are supposed to be posted, stages a sit-down strike on a plot of land to prevent its being used as a practice firing range by the army, holds protest demonstrations that have not been approved in advance by the police, or sends squatters into an empty building to prevent its being torn down by its owners who want to replace it with a high-rise for commercial purposes.

Simultaneously, it also reflects a greater willingness on the part of Germans to accomplish for themselves, more quickly and efficiently, I might add, what traditionally has always been left to the state, to "them up there" to do. It is important to bear in mind that Germany, at least going back to the days of Bismarck, if not before, has been a highly centralized welfare society. The state was charged with responsibilities which in other societies were the province of private initiative. As a price, it arrogated to itself a measure of control over the citizen's daily life which would be regarded as unacceptable interference in other countries. For, as the Prussian historian Heinrich von Treitschke contended in the nineteenth century, "The state is not there for the citizens but is an end in itself." Toward that end, von Treitschke argued, the state is entitled to control human life to the greatest extent possible.

Today all these traditional values are being questioned and challenged, not necessarily by conscious or organized design but as a consequence of democracy taking roots and of the maturing of the German citizenry. The degree, for example, to which parents in both West and East Germany now demand a decisive voice in the state's education of their children would have been unthinkable a decade or two ago. West Germany's 1949 constitution does say that "educating and bringing up children is the parents' natural right and a duty that is first and foremost theirs." But as recently as the mid-1960s that duty was more or less left entirely to the state to perform. No German parent would have seriously considered questioning the quality of that education in general, let alone such concrete matters as the size of classrooms, the location of schools, the content and reorganization of curricula, or the attitudes, abilities, and behavior of teachers who, after all, are *Beamten*, that is, civil servants representing the power and authority of the state, with life tenure. But this happens with growing frequency these days.

Or who, even a decade ago, could have imagined a father, such as Christian Duevel in Munich, who sued all the way to the German supreme court for the right to keep his two children out of school and to tutor them himself because aircraft noise over their school, located close to Riem Airport, violated their constitutional right to "protection of health."

In Munich, too, a group of eighty parents formed an association, with their own money and on their own initiative, to fight drug abuse among teenagers. The aim: to educate other parents about the dangers and to set up a house in a residential section where up to ten young addicts could be treated. As one parent in the group explained: "Since the problem is growing and the state's measures are inadequate, we felt we had to take matters in our own hands."

Municipal governments and the highly structuralized church organizations do not provide enough preschools and day-care centers to satisfy the demand. Often those that do exist fail to meet the anti-authoritarian pedagogical expectations of modern parents. And private schools and kindergartens are just too expensive. The result: all over West Germany, in hundreds of cities and towns, parents have banded together and formed cooperatives to start their own nursery schools, often with professionally trained mothers and fathers taking turns to supervise the children.

In Frankfurt one citizens' action group armed itself with pickaxes and began ripping up city sidewalks around 120-year-old, but environmentally endangered, linden trees so that the trees would get enough moisture and "be able to breathe again."

"Gone are the days," said Martin Neuffer, the city manager of Hanover, "when the public would simply accept bad government and substandard political performance without protest."

Indeed, there are few issues against which West Germans will not protest, and few for which they will not demonstrate these days. A proposal to build a nuclear power plant near the quaint medieval town of Breisach drew fifty thousand signatures on a protest petition within two weeks after a citizens' action group had launched its campaign. Some sixteen thousand signatures halted (albeit only temporarily) the construction of a twenty-four-story hotel and apartment building on the North Sea resort island of Sylt.

All 1,437 inhabitants of Klausheide—grandparents, parents, children, and grandchildren—came out to stage a sit-in on NATO's Nordhorn Range, a scant mile from their village, in an abortive effort to prevent its continued use for practice bombing. "For years, day in, day out," complained the village schoolmaster's wife, "we have been plagued by the unbearable noise of low-flying jet fighter-bombers. Enough is enough." Helmeted police, armed with shields, tear gas grenades, and water cannon, arrived and blocked off two bridges over the Ems-Vechte canal leading to the target range. The demonstrators built a pontoon walkway of wooden barrels and planks to bring in reinforcements and a day-long supply of sausages and beer. Though eventually the cops won, driving the protesters from the range, and the planes returned the following day, the demonstration, described as a "mixture of Woodstock and Paris Commune," was unique by German standards.

The techniques employed by action-minded citizens have been borrowed from those used by demonstrating students and the APO, the extra-parliamentary opposition, in the 1960s. These in turn had been borrowed from the protest arsenal of American youth: marches, posters, handbills, sit-ins, political happenings, and a heaping dose of ridicule and humor.

The organizers and activists are mostly young, white-collar, and educated. Many are veterans of the student demonstrations and quite a few are members of the Social Democratic party's militant Juso, that is, young socialist organization. Neither age, political leanings, or social standing are bars to participation, however. The oldest "active citizen" identified to date was also an aristocrat—Margarete von Gevernits, seventy-five, proud grandmother of twelve. A Munich police patrol picked her up late one night as she was surreptitiously pasting black-bordered "mourning posters" on building walls to protest the incursion of banks and office blocks into what had once been one of the city's most idyllic residential areas.

The movement—if it can even be called that, for it is so spontaneous, disparate, and varied in aims and objectives—has caused no end of controversy and discussion. Books have been written, lectures delivered, and seminars held, all with several basic questions in mind: What does it really signify? Is it proto-revolutionary? Is it progressive or retrogressive?

By circumventing their elected representatives aren't citizens jeopardizing democracy and encouraging anarchism?

Sebastian Haffner, the Anglo-German publicist, may have come closest to the answer in a book about Buergerinitiativen published in 1974. In contrast to American democracy, he pointed out, most of the European democracies, including Germany's, replaced existing monarchies and simply assimilated the bureaucracies and administrative structures of those monarchies. These administrations were accustomed to controlling from the top on down and still do. Hierarchical and very formalized, they administer in a very authoritarian manner, and the power of the parliaments is largely limited to exercising some control over them. The European democracies are indirect democracies, in sharp contrast to America's, which is very direct and in which nearly all public officials, from the president on down to the local dogcatcher are elected rather than appointed. Whereas the American citizen's control is often direct, the German's passes through so many filters that, in the end, he stands as helpless and powerless before the authority of whatever civil servant he is dealing with as in the kaiser's days.

"This," says Haffner, "is the condition which the Buergerinitiativen are trying to change. Not always consciously and certainly not always with success. But if there is any ideology behind them, then it is the concept of total or direct democracy based on the American model. Again and again you will hear from the initiators of these actions the argument that merely filling in a ballot every four or even two years, only to be subordinate to authority in the meantime, does not suffice. Democratic principles, they contend, must prevail in daily life; the citizen must have a say in the administrative decisions that concern him, and the officials that make such decisions must be as accountable to the citizen as the elected member of parliament."

In the process these Buergerinitiativen may break the law, not to mention the holy principle of majority rule, but as Wolf Dieter Narr, a Berlin University political scientist, has stressed, "they do so only temporarily and not with anarchistic lawlessness in mind, but in order to have better laws."

This German longing for more participatory democracy, for a larger and more influential voice in the decision-making process, has found expression not only in government but in business as well. The most striking example is the corporate annual general meeting. Unlike the somber, businesslike sessions in the United States or Great Britain, the annual shareholders' meetings of large German corporations are action-packed dramas—something of a cross between a public forum and a political convention. They are replete with fiery oratory, grass-roots democracy, lectures by little old ladies in tennis shoes, frequent outbursts of temper, occasional violence, and invariably, rivers of free beer and mountains of free sausages.

The price of admission is a minimum of one share, and inevitably hundreds, often thousands, of such small shareholders attend. In fact, an annual meeting attended by less than 1,000 is considered small. The Volkswagen corporation rents the Wolfsburg municipal auditorium for its yearly show and usually draws a capacity crowd of 2,500. AEG-Tele-funken generally fills Berlin's 3,000-seat Congress Hall. And the reason "only" 1,700 shareholders turned out for the Bayer Chemical Corpora-tion's 1974 meeting was because the meeting was competing with a decisive game between West Germany and Poland in the World Cup soccer championship that day.

Since everyone is entitled to a say, shareholders' meetings go on interminably. They are considered short and businesslike by the financial press if they last only six hours or so; ten is considered average and the all-time record was set by Audi-NSU Motor Works, whose 1971 meeting ran for a solid twenty-seven hours.

Widespread public buying of shares is a development almost as remarkable as Buergerinitiativen. Until the early 1960s, it was almost unheard of in West Germany. It increased in popularity with the partial denationalization of Preussag (the Prussian Mining and Milling Corpora-tion) and Volkswagen (West Germany's largest single enterprise) and the issuance of so-called *Volksaktien,* literally "people's shares." With diversified ownership came a growing desire to have some say in the running of the companies, even when ownership was limited to just a few shares.

Thanks to changes in West German corporate law prescribing more transparency and accountability, and thanks, also, to the gradual democra-tization of the society as a whole, company managements appear determined to stage the annual meetings as openly and democratically as possible. In fact, the annual general meeting is becoming a kind of corporate parliament in which minority shareholders act out the role of—not always loyal—opposition to the "government," that is, to the supervisory board and management. Though loud, boisterous, and critical, they never, or rarely, win. Ultimately, management can always count on the support of the large and majority shareholders and the representatives of the big depository banks with their huge blocks of proxy votes.

But invariably the point of opposition to company policies is made, usually most effectively and eloquently by representatives of small-shareholder groups—investment counsellors speaking for their clients and paid executives of such organizations as the Association for the Protection of Stock Owners or the Bonn-based German Society for the Protection of Savings. These men, who travel the annual meeting circuit and take the floor at nearly every session, have been called the "brimstone-and-fire preachers of capitalism."

By far the best known and most vociferous among them is Kurt Fiebich, a Duesseldorf money manager who, armed with a briefcase full of proxies, descends on every major meeting to give managements and supervisory boards hell. Renowned for his sharp repartee and quick mind, he will pass judgment on executive performance with such quips as, "When are you going to stop milking this sacred cow?" Or, "It's time to fatten this Christmas goose again." But Fiebich, for all his colorful oratory, has no illusions about the power of the small shareholder and the annual meeting. "The elections of corporate supervisory boards in this country," he said in an interview, "are about as democratic as those to Russia's Supreme Soviet." And that is what he has set out to change.

Unlike corporate meetings elsewhere, those in West Germany are also decidedly political affairs. Board chairmen and chief executives seem to make a special point of lacing their reports on company performance with their partisan political views. Attacks on or praise of government foreign and economic policies, tax and trade legislation, and environmental control regulations are commonplace.

As managements have politicized the meetings, so have many of the shareholders, especially the younger ones. In fact, among some political activists it has become fashionable to buy one or two shares as an entrance ticket to a corporate meeting which they can then transform into a political clambake for attacks on company policy. One of the best known among them is Dr. Wolff Geisler, a Bonn physician born midway through World War II, who, together with a group of "new left" political soulmates, launched a mini-war against all large German corporations involved in the construction of the Cabora Bassa dam project in Portuguese Mozambique. Their main argument, at least until the collapse of the Caetano regime in Lisbon in the spring of 1974, was that these corporations are abetting murder and genocide through their entrepreneurial support of the Portuguese colonial administration.

In 1972 Geisler and some of his friends, each owning one share, attempted to storm the annual meeting of the Siemens Electrical Corp., one of the principal contractors in Mozambique, and to physically wrest control of the podium and public address system from the company's chairman, Peter von Siemens. Police were called. Geisler and his supporters were removed from the hall and subsequently convicted of breach of the peace by a Munich court. Although he was fined four hundred deutsch marks (DM 400), the judge stressed that Geisler had been "motivated by pure and noble ideals." Similar demonstrations and attempts at filibustering have been staged at other meetings, especially those of companies whose environmental policies are open to attack.

Incongruous as it may sound, there is also a trend toward participant democracy in East Germany. In fact, while the GDR is anything but the democracy it pretends to be, neither is it as undemocratic and regimented as it is made out to be.

Germany's repudiation of Hitler was not a spontaneous uprising against tyranny but a renunciation forced upon it in the throes of defeat. In the wake of conquest each victor attempted to rebuild Germany in his own image. In the West this represented an endeavor—differing somewhat, to be sure from British to French to American zones of occupation—to transplant the great tenets of Anglo-Saxon democracy and the ideal of the Enlightenment upon a society that had misunderstood the Age of Reason and had turned its own century of nationalism into an aberration of myths that bore the fruits of Prussian hegemony. In the East the situation was analogous. East Germany's population did not stage a revolution. It neither revolted against the Nazis when they were in power, nor participated actively in the reformation of society imposed upon it by the Soviet conquerors and the German Communists who assisted them. Backed by Soviet tanks and bayonets, Walter Ulbricht and his followers expropriated the holdings of Junkers and industrialists. They subjugated the upper-middle class. They convulsed the civil service and the judiciary, both festering with the mold of reaction. But it was not a revolution, for the social-political upheaval of East Germany was imposed from outside.

However, the instability of Ulbricht's position as Soviet proconsul in a Germany whose ultimate fate remained in abeyance, and the messianic nature of communism itself, compelled him to attempt a "revolution" of his own. It demanded far more than simply expropriating capitalists, nationalizing the means of production, collectivizing agriculture, and securing the Socialist Unity party's monopoly over the state. It required a metamorphosis of the character of East German man—his sense of values, views on property, notions about God, perspective of history, relationship to fellow beings, concepts of morality, and his attitude toward authority. This transformation of East German man, of course, had to conform to basic Marxist-Leninist tenets; that is, rejection of a permissive social order in which everyone follows his own pursuits and impulses, with the emphasis instead on collectivity and subordination of individual interests to that of the group, the collective. Moreover, Communist dogma seems to demand inner approval of this transformation, so the East German regime badgered its subjects with incessant propaganda in order to persuade them to embrace their new world voluntarily.

The result is a society in which labor, the factory, the collective, and the building of socialism have become raisons d'être—the end, not the means, to a better life; a society which demands acquiescence and promises the rewards of absolution and socialist salvation. But above all, it is a society committed to the principle of collectivity, to a new philosophy of togetherness. This has produced a unique way of thinking.

East Germans have been taught to think in terms of "our team, our comrades, our factory, our collective." Newspapers are published by "editorial collectives." Waiters in restaurants are organized into "service collectives." Scientific work is conducted by "research collectives." Apartment houses are run by "housing collectives." Children are taught by "teaching collectives." And of course, repeated attempts are made to organize artists, writers, and composers into "collectives," usually with devastating artistic and literary results.

Alien as all this may sound, repugnant as this induced collectivism may be to those nurtured on the principle that the rights of the individual are inviolable, the "collective spirit" must be seen as a uniquely East German form of teamwork, indeed of participatory democracy. The degree to which older East German citizens merely give lip service to it and the degree to which they actually believe in it—that is open to speculation. As open, perhaps, as the question of the degree to which West Germans of the older and middle generations are really imbued with the spirit of democracy. But among the young, those who have known little else other than the East German system of communism into which they were born, the spirit of collective democracy has taken root and forms a generational attitude today. They really consider the state as "ours." And despite its totalitarian nature, their attitude toward that state and its official representatives is, in a sense, more constructive than the West Germans' to theirs. And why not, when every East German has been taught to address those representatives as "Comrade." There is more than a mere formalistic difference between addressing the cop who tickets you for speeding as "Comrade Policeman" and "Herr Hauptwachtmeister."

Ultimately, of course, the test of any democracy is the willingness of its citizens to reject and protest against injustice. East Germany was put to the test in August 1968 when its troops joined those of the Soviet Union, Poland, Hungary, and Bulgaria in the invasion and occupation of Czechoslovakia. In contrast to most of Eastern Europe and the Communist bloc, the East Germans were able to get an uncensored impression of what had transpired in Czechoslovakia before and after the invasion. While the Russians had been forced to extract their information from between the lines of *Pravda* and *Izvestia*—Western radio broadcasts having again been jammed—and other East Europeans were largely dependent on scraps of news and truth that had passed through the censorship screen, the East Germans had gotten a close-up view of developments in Czechoslovakia, thanks to West German television which reaches 75 percent of the population of the GDR.

The East German reaction to the invasion came as a surprise. The majority were obviously apathetic, most likely because they had failed to understand the real meaning and significance of the reforms initiated by Alexander Dubcek or because they simply did not care. Not a few actually approved of the invasion and suppression of the Prague spring. But a vast number condemned the invasion on principle, and East Germany's participation in it specifically, on moral grounds.

Within the first week an estimated five thousand East Berliners had gone to the Czechoslovak embassy on Schoenhauser Allee to sign protest petitions against the occupation and to declare their solidarity with the Prague reformers. Some even brought flowers and gifts of money and jewelry. In the southern regions of the GDR there were numerous incidents of anti-regime and anti-Soviet slogans being painted on walls and the distribution of clandestine oppositional leaflets. In Frankfurt-on-the-Oder, three days after the invasion, police were busy removing signs reading Long Live Dubcek! Down With Ulbricht! and Russians Out of Czechoslovakia! from a downtown building wall. Similar slogans were painted in other cities. In Karl-Marx-Stadt swastikas had been painted on Soviet tanks bivouacked there. Between August 22 and 25 platoons of Volkspolizei went on patrol in downtown Erfurt to forestall planned protest demonstrations. In Leipzig motorized and dog-walking police patrols were called out to protect the Soviet consulate. In Schwerin police with water cannon were used to disperse a demonstration on the market square.

And from all over East Germany came reports of arrests and trials. Significantly, those apprehended, indicted, and subsequently convicted could not be classified as "opponents of the regime" but as loyal Communists themselves, who had seen in the Dubcek policy the hope and salvation of the political system to which they were committed. Most of them were young—in their late teens or early twenties. And a large number were the children of some of the most prominent officials and intellectuals of East Germany: for example, Sandra Weigel, the niece of Bertolt Brecht; Erika Berthold, the daughter of the director of the Institute of Marxism-Leninism; Inge Hunziger, daughter of a prominent sculptor; and the two teenage sons of the noted, dissident chemist and Marxist philosopher, Robert Havemann.

What surprised most observers was the scope and intensity of the East German protest. Moreover, it demonstrated that despite many years of suppression, the spirit of "reform communism" and "democratic social-ism" continued to flourish. On the other hand, the massiveness of the repressive measures against the protesters left no doubt about the totalitarian nature of the Germany that is on the other side of the Berlin Wall. On paper, of course, that Germany appears to be a democracy. At least, it has all the formal attributes of one: a constitution which guarantees its citizens all the basic human rights; a government elected by and accountable to parliament; a parliament, the *Volkskammer*, answerable to and elected by the people with a secret ballot. There is even a multiparty system, for in addition to the Socialist Unity party, East Germany has a Christian Democratic Union, a Liberal Democratic, a Peasant, and a National Democratic party.

But it is all on paper. The parties do not compete against each other.

They nominate candidates according to a predetermined formula for a "national front" list of which the voter can either approve or disapprove. And approval is usually 99.9 percent "Ivory pure." Despite proportional representation for the other parties in parliament, none of their members has so much as a whisper in the actual decision-making process. The government is composed entirely of members of the SED, that is, the Socialist Unity party.

On the other hand, in 1967 East Germany did become the first Communist country to present the voters with ballots listing more candidates than positions to be filled. The East German electoral system calls for placing 20 percent more names on the list than needed. All candidates are still on the same "national front" ticket, but voters can choose them individually. The preferred candidates are at the top of the ballot. If one of them receives less than 50 percent of the votes cast, he is disqualified and the "reserve candidate" with the highest number of votes moves up a slot to take his place and becomes a member of the Volkskammer. Though hardly what we would consider a choice, it is at least more than a mere echo, and while not yet an election, it is at least a selection process.

Some East Germans, moreover, claim that they exercise far more influence over their elected representatives than is generally assumed by Western observers. "We may not have a choice of parties," an East German steelworker once told me, "but we know who the candidates are, and they are subjected to a careful screening from everyone before they are even listed on the ballot. They have to answer questions in factory and neighborhood meetings and the cross-examination is often quite stiff. In West Germany," he added, "what choice does the voter really have? He can pick between parties, but he has little influence on the candidates they have proposed. These are nominated by a party machine over which the members, not to mention the vast majority of voters who do not belong to a party, have no control. Ninety-nine times out of a hundred, the voter won't even know anything about the candidates when the time comes to cast a ballot. The West jokes about our single ticket and the 'national front,' but plenty of people here prefer knowing all about the candidate before the election than having to choose between names which mean nothing and being represented by men and women over whom they have no leverage."

As anyone who has watched an East German pre-election campaign can attest, there is a considerable measure of truth in this. Candidates, or those proposed for a spot on the ticket, are taken through the mill before the final decision is made. They will be asked detailed and specific questions: What does he propose to do about improving the transit system? Why aren't there more playgrounds for children? And why not more nursery schools? Why is the supply of fresh meat so sporadic? What will he do to get more fresh vegetables to market?

"My constituents seem to think I'm Santa Claus," one young member of the Volkskammer, thirty-five-year-old Rolf Poche, from the town of Zahna, north of Leipzig, once complained to a Western correspondent. "I can't afford to make empty promises in a campaign."

And the East German monthly *Weltbuehne* says: "There is no noisy competition between political opponents here. We have no need for the meaningless falderal that accompanies bourgeois-capitalist elections in order to dupe the voter into thinking he is a decision-making subject rather than a manipulated object."

These arguments might even have some validity if East German parliaments had any power or influence. But in fact, the Volkskammer is basically a rubber-stamp legislature. It meets no more than three or four times a year, and then only for a few days each time, and generally approves all proposed legislation unanimously and without debate. What it does, in effect, is ratify and codify decisions reached and implemented long before by the leadership of East Germany's ruling Socialist Unity party. Only once in its twenty-five-year-history has the Volkskammer passed a bill without the usual obligatory unanimity. That was in March 1972, when the regime freed all deputies to vote according to their conscience on a measure legalizing abortion-on-demand. Some fourteen voted against the bill, another eight abstained—a precedent-setting example of democracy in action for any Communist parliament anywhere. Unfortunately, it has not happened again since then.

West Germany's elections may be, as *Weltbuehne* put it, "bourgeois-capitalist falderal." But the Bundestag rubber-stamps nothing. On the contrary, over the decades since its constitution in 1949 it has grown steadily into the supreme law-making and policy-setting instrument of the country. As it has flexed its muscles of legislative power and control over the administration, public confidence in the electoral process, parliamentary democracy and the separation of powers has grown too. Three-fourths of adult Germans may still harbor the suspicion that despite periodic elections, "politicians do more or less what they want to do anyhow." But conversely, three-fourths also believe a democracy to be the best possible form of government, a scant 4 percent think some other form would be better, and the rest have no opinion. An overwhelming 80 percent would oppose attempts by either a neo-Nazi or radical left-wing party, such as the Communists, to come to power.

In 1951, according to the Allensbach Opinion Research Institute, only 32 percent of West Germans believed that if they wrote their Bundestag deputy a letter, he would actually read it. Today nearly twice as many express confidence that their letters would be read and even acted upon. And they know who that deputy is. More than 60 percent were able to identify him, at least by political party or name.

As confidence in democracy has taken roots, so has West German awareness of basic rights and the rule of law, as well as the readiness to defend them against encroachments. This, it is important to bear in mind, could not have been taken for granted, because these are rights which are new to German society and which up to a generation ago were still quite alienable.

In May 1969 Allensbach researchers asked a representative sample of West Germans which basic rights—for example, freedom of speech and the press, the secret ballot, secrecy of the mails, the right to choose one's place of work, and others—they would be prepared to surrender as the price for Soviet-approved reunification with East Germany. Some 12 percent of those polled cited secrecy of the mail; 10 percent, freedom of assembly; but an overwhelming 56 percent said they would give up no rights or freedoms at all. Probing deeper, the interviewers alluded to violent student demonstrations taking place at that time and suggested that the constitution allows too much freedom and that the right to demonstrate should be curbed. Some 39 percent agreed, but a majority of 53 percent said flatly that the freedom to demonstrate should not be restricted, even when it is misused by some people.

Deep-seated as the principle of parliamentary democracy may now be in the West German psyche, there is no shortage of proposals—some overdue, some misguided, and some potentially dangerous—to change and improve the system. These range from altering the seating arrangement in the Bundestag so as to encourage freer and more spontaneous debate, to the demand of the more radical Young Socialists for the introduction of the "imperative mandate" which would bind deputies to the decisions and orders of their local party organizations. All the proposals, in a sense, stem from an inherent contradiction in the electoral system and the structure of the Bundestag: namely, that it is only partially representative of, and accountable to, the people.

To avoid the mistakes of Weimar and to prevent the tragic history of Germany's first democracy from repeating itself, the Federal Republic's founding fathers introduced a mixed system of direct and proportional representation, protected by a number of important safeguards against the multitude of tiny parties and factions that had turned the old *Reichstag* into a powerless, ineffectual debating society.

Of the Bundestag's 496 members, only half are elected directly from 248 constituencies in which the candidate who obtains a plurality is the winner and becomes a deputy. The other 248 deputies entered parliament because they were listed on their party's ticket. In a federal election, each voter has two votes: one for the candidate in his district, one for a party ticket, called a *Liste*. When the polls close and the ballots are counted, a highly complicated mathematical system is employed to apportion seating in accordance to the percentage of the total vote cast for each party. This system enables a small party, such as the Free Democrats, which fails to win a plurality in any of the 248 constituencies, to enter parliament anyway, with a delegation of *Listen* deputies proportional to its percentage of the total popular vote. The principal safeguard is that a party must obtain at least 5 percent of the total vote before it can be represented at all (unless, of course, one of its candidates should win a plurality in one of the 248 districts).

This system has led to what now appears to be a fairly stable three-party parliament and has excluded dangerous fringe groups and small radical parties. It has undoubtedly made West Germany eminently safer for democracy than the Weimar Republic was.

But it also has some distinct disadvantages, aggravated in part by the tightly organized, machine nature of the principal political parties and by the nature of the parliamentary system itself. Because of his dependency on the party organization and the requirement for factional cohesion in order to pass legislation on the floor, the Bundestag deputy enjoys far less autonomy, not to mention prestige, than, for example, a British MP or an American congressman. He also tends to be less responsive and accountable to his constituents than to the party which either nominated him as a candidate in the district he represents or gave him a "safe" place on the ticket. Moreover, because the administration, or government, is composed of deputies from the party or coalition which has a majority in parliament, the legislator who belongs to that group is more likely to support it unequivocally, and the deputy who belongs to the minority is more likely to oppose it, regardless of the merits of the issue up for discussion or vote. Debate on the floor tends largely to follow the patterns and directions laid down by the powerful front-benchers and party whips. When it comes to a vote there is virtually no crossing of party lines unless deputies have been specifically freed to vote according to their conscience, as was the case with the extension of the statute of limitations for Nazi crimes in 1965 or a bill legalizing abortion in the spring of 1974.

Given the relative unchangeability of the system itself, numerous members of the Bundestag, especially its younger, freshmen deputies, have been proposing ways to "democratize" and to enliven it and at the same time to enhance their own prestige and influence. One of the most active in this regard was Dr. Eugen Gerstenmaier, for fifteen years the Bundestag's president, a position equal to that of the speaker of the U. S. House of Representatives. What worried Gerstenmaier in the 1960s, for example, was the possibility that the Bundestag's lackluster sessions, frequently marked by tedious, schoolmasterly monologues to a near-empty house, would stifle West Germany's embryonic democracy. The years during which foxy, imperious Konrad Adenauer reigned as chancellor, had undermined the will of most deputies to disagree. And the tenure of Ludwig Erhard, renowned for his indecision, had given even the most argumentative members of the house little meat into which they could sink their debating teeth. Instead of talking things out on the floor of parliament, deputies fled to the infinitely larger and more rewarding platform of interviews and columns in the press. It was a period which one CDU back-bencher described to me at the time as "the era of the illustrated-magazine parliament and legislation by interview."

Gerstenmaier, first of all, arranged to have more Bundestag debates televised live and nationwide. Then he introduced the "topical hour," a sixty-minute debating period which could be called virtually at a moment's notice at the request of at least thirty members of the house. The ground rules were designed to compel members to think and speak on their feet and to get their ideas across quickly. Each speaker was limited to five minutes and not permitted to use a script. To prevent the five minutes from being exceeded, Gerstenmaier ordered a liveried house messenger to deliver a note to each speaker after four minutes with a warning that read: "You have one minute left." Members of the administration were exempted from the time limit, but to assure they didn't misuse their freedom to dominate the period with monologues or filibusters, their time was not counted against the total hour. "This is sure to benefit parliamentary procedure," the usually conservative and stodgy *Frankfurter Allgemeine Zeitung* editorialized on its front page. And it did.

Gerstenmaier also imposed heavier penalties for absences, in the hope that a full house would stimulate more discussion. He enlarged the powers and enhanced the prestige of parliamentary committees, though to this day the practice of open hearings has still not really taken root. They are exceptions rather than the rule. And for years he tried to rearrange the deputies' desks in the plenary chamber. Instead of sitting like obedient schoolchildren in classroom-amphitheater style, with the government seated teacherlike on a raised bench at the head of the hall, he wanted government and opposition parties to face each other as they do in England. But the chamber was too small. Now a new parliament building is to be constructed, with completion scheduled for 1977. Though the government will still be seated at the front of its chamber, deputies will be placed in a horseshoe that will enable minority and majority members to face each other.

All Bundestag deputies seem to agree that what parliament needs are better working conditions for its members. For the first twenty years or so of the Federal Republic these were catastrophic. Parliament was located in the same old teachers' college on the banks of the Rhine in which the constitutional convention had given birth to the Federal Republic in 1949. The only addition was an office tract in which deputies were often housed two and more to a cubicle-sized office and shared the services of a typing pool.

The facilities seemed deliberately designed to underscore the role of Bonn as a *provisional* capital. And for many years proposals to build more spacious quarters were rejected on the grounds that they would contribute to making Bonn a permanent seat of the government and, in effect, hinder the goal of German reunification and undermine claims to Berlin as the capital of a united Germany. Finally, even the most dedicated reunificationists began to realize that it might take decades to fulfill their goals, if they could ever be met. Work began on the twenty-two-story parliamentary office building, nicknamed "tall Eugene" for its planner, Gerstenmaier, in which deputies now conduct the increasingly complex business of making laws.

By American standards, the Bundestag deputy is still grossly under-privileged. His office is barely large enough for a desk, a few file cabinets, a divan, and a couple of easy chairs for visitors. If he is lucky enough to have an administrative assistant, he must pay for him out of his meager expense fund and share with him the office as well as the single phone to which each deputy is entitled.

"But it's opulent compared to what we used to have," said a former member of parliament, now the administrative aide to Helmut Sauer, the CDU's youngest deputy.

"I am not suggesting that we need or even want the pay or vast superstructure of the average American congressman," one young Social Democratic deputy told me. "But the physical and financial restrictions under which we operate presently make it impossible for us to do our constitutional duty, much less meet our democratic obligations. Just consider that nearly a kilogram of parliamentary papers and documents lands on my desk every day. That is more than I and my assistant can read. But they should be read—in addition to all the other things we should read to keep us abreast of developments. We do not have time to prepare for committee meetings and we do not really know anything about the bills on which we are supposed to vote.

"A primary function of parliament," he added, "is to exercise control over the government and the administration. That function is not being fulfilled. We lack the power, prestige, and authority with which to penetrate the labyrinthine, bureaucratic administration and to retrieve the information we would need. Even assuming we could retrieve it, no deputy, no group of deputies, no committee, has sufficient trained and specialized manpower to digest and analyze it.

"This is my first term and I'll probably run again. But I can tell you I am already sorely disappointed and frustrated. I am no more than a small cog in a vast machine over which I exercise no control. I owe my constituents something more and something better. This is not what they sent me here for."

If some members of this young deputy's party had their way, he would enjoy even less independence than he does today. These are the most radical among the SPD's Young Socialists (Jusos) who advocate introduction of the "imperative mandate" to compel the deputy, under penalty of recall or impeachment should he fail to comply, to vote according to the dictates and directives of his constituents. As constituents, however, they see, not the voters in the district, but the local party organization that nominated and placed him on the ballot.

"Each deputy," says Hubertus Schroer, twenty-nine, a Munich Juso, "should have his orientation among the grass-roots group that elected him and should subordinate himself to their control." Heide Wieczorek-Zeul, thirty-two, the Juso national chairman, once went so far as to insist that this principle of "instruction" should apply not only to basic policy questions but to day-to-day parliamentary work. Reinhart Klimmt, thirty-one, state Juso chairman in the Saarland, regards the "instructed deputy" and the "imperative mandate" as "important means to break down establishment structures."

The proposal is not all that new, and to support their argument the proponents will quote at length from both Jean Jacques Rousseau and Karl Marx. Nor, at first glance, is it all as abhorrent as its opponents suggest. Certainly it raises some basic questions of what democracy is all about. Should the deputy be a "servant of the people," or should he, as Max Weber, the German sociologist once insisted, be "a sovereign elected by the people"? In theory, at least, the imperative mandate, as proposed by the Jusos, is the acme of democratization, for it would make the parliamentary deputy directly accountable and responsive to the instructions and wishes of his voters. Though, as Marx's friend Friedrich Engels pointed out a century ago: "Were all bodies of electors to impose an imperative mandate on their delegates, the assemblies of delegates and the debates they hold would be quite superfluous."

In practice, of course, the Juso proposal would spell the end of representative and parliamentary democracy, for what these young theoreticians demand is a deputy who would be wholly answerable, not to the voters in his district, but to the party organization, which, of course, they hope ultimately to control. Instead of leading to more democracy it would lead to an even more intensified form of "party democracy"—a huge step toward the system in East Germany and the Soviet Union. Moreover, it would violate the West German constitution which states that a deputy must not be bound by instructions, must act only according to the dictates of his conscience, and must represent "all the people [in his constituency], not a single party or group."

Misguided and potentially pernicious as the imperative-mandate concept may be, it is, however, a further manifestation of the West German longing for more and better democracy.

That longing has found especial expression in recent years in growing interest in those periods and events of German history which can be held up as ideals of democracy, as examples of "maturity of citizenship."

No citizen has done more to stimulate that interest than former President Gustav Heinemann, whose maternal great-grandfather, Gustav Jakob Walter, was one of the revolutionaries of 1848–49. It was Heinemann who provided the impetus for a revision of schoolbooks in order to "bring to light those episodes in our history which deserve to be imbedded more strongly in the consciousness of our people." Heinemann instituted the yearly school-essay contests devoted to the "democratic events" in German history. And it was Heinemann who, in the early 1970s, motivated the founding of a museum devoted to German revolutionary and freedom movements. It is located in the Palace of Rastatt—the building in which the last of the 1849 rebels surrendered to Prussian troops and were executed.

The revolution of 1848–49 was indeed one of the shining moments in German history, one that has not been given its due, but whose legacy has survived to the present. It gave Germany its first elected parliament, a constitution, and principles of human rights such as freedom of the press, freedom of religion and conscience, and the right to education and equal opportunity, which were adopted in both the constitutions of the Weimar Republic of 1919 and the Federal Republic of 1949. Like so many epochs of freedom and democracy in German history, it was short-lived, and those who had launched it were either executed, imprisoned, or forced to flee abroad—the vast majority of them to the United States, where many took a leading role in the struggle to abolish slavery and acquitted themselves heroically on the Union side in the Civil War. But despite its failure, that revolution is proof that the juices of democracy run deeper in German veins than has generally been believed.

"That revolution produced a constitution," Heinemann said at the opening ceremony of the Rastatt Museum in June 1974. "It was Germany's first constitution. It was also the only one which a mass popular movement attempted to defend with arms. Men and women fought for it here in Rastatt. They bled and they died for it. . . .

"It is often said that history is written by the victors. It is true that the German revolution of 1848–49, like others in our history, was crushed.

And it is also true that the victors—the kings, the princes, and their lackeys—did everything in their power to slander that revolutionary movement in the history books, to obliterate it, and distort it in the minds of the people.

"But who are the victors and who are the defeated? Are those who shot down German unity and democratic freedoms one hundred and twenty-five years ago really the victors? Weren't they the ones who ultimately led our nation to shame and to total collapse? Ultimately, were not they the losers, and the winners those who fought for what today we regard as our free, democratic system? . . .

"As federal president I am not the nation's history teacher. My aim is only to draw attention to those movements in our history which provided the foundations for our democracy today, to bring them out of hiding, and to interweave them with the present. My aim is to demonstrate that our constitution of today does indeed have roots in the past and is more than merely a document imposed upon us by the victors after 1945. . . .

"This museum," Heinemann stressed, "is not intended as a hall of fame, as a Walhalla of German freedom. It should not evoke silent reverence. Instead of providing answers, it should provoke questions, not the least of which is why so many freedom movements in our history failed."

Thirty years after the defeat of the Third Reich, Germans, especially those of the younger generation, have at last begun to ask those questions. And in asking, they are at last making Germany safe for democracy.

3

The New Order

IT WAS a sunny day in August 1950 when John J. McCloy, then U. S. high commissioner for Germany, called together some dozen American news correspondents at his hideaway in Koenigstein near Frankfurt. The purpose: a secret briefing on Secretary of State Dean Acheson's decision to push for a West German military contribution to the recently created North Atlantic Treaty Organization and the defense of the West.

Over a convivial brunch with Pilsner beer, McCloy was asked by one of the newsmen whether he thought the Germans would go along with the scheme.

"Why, just give me a brass band and a loudspeaker truck," he replied. "Then let me march from Lake Constance in the south to the Kiel Canal up north, and I will have a German army of a million men behind me—all eager-eyed."

No reading of postwar German public opinion was ever quite as wrong. None has proven to be as consistently wrong for so long a time. Yet it was on the basis of that misreading that the West German "un-army" came into being. It was from the start, and remains to the present, a *"ja-aber"*—a "yes-but"—army which has nothing whatsoever in common with the lingering world image of a strapping, jack-booted, helmeted force of arrogant young warriors who goosestep with mechanical precision and follow orders with puppetlike obedience. For, in ultimately saying "yes" to rearmament, the West Germans also said, "but" only under conditions which would protect the state from the soldier while the soldier would be busy protecting the state from its enemies. That was new to Germany, and the historically founded contradiction has to this day not been entirely resolved.

The idea of West German rearmament was born in the hysterical weeks and months of the American retreat in Korea and Soviet sabre-rattling in Europe. Seeing a Western Germany entirely dependent on limited American, British, and French occupation forces and a Western Europe virtually naked before a putative Soviet armed thrust across the Rhine, American strategic thinkers in those last years of the Truman administration were convinced that a West German defense contribution was absolutely necessary.

But not the Germans who, remembering the last war barely ended, were either passive, indifferent, or opposed. Moreover, as chancellor of their new government they had Konrad Adenauer, a man whose favorite quote was, "I am proud of the fact that I have never worn a uniform." Of him it had been said that he avoided joining an anti-Hitler plot because when he arrived at an organizing session he noticed two German generals' caps hanging in the cloakroom. "This isn't for me," he said. "Anything that two or more German generals are involved in is certain to fail."

It was a Germany in which a bright, up-and-coming young Bavarian politician, Franz-Josef Strauss, had made his first mark in a 1947 local election by proclaiming: "Any man who takes up a gun in his hand again ought to lose an arm." By 1950, when the pressure to rebuild an army was on, he was saying: "Why should we shed our blood to defend a border set up by the stupidity of others?" Six years later, of course, the same Franz-Josef Strauss was minister of defense and the new army's peacetime commander-in-chief.

Not only were the Germans war-weary, but feeling that their patriotic fervor had been so badly misused and betrayed by the Nazis, they were unwilling to don uniform again for any cause. Moreover many of them, in particular the Social Democratic opposition, predicted—correctly as history has shown—that rearmament under the Allied aegis would result in the country's permanent division between West and East.

The generals in the Pentagon, however, panicked by predictions of Soviet aggression, were mesmerized by the vision of West German divisions. They were determined to have a German army, no matter what anyone might say. And eventually they swung Adenauer around to their point of view.

Not that he required all that much persuading. Der Alte, a crafty political fox who had twice been offered the chancellorship of the Weimar Republic and twice turned it down, soon recognized the political potential in rearmament.

He too was aware of the possibility—more accurately, perhaps, the likelihood—that rearmament would seal the partition of Germany. Looking backward, we now know it was a possibility he was only too happy to explore. Adenauer had always had somewhat of a separatist streak in him, plus a dyed-in-the-hide contempt for Prussia and Prussia's dominant role in the German Reich. On several occasions as lord-mayor of Cologne in the 1920s he had toyed with the idea of creating a separate German Rhineland republic. It would be Catholic in its religious orientation, pro-French and Western in its foreign policy, and free of domination by Protestant, eastward-looking Prussia. Nothing ever came of these various schemes, but the idea lingered in his mind right through Nazi-enforced retirement from public life, and it was still there when he reentered the political stage in 1945. At that time he told an American journalist: "A Prussian is nothing but a Slav who has forgotten who his grandfather was." In a newspaper interview in 1946 he said: "It is my belief that Germany's future capital should be situated in the southwest rather than in Berlin which is far to the east. The new capital should lie somewhere where Germany's windows are wide open to the West. Whoever makes Berlin the new capital will be creating a new spiritual Prussia." Moreover, his political astuteness also convinced him that his predominantly Catholic Christian Democratic party could best survive in such a rump, Western Germany: a Germany in which the Protestant Prussians and the left-leaning Protestant Saxons would have no vote with which to defeat the CDU at the polls. Beyond that, Adenauer also recognized in rearmament a powerful lever with which he could extort ever more independence for the infant Federal Republic from the West, especially from the Americans.

Thus, the West German army was conceived—not without massive political opposition, of course, which culminated in the resignation of Adenauer's minister of the interior, Gustav Heinemann. Not without powerful international opposition, either—particularly from France, which finally agreed to German rearmament only within the framework of the then-popular idea of a European Defense Community and a European army. It took until October 1952 for the complex of treaties to be signed. Then the French parliament suddenly rejected them, and the European Defense Community was stillborn. The only thing left to do was to integrate the proposed German force into NATO, which was finally done in 1955. And then there were countless delays so that it took until the mid-1960s, when the cold war was virtually over, before the Bundeswehr reached its projected strength of the twelve divisions which the United States had called for in 1950.

From the outset the average West German responded to the new army in the manner of a porcupine under attack. He was opposed and raised his quills in an attempt to keep it at maximum distance. Instead of flocking to the colors a million strong, as McCloy had predicted, vast numbers of young Germans registered as conscientious objectors. The first volunteers were jeered when they appeared on the streets in uniform and, in some cases, were even physically attacked. That was a unique development among a people who in the past had been so proud of their armies, whose pride in nationhood had found almost exclusive expression in militarism and soldiering.

From the outset, too, West Germany's leaders did all in their power to prevent the army from again becoming the focus of what they regarded as false national pride and free of the trappings that might make it the object of false hero-worship.

It was, first of all, to be a "democratic army" composed of "citizens in uniform." In crushing the revolution of 1848–49 the Prussians had coined a slogan which became the virtual motto of German society for a century: "Soldiers are the only effective defense against Democrats." More than a hundred years later, when the Bundeswehr was founded, its ideological leitmotif was the reverse of that slogan: "Democrats are the only effective defense against soldiers."

Above all, it was to be an army under tight political control, an army that could never again become a state within the state. The immensity and complexity of that goal can be understood only in the context of German history.

Prussia, as the French used to describe it, was not a state with an army but "an army with a state." The army set the tone, determined the style of life, and laid down Prussia's national goals. The king, like the kings of other states, was the army's leader. But unlike other kings he was regarded—and regarded himself—as an officer first, and only after that as a political figure. In both power and prestige, generals ranked above the king's ministers and diplomats. Prussia's victory on the battlefield against France in 1871 provided the basis for the unification of the German states—under Prussian hegemony. The king of Prussia was crowned kaiser of the German Reich and both he and the army assumed the same roles in the Reich as in the kingdom. If anything, the army's role was even more pronounced. It gave the Reich its might and fame, becoming the very foundation of the imperial German state and Wilhelminian society. Its officers were a caste of the rich and educated elite—members of a hereditary establishment with its own code of conduct, acutely aware of its importance and authority, and dedicated to the principle of self-perpetuation. The general staff was revered and regarded as infallible. Military service was like service in a privileged priesthood and the parade ground became as sacrosanct as a temple.

In 1918, when the empire collapsed—largely because the field marshals and generals had proven themselves very fallible indeed—the army was deprived of its traditional role. Not only were its numerical strength and arsenal sharply truncated by the terms of the Versailles Treaty, but the rulers of the new Weimar Republic regarded the army as, at best, a necessary evil. Two factors contributed toward making it the "state within the state" which it eventually became.

First of all, the officers, for the most part aristocrats, continued to pine for the monarchy and kept its spirit alive behind the gates and guarded fences of their barracks and in the seclusion of their clubs. Theirs was a closed society in which the *Reichswehr*'s chief-of-staff, General Hans von Seeckt became a sort of ersatz kaiser.

More importantly, however, the politicians soon depended on the army—not to protect Germany from enemies abroad or to extend again Germany's power and boundaries, but to enforce law and order at home. In the chaotic circumstances of the early 1920s the leaders of the government soon realized they could not govern without the army, and the more they needed it, the more the Reichswehr generals profited. In the tumultuous weeks before Hitler's abortive November 1923 Munich beerhall putsch, when Communist governments were establishing themselves in Saxony and Thuringia, when Bavaria was threatening to secede and form a South German union with Austria under the Wittelsbach monarchy, President Friedrich Ebert nervously called on Seeckt and asked him where the army stood. Bluntly, Seeckt replied: "The army, Mr. President, stands behind me." And subsequently he declared arrogantly: "If there is going to be a putsch, then I'll do the putsching."

In the Third Reich Hitler restored the armed forces to fame and glory, but he simultaneously made them an instrument of his dictatorial power and used them to realize his dreams of world conquest. Compelled to swear personal allegiance to the Fuehrer and subjected to intense ideological and political indoctrination, the officers and men of the Wehrmacht became the incarnation of all the evil ascribed to Germany.

It was upon this historical foundation that a new, "democratic," but at the same time professionally competent army was to be built in 1955. To accomplish that, numerous safeguards and restrictions had to be written into the legislation. Officers free of the pernicious legacy of the Reichswehr and Wehrmacht had to be found, and once found they had to be encouraged to serve. An entirely new attitude toward military service had to be cultivated. The military's role in the state had to be redefined; so did the relationship between officers and men. Modern training methods, new and alien to traditional German military thinking, had to be introduced. And ultimately, the public, skeptical and patently weary of all things martial, had to be persuaded of the political necessity for the new armed forces.

In the process of establishing the Bundeswehr, West Germany went considerably beyond the concepts originally envisioned by the occupying powers. The Bundeswehr is not only entirely different from all previous German armies, it is almost too civilian and too democratic for the tastes of American military leaders. Civilian control was firmly established. The Bundeswehr's commander-in-chief in peacetime is the minister of defense—a political figure, responsible to the federal chancellor and parliament. His second-in-command is the equally political parliamentary secretary, a German version of the British "junior minister" concept. The traditional general staff was abolished. There are no service chiefs-of-staff nor is there a chairman of the joint chiefs. Instead, the top-ranking officers of the three services and of the Bundeswehr as a whole are called inspectors general, and the title is more than semantic eyewash, for none of the four has either command or disciplinary authority. Finally, the armed services committee of parliament was given wide-ranging powers of investigation into military affairs, including the right to "screen" all aspirants to officers' commissions.

The army's place in society was thus completely contradictory to German tradition. Even more revolutionary in concept was the soldier's place in the army. As a "citizen in uniform" he was upgraded to being a person while the officer corps was hauled down from its traditional social pedestal. The first principle was that the citizen soldier would lose only those constitutional rights absolutely necessary for effective administration of an army. Although the soldier, of necessity, had to lose the right to live wherever he pleases, he retained the right to vote and to run for office—neither of which he had in the Wehrmacht. Troops were also allowed to join labor unions, though not to strike, and union organizers were permitted to recruit members on military bases. Union activity among career officers and noncoms is not extensive and the majority who do belong are members of the German Teamsters' and Public Service Workers' Union. But the very thought of union-organized soldiers must make the Hindenburgs and Seeckts of German military history turn in their graves. It is revolutionary even by "democratic" Anglo-American standards.

Furthermore, a variety of safeguards for the soldier was established. Soldiers, for example, are expressively instructed by the law to *refuse* to obey orders which violate the German criminal code, notably its sections on homicide and genocide. The soldier is also free to refuse orders not directly related to the military mission, for instance, if an officer asks him to do his personal grocery-shopping or to move his family furniture around the living room.

Another important measure was the establishment of civil court jurisdiction over military law. The Bundeswehr is virtually the only army in the world that has no courts-martial or a judge advocate's division. All crimes committed by West German servicemen—including violations of military law such as insubordination, absence-without-leave, or desertion —are subject to civilian jurisdiction and must be tried in civilian courts by civilian judges.

The more demeaning aspects of the old Prussian drill were eliminated. Soldiers no longer had to wear uniform off duty. They were no longer required to salute "everything that moves"—merely generals and immediate unit officers, and these only once daily on their first encounter.

Der Spiess—the company first sergeant—was deprived of the power and aura that had made him a virtual demigod in German armies of the past. Harassment of recruits—called *schleifen* in German and known as "Mickey Mouse" in the U. S. Army—was forbidden. No longer could officers and noncoms order recruits to perch atop wall lockers to sing repeated strains of "The Watch on the Rhine" or to clean the latrine floors with a toothbrush.

A new uniform, guaranteed to evoke no martial instincts, was designed. It was so baggy and unmartial that an American general once described it as a "hicktown movie doorman's outfit." The source of much ridicule, it was eventually restyled and trimmed with the accouterments of braid and brass which all military men, regardless of nationality, seem to prefer. But it is still a far cry from the jackbooted, razor-creased, stiff-collared dress of the Wehrmacht or, for that matter, the uniform of the *East* German National People's army which, except for its Soviet-style helmet, looks like a hand-me-down from imperial and Nazi days.

Soldiers were also guaranteed maximum freedom in their personal appearance. Instead of Prussian-style crew cuts, they were permitted to wear their hair long: so long, in fact, that the Bundeswehr eventually turned into the most hirsute army in the world. Nicknamed the "German Hair Force," it became so long-maned by the early 1970s that Helmut Schmidt, then the minister of defense, ordered the purchase of thousands of hairnets which were then issued to the troops. The battle against the long tresses, waged by numerous officers and noncoms, did not, in fact, reach a turning point until May 1974, when a civilian court in Koblenz ruled that soldiers could be forbidden to wear their hair below their collars. Suit had been brought by one young conscript who contended that a haircut order given him by his company commander had violated his "constitutional right to freely develop my personality." That right, the court decided, was superseded by the soldier's constitutional duty to serve in defense of the country. Shoulder-length hair, the court ruled, was not only a safety hazard but a hindrance in performing that constitutional duty.

The most significant innovation, however, was the effort by reform-minded officers such as Count Wolf von Baudissin to create a completely new, self-reliant, independent-thinking type of soldier. Rejecting the old Prussian and Nazi notion that the ideal recruit is "big, strong, dumb, and waterproof," General Baudissin and other progressive World War II veterans called for a modern soldier capable of thinking on his own and thinking fast; a soldier who, instead of following orders blindly, would understand and even question the reasons why they had been issued; a soldier who, above all, would be intellectually equipped to handle the sophisticated weaponry of technological warfare. Baudissin, whom some already rank in German military history with such towering figures of abortive nineteenth-century reform as Gerhard von Scharnhorst and August von Gneisenau, is the architect of the concept of *Innere Fuehrung*. Translated loosely, it means "internal leadership." There is a defense ministry department by that name as well as a Bundeswehr training school for Innere Fuehrung whose officers and career noncoms are indoctrinated in and taught to implement all the new principles with which the Bundeswehr was conceived—that is, the concepts of a democratic army of independent-thinking soldier-citizens serving their country.

Finally, to assure that the new army would abide by all these lofty principles, the office of a "parliamentary inspector" was established. Comparable to Sweden's ombudsman, he is a civilian elected by the Bundestag and answerable only to parliament. He has far-reaching authority to check on soldier grievances and must prepare an annual report informing parliament of the state of democracy, discipline, integration, and the observance of basic civil rights within the military. Servicemen have the right to report and appeal to him directly without going through "military channels," and he in turn has the power to inspect military bases at random and unannounced and to interrogate commissioned and noncommissioned officers accused of wrongdoing. A number of former high-ranking officers have had the job.

Twenty years after its launching, what kind of army is the Bundeswehr really? How democratic is it? How effective a fighting force would it be? What is the public attitude toward it and toward the military?

Although an integral and established institution of postwar West German society, the Bundeswehr is still not entirely accepted by a people who, the legacy of their history notwithstanding, are now so antimilitary that their mood borders on pacifism. The majority of West Germans, while no longer so exercised as to take to the streets to protest against it, regard the army as, at best, a necessary evil. Their attitude toward it can be described as totally indifferent. Only a third of those questioned in a number of recent surveys had a "good" opinion of the Bundeswehr.

One-fourth replied with an equivocal "so-so," while 27 percent said categorically that their opinion of it was "not good."

The career officer, once so esteemed and considered the cream of German society, now ranks second-lowest on the status and prestige scales of principal professions—scales on which physicians, university professors, and atomic physicists rank highest. The handsome, dashing cavalry lieutenant may have been the dream of German maidens in the Wilhelminian era, but the average young *Fräulein* today wouldn't consider dating an officer, no matter how dashing. And even assuming she would, he would be well advised not to pick her up in uniform. Less than 10 percent of Gymnasium graduates express an interest in applying for commissions and pursuing military careers. The Bundeswehr faces a persistent shortage of younger officers (not to mention a drastic deficit of sergeants and corporals), which it tries to meet with lucrative offers of pay and education and four-color advertisements in national magazines promising the dubious that being an officer is "More than Just a Job."

No country in the world has as many draft resisters and conscientious objectors—37,000 new ones in 1974—as the Federal Republic. In no country is the objector's social prestige as high. Indeed, nearly half of the people queried in one recent opinion poll expressed "a great deal of respect" for young men who refuse military induction on grounds of conscience. And in no country is it easier to resist military service, for the right to conscientious objection is firmly secured in the constitution. A bill introduced in the Bundestag in the spring of 1975 will make it even easier than before. Under previous regulations, draft-eligible men registering as objectors had to face interrogation by local evaluation boards empowered to decide whether the applicant was sincere and really motivated by considerations of conscience. Under the new law, simply registering as a conscientious objector will automatically free anyone from military service. The resisters, instead of spending fifteen months in the Bundeswehr, must do eighteen months' compulsory "substitute service," usually social and welfare work as orderlies and nurses' aides in psychiatric hospitals and homes for the retarded or as laborers on reclamation and conservation projects.

The development of a new, "democratic" army was not, of course, without crises and problems. Older, more tradition-bound officers and noncoms were skeptical about all the experiments. "An army that doesn't drill, an army that can't march, an army that has no discipline and whose men are not taught obedience," one disgruntled battalion commander told me shortly after the first batch of postwar draftees reported for duty in 1957, "is also an army that will not be able to fight when it has to."

It was an army which by political design and in response to the public will was a "nonarmy." It could have neither traditions nor heroes because all the heroes and traditions of the past had stood for the wrong ideals. Its generals were treated like lepers and were subject not only to civilian political control, which they might have accepted, but also to the authority of nonelected civil servants who had neither democratic political nor military experience to offer. The generals regarded those civil servants as incompetents, and while the generals had no real authority to carry out their duties, they were the ones who were blamed when things went wrong.

And plenty went wrong for a long time. First the "internal leadership" program suffered a serious blow at the hands of traditionalist officers who were opposed to it and arranged for the transfer of its author, Count von Baudissin, to a field command in 1958. Almost a dozen years were to pass before a group of younger, more progressive officers took charge of the department and the school, and Baudissin's ideas became operative again. Effective parliamentary control was weakened because the first two ombudsmen had to resign: one following his alleged involvement in a homosexual affair which drove him to attempt suicide, the other because he was too outspoken in his criticism of the top brass. And even the fourth, Fritz Rudolf Schultz, a World War II tank officer and former FDP member of parliament, whose term of office ended in May 1975, complained upon retirement that his watchdog role had often been subverted by the brass and that many of his instructions and warnings over a five-year period in office had been ignored. Ranking generals were sacked and others quit in anger. There were arms-purchasing scandals too numerous to recount. There was a series of incidents of brutal recruit harassment that raised the ominous spectre of the bad old days.

And there was the Starfighter crisis—a seemingly endless chain of crashes (171 resulting in the death of 84 pilots since 1962 when this supersophisticated aircraft was first placed in service). A single, satisfactory explanation for the losses of the F-104G's has never been found. When the decision was made in the late 1950s to purchase the franchise for this American-designed weapons system, the Germans were looking for an airplane of highly advanced design which they could build themselves on license. It was to be a multipurpose aircraft capable of operating either as a high-speed fighter, a low-flying bomber able to slip under enemy radar, as well as a high-altitude reconnaissance vehicle. That may have been asking too much of a single airplane, especially by an air force whose pilots and service personnel had inadequate experience; whose development had been stopped abruptly in 1945, and whose flying generals and colonels still had, for the most part, a propeller-driven mentality.

At the height of the Starfighter crisis in 1966 one American observer remarked caustically to a fellow correspondent in Bonn: "The Bundeswehr has all the qualifications of a duck. It flies a little, swims a little, and walks a little—everything just a little."

I mention the Starfighter tragedy because, in retrospect, it was the turning point of the Bundeswehr's path to becoming both a democratic army and an army that could fight. The crisis resulted in a top-level command shakeup, with the resignation of a number of generals, including the air force chief and the Bundeswehr's inspector general. Those who replaced them were generals of a different generation, cast from a different political and ideological mold. The most striking examples of this change were Heinz Trettner, the outgoing inspector general, and his successor Ulrich de Maiziere.

Trettner was certainly not the war criminal East German and Soviet propaganda had made him out to be. But his record in the Third Reich had hardly been savory. A volunteer for Hitler's Condor Legion in the Spanish civil war, his rise from a 1937 captaincy to a lieutenant-generalship by 1944 was spectacular even by the fast promotion criteria of the Nazi era. Trettner got his promotions largely by being the sort of officer the Fuehrer adored. An "old sweat," his 1964 appointment as the top officer of the Bundeswehr was a political blunder and an affront to all those who had hoped to make the new army different from the old.

De Maiziere, who replaced Trettner in August 1966, stood for virtually everything that was right. A participant in the unsuccessful July 20, 1944 plot to assassinate Hitler, he entered the Bundeswehr with the reputation of being a keen reformer. In fact, de Maiziere was one of Baudissin's closest associates, and along with him, one of the innovators of the "citizen in uniform" concept. A military egghead and an accomplished pianist who had spent the postwar years managing the music department of a large Hamburg book store, de Maiziere was also highly competent. He reimbued the Bundeswehr with some of the spirit of reform in which it had been conceived, and also instilled in it a degree of efficiency it had not previously displayed. His stewardship as Bonn's top general lasted until his retirement in mid-1972—the longest period any inspector general has been in office. Those six years were crucial, for they brought the Bundeswehr closer than ever before to being the kind of army originally envisaged.

Problems persist, to be sure. Some high-ranking officers still believe that the army's effectiveness depends on spit-and-polish and blind obedience. The shortage of qualified junior officers and the even greater lack of competent noncoms has not been alleviated. That may change if West Germany's unemployment rate continues to rise, but to meet the deficit in leadership with the spillage of an economy in recession is hardly conducive to building a better army. No one really knows how efficient a fighting instrument the Bundeswehr would be when needed, though fortunately, the need appears to be diminishing from year to year. Its efficiency, according to NATO experts, has certainly improved since the mid-1960s, despite a pronounced decline in discipline. In fact, what worries many officers—even the young and reform-oriented ones—today is not the danger of too much old-style discipline but the almost total lack of any. Made up largely of conscripts who serve their compulsory fifteen months, the Bundeswehr fills each year with recruits who are members of a rebellious generation and the products of anti-authoritarian and affluent society. Their attitude toward their uniformed superiors, to the military establishment, to the whole idea of service, ranges from indifference to contempt.

As one rear admiral put it, reviewing a detachment of long-haired West German sailors in Kiel a couple of years ago: "The idea of citizens in uniform isn't really going to work until the young people we get as recruits already regard themselves and behave like citizens."

Of one thing, however, virtually all West Germans sound confident. Twenty years after its conception, the Bundeswehr is at last firmly integrated *into* democratic society. That was not always so certain. A decade ago Hellmuth Heye, then the parliamentary ombudsman, stirred a nationwide and international controversy with his dire warning that the army was again threatening to become a state within the state. And for a while, as the generals balked and revolted at civilian control, it seemed as if Heye's prediction was about to come true. But those generals were put to pasture and replaced by better men. Meanwhile, the replacements, too, have retired, to be succeeded by generals and admirals who were barely out of their teens when World War II ended and still in diapers when Hans von Seeckt believed that his Reichswehr actually *was* the state. Those ten years since Heye expressed his fears have wrought sweeping changes. The danger is over.

For some young West Germans, however, that is not enough. "Of course the Bundeswehr is politically neutral," says SPD Deputy Uwe Holtz, "and I have no doubt that it would remain neutral in the event of some radical coup against the democratic state. But I expect more from it. I expect the Bundeswehr to come down hard and unequivocally on the side of democracy and to defend it should it ever be threatened. When I feel confident that it would do that, we will have the kind of army I am looking for. Eventually we will have it, but it will take some time."

If the Bundeswehr is ever called upon to fight, a reasonable assumption is that its initial opponent would be East Germany's Volksarmee, the GDR's People's army.

A force about one-third the size of the Bundeswehr, it is an army of an entirely different kind. In raising it, East Germany's leaders had to answer none of the uncomfortable questions about German armies of the past. The past, in their view, being West Germany's exclusive headache, they were not dogged by the need for a great deal of agonizing historical introspection. Their regime being totalitarian, they had little need to sound out the public mood regarding rearmament. Moreover, tight discipline also being the way of civilian life, such issues as the abolition of Prussian-style drill, refusal to obey illegal orders, democracy versus strict obedience, and the preservation of civil rights while in uniform did not even arise.

To me and others with long memories it is always a chilling sight when detachments of the Volksarmee—jackbooted, wearing a uniform indistinguishable from the Wehrmacht's except for the Soviet-style helmet, preceded by brass bands and officers hoarsely snapping commands— goosestep along East Berlin's Unter-den-Linden.

But whether or not that image of a reincarnated Prussia and the Third Reich unnerves me, it doesn't seem to embarrass East Germans, especially officials, in the least. "West Germany changed the uniform but kept the old generals," a Leipzig political scientist once told me. "We kept the uniform but changed the generals."

And he had a point. Not only were the generals and admirals who built up the Volksarmee younger than the Bundeswehr's—ergo, less likely to have been steeped in German military tradition—but they had completely different sociological origins. The majority had served in the ranks of the Wehrmacht, if they had served at all, and were the sons of workers and peasants rather than sons of aristocrats, other officers, or civil servants. Moreover, when the Bundeswehr was organized, professional competence was the primary standard for the selection of its senior officers, with political reliability and adaptability to the new concepts of a democratic army ranking second and third. In the GDR it was just the opposite. Political reliability was the primary criterion. Once *it* had been met, professional competence was considered.

An analysis of the personal histories of 180 West German and 50 East German generals and admirals, undertaken at Tuebingen University in the mid-1960s, revealed some striking data. Of the 180 Bundeswehr officers, all had previously served in the Wehrmacht as general or field-grade officers. Of the 50 Volksarmee generals, only 12 had been officers and of the 12, only five had been colonels or generals.

The majority of senior East German officers are veterans of the German Communist movement. Many of them spent the twelve years of the Third Reich either in hiding, in prisons and concentration camps, or in emigration. And the emigration, more often than not, had been to the USSR. A number of those who had been either too young or politically too unimportant to get caught in the Gestapo dragnet were drafted as enlisted men into the Wehrmacht. A few acquired their military experience by fighting with various resistance groups in Western Europe. Some, such as General Karl-Heinz Hoffmann, the East German defense minister, received solid professional training in the Soviet Union. Hoffmann, a mechanic before he fled Germany in 1935, was educated at Moscow's Frunze Academy (the Soviet West Point), served as a battalion commander with the International Brigades in Spain, and spent most of the war years as a student at the Comintern School in Kushnarenkovo and as a Soviet propagandist, indoctrinating German prisoners of war in Russia.

What these men have created is a tightly disciplined, highly efficient, no-frills army—despite the defection of 2,650 of its members to West

Germany since the building of the Berlin Wall in 1961 (and almost ten times that many before it was built). It is regarded, by Western and Eastern strategists alike, as the most effective and reliable fighting force—next to the Soviet Union's—in the Warsaw Pact.

Its penchant for Prussian drill and spartanism may evoke unpleasant memories. However, it is important to keep in mind that these attributes of the Volksarmee are not as exclusively German as they may seem but also Soviet, though on the other hand, much that is Soviet is also Prussian, for the Prussian tradition runs deep in Russian military veins—back to the days of Peter the Great and Catherine the Great (herself a German princess). Can anyone really say whether the Volksarmee goosestep is Prussian or Russian, or both? To the casual observer, at any rate, there is little difference between a parade on Moscow's Red Square and East Berlin's Max Engels Platz.

With all the means of ideological propaganda and patriotic indoctrination at the disposal of the East German regime, it would seem that the Volksarmee is a totally compliant force, unburdened by any of the problems facing Western armies, especially the Bundeswehr. But in fact, behind the facade of parade-ground precision it too has had to face the challenge of a more critical young generation and the complications arising from modern warfare.

Technological warfare simply requires a more intelligent and independent-minded soldier. And that kind of soldier is more demanding of his officers and noncoms. He is less patient with traditional military practices such as parade-ground drill, less inclined toward blind obedience, and less receptive to simplistic ideological indoctrination. Above all, being better educated and having been raised in a society with rapidly rising expectations, he is more inclined to grumble and complain when confronted with barracks conditions which, as is frequently the case in the GDR, have not improved perceptibly since the 1930s. These complaints are rarely made public and even more rarely do they reach the West. But the exceptions offer useful insight. In July 1973, for example, East German authorities made public a survey of canteen facilities in Volksarmee barracks. Among a cross-section of soldiers queried, only 10 percent rated the facilities in their casern as "good." Another 30 percent described them as "sufficient," and the remainder categorized them as "poor." They complained about the small choice of food and drink, the drabness of the surroundings, 53 percent charged that the counters, the tables, and the serving staff were dirty.

Like the Bundeswehr, the Volksarmee also faces the problem of recruiting competent volunteers, either as reserve officers or noncoms. For many years it relied on appeals to patriotism and when that failed to produce results, on bribery and extortion. The bribery manifested itself in promises of educational benefits for signing up; the extortion amounted to threats of blackballing from colleges and universities against those refusing to serve for longer terms. But these methods are no longer sufficiently effective, and increasingly the Volksarmee is resorting to material incentives; housing and off-post living allowances; free train travel; furloughs at low cost in plush army-owned recreation areas, and numerous other perquisites to which civilians are not entitled.

In 1974 the Volksarmee even reintroduced the old Wehrmacht warrant-officer ranks in an obvious attempt to induce noncoms, who may be barred from obtaining commissions because they have no secondary school diplomas, to remain in service. The basic pay scales are comparable to those of junior executives in industry and well above the East German average.

But no amount of emoluments and incentives seems to bring the desired results. As the East German trade union weekly, *Tribune*, pointed out in July 1974: "There is a disturbing lack of interest among young people in pursuing military careers."

To keep the Volksarmee at full strength, East Germany also depends on universal conscription. But increasingly, it seems, the draftees are a source of frustration and disappointment to their officers. As one East German colonel complained quite publicly: "Too many of the young men lack military consciousness . . . and spend too much time counting the days until their discharge."

Above all, young recruits seem to be balking at old values. Articles and letters-to-the-editors in *Volksarmee* and *Armee Rundschau*, official organs of the GDR defense ministry, suggest that East German soldiers are too "independent minded," "sloppily dressed," "undisciplined," and definitely too "long-haired" for the comfort of their commanders. "Men who lack discipline in the little things [of military life]," wrote one battalion commander, "cannot be depended upon in serious situations. Military discipline begins with the neatness of your hair and the sharpness of your trousers crease."

East Germany's brass would have little to worry about if disciplinary problems were limited to such trivialities as unpressed trousers and overly long locks. But the troubles seem to go deeper. According to the *Oesterreichische Militaer Zeitschrift,* an Austrian military publication with exceptionally good contacts in East Germany, serious breaches of discipline have been multiplying at a steady rate in the Volksarmee. In 1972 there was a 14 percent increase over 1971 in the number of East German soldiers serving "probationary" terms in construction battalions, and the rate of increase for 1973 has been reliably reported to be equally high. In 1972, too, according to the Austrian paper, there were more than a hundred courts-martial for serious disciplinary violations in a single garrison—East Berlin's. These ranged from drunkenness on duty and refusal to obey orders to assaults on superiors.

Developments such as deteriorating discipline, rebelliousness among youth forced to serve, lack of patriotic fervor, and apathy, if not outright contempt, for themes martial—these are phenomena which are by no means exclusive to the two Germanys today. They are characteristic of nearly all more or less affluent industrial societies—East and West. Like the United States, to mention one very applicable case in point, the Soviet Union currently also faces the perplexing dilemma of a "new army" whose soldiers refuse to play by the rules laid down in times past. But in Germany, whose image for so long was a strident and ardent militarism, it is a remarkable development indeed. Thirty years after the end of World War II, militarism in Germany is a dead issue. Deader, to be sure, in West than in East Germany, but dead nonetheless.

Just as the German attitude toward the army has undergone a transformation, so has the attitude toward the police. And just as the German soldier has changed, so has the German cop.

In the days of the monarchy the policeman on the street was the monarch's most visible and omnipresent representative. The police, organized on a state rather than local basis, were in Bavaria, Saxony, and Wuerttemberg the executive arms of the respective kings and in Prussia, by virtue of the fact that the king was also the kaiser, the symbol of his power. The policeman was, and regarded himself, less a guardian of law and order than the embodiment of state authority. He was respected and feared accordingly.

Like the soldier, the policeman's world collapsed with that of the monarchy in 1918. And just as the army's role had been thrown into question with the advent of the Weimar Republic, so was that of the police. The kings and kaiser to whom they had sworn allegiance being gone, the police were expected to be loyal to the men who had toppled them and to enforce the laws of a democratic government, many of whose members had long been regarded as being on the fringes of legality. In a sense, the police, even less than the army, never found itself or its proper place in society in those turbulent years. Nor did the German people seem to find a place for the police.

Lacking the class consciousness of the army, its traditions of hereditary service, and the status that accrued to the Reichswehr aristocrats even after the aristocracy had been abolished, the police never became a state within the state. But on the other hand, it failed to support democracy. More than that, it was contemptuous of it. Ultraconservative, paramilitary in its structure (as it tends to be to the present day, for police recruits in most of Germany spend the first two years or so of training in armylike barracks), and supernationalist in their outlook, the police of the Weimar era yearned for nothing more than return of the "good old days." Although legally bound to political neutrality, it followed only logically that the police would sympathize with, and when circumstances afforded or required it, favor those forces offering the closest substitute for those days—the Nazis.

And when the Nazis finally took power in 1933 they wasted little time before making the police the chief instrument for preserving their power. Two names figure prominently in what was undoubtedly the Nazi leadership's shrewdest but most diabolical plot: Hermann Goering and Heinrich Himmler. What they did with the police has to be understood in order to understand the role of the police and attitudes toward it today.

Goering had been one of Hitler's earliest supporters and had played an instrumental role in transforming the gangs of thugs and sluggers who protected Hitler's political rallies into the *Schutzabteilung*—literally "protective department" of the Nazi party. Called SA for short, these were the brown-shirted storm troopers who became the party's private army under the leadership of another early supporter, Ernst Roehm.

Notwithstanding its size—several hundred thousand men—the SA never became much more than a mob of brawlers. A number of its top leaders, beginning with Roehm, were notorious homosexual perverts who quarreled and feuded incessantly. To have a more dependable band, Hitler created the *Schutzstaffel*—literally, "protective squadron"—as a division of the SA. Called SS for short, its members wore black uniforms similar to those of the Italian Fascists. Initially the SS was little more than a bodyguard for Hitler, who made its members swear a special oath of loyalty to him personally. Hitler dumped two successive leaders of the SS until, in 1929, he found the right man to run it—Himmler, a pince-nez-wearing Bavarian chicken farmer. At the time the SS numbered two hundred men. Himmler developed it into an organization that soon rivaled the SA, and ultimately into a police force that terrorized an entire continent.

On January 30, 1933, when the Nazis came to power—that is, when Hitler was named chancellor of Germany—Goering entered the coalition government in two capacities: as minister-without-portfolio in the national cabinet and as minister of interior of Prussia, the largest of the German states, which encompassed two-thirds of the country's population and territory. As Prussia's interior minister he was also the de facto head of the Prussian police whose staff and ranks he soon filled with Nazi party members, most of them drawn from the SA and SS. For good measure he also created an auxiliary police force of fifty thousand men, nearly all of them SS and SA troopers.

In April 1933, once he had the uniformed police firmly in his and Nazi control, Goering turned his attention to the old Prussian political police, abolishing it and replacing it with an organization called the Gestapo—the secret state police. One year later, in April 1934, Goering appointed Himmler, the head of the SS, to be deputy chief of the Prussian Gestapo. Thus began the symbiosis of those two dreaded organizations—one originally conceived as an upstart politician's personal bodyguard, the other as a secret service. Increasingly, the Gestapo became an arm of the SS to which Himmler had previously added a private secret force of his own—the *Sicherheitsdienst*, or security service, known as the SD and operated by Reinhard Heydrich.

Two years later, in June 1936, the Prussian police and those of the other states were unified into a police force for the whole of the German Reich, with Himmler as its chief. For all practical purposes SS, SD, Gestapo, and all the police in all of Germany became one—under the personal command of Heinrich Himmler. Himmler was in charge of the cop on the corner, the guard in the concentration camp, the detective investigating a larceny, the agent in civvies eavesdropping on people opposed to the regime, and the executioner of resistance fighters in occupied territories. And to those who might question the legality of it all, Dr. Werner Best, one of Himmler's right-hand men in the Gestapo, had a ready answer: "As long as the police carries out the will of the leadership, it is acting legally."

At war's end this vast police superstructure posed a bigger dilemma than any other for the victorious Allies. All four powers agreed that some kind of police was necessary and that their own military police could not do the job without local German help. But they were also agreed that the vast apparatus left by Himmler would have to be dismantled and carefully screened and sifted for Nazi criminals and accessories to Himmler's crimes. They were also determined that no German police force should ever again become the awesome, omnipotent instrument of state authority which it had been under both Hitler and the Kaiser. The beginnings were a pitiable parody of police power: hungry, scrawny-looking men—too old or too sick to have been drafted into the Wehrmacht—wearing ragged and shabby odds and ends of civilian clothing, armed only with billy clubs and identified by hand-painted armbands on their sleeves reading "German Police."

As with so many other issues pertinent to the administration of defeated Germany under four-power military government, agreement among the Allies did not go much beyond knowing what they did *not* want. With totally dissimilar police traditions of their own, each began rebuilding the police forces in its respective occupation zones in accordance with its own police experience. While the British tried to create a force of German bobbies, the French attempted to cultivate sort of a Teutonic gendarmerie. Cops in the American zone began looking and acting like versions of Officer Clancy on the corner of First and Main streets, and in the Soviet zone they were developed as Saxonian retreads of the *militsionery* on Red Square.

The British and French, steeped in the tradition of centralized, national police forces, organized theirs on a statewide basis, whereas the Americans, accustomed to the system of autonomous city police departments, set up local municipal forces in their zone. The result, thirty years later, is the most decentralized and disparate police organization in Europe. Not only do administrative structures and uniforms differ markedly from state to state—and until recently, in the case of the three states formerly under American occupation, from city to city—but even the duties, powers, responsibilities, and functions of the police vary greatly from area to area.

But by far the most pronounced transformation has been the role of the police in a changing society and the society's attitude toward the police. And at no time in German history have that role and attitude been more ambivalent and equivocal or the subject of as much discussion and controversy than at present—in the mid-1970s. Although this phenomenon is by no means exclusive to West Germany—the role of the police and society's attitude toward it being the subject of much discussion in other countries too—it seems to have a greater urgency and immediacy here than elsewhere.

The reasons are numerous and complex—linked to Germany's political history as well as to its emergence as a superaffluent, consumerist society. First of all, the crime rate has been rising dramatically in recent years. Moreover, both the nature of crime and its types have changed radically. Whereas the bank robber or kidnapper of yesteryear was invariably a plain and simple gangster, easily categorized, today he is just as likely to be a political terrorist trying to finance or enforce his cause. While shoot-outs were once staged between "cops and robbers," today, in all probability, they are between police and guerillas of one political persuasion or another.

"Even the leather-jacketed rocker gangs which terrorize this city have gone political," Dr. Manfred Schreiber, police chief of Munich and president of the German Association of Chiefs of Police, once told me. "As they beat up innocent people on the street they shout, 'Ho, Ho Chi Minh.' I asked one of them if he even knew what it meant and he replied: 'Oh, sure. I think it's a laundry detergent.' The problem facing our police today is that the traffic cop of yesterday now also has to be taught to be a 'Green Beret.' "

He has had to be taught far more than that, for during the past decade the once clear lines between right and wrong, between justice and injustice, have become dimmer and more blurred. As democratic concepts have taken root in Germany, though often not yet fully understood, the roles between the citizen and the state, between society and the individual, have changed. Where once the individual's duties to the state and the state's rights vis-à-vis the individual were clearly defined, these have become juxtaposed and the policeman today increasingly finds himself in situations where he cannot decide whose rights come first and who needs most to be protected.

The German cop today is at sea—morally, psychologically, and in daily practice on his beat. He is never sure whether he should pull his billy or simply look the other way; whether to shoot first, or perhaps let himself be shot at; whether what appears to be a crime is not in fact a more modern, less puritanical form of behavior. He does not know—and society cannot make up its mind—whether he is "a friend and helper" or a "pig." Although he does not yet regard himself as a "servant of the people," he is, on the other hand, well past considering himself, as did all previous generations of German police, their master. And while the average German no longer fears the cop or defers to him as the incarnation of state authority, neither does he look to the police for protection.

"The police today," says Schreiber, "has to be sold to the public—like a breakfast cereal." And since 1965 Munich's top cop has spent more than five million dollars on advertising and public relations to make his force more palatable to the citizenry.

Professional image-building is but one of numerous strange things happening to and in the German police today. The majority of policemen in West Germany are unionized, but being tenured civil servants they do not have the right to strike. They do, however, have the right to demonstrate for more pay and better working conditions, and in Duesseldorf several years ago some eight thousand officers did. Carrying the black flags of anarchy and banners which read "We Are the Stepchildren of the State," they marched through the city's downtown streets to the total astonishment of local burghers and the anger of their supreme chief, Northrhine-Westphalia's minister of the interior Willi Weyer. "That was a blatant misuse of the uniform," he said, "and a challenge to the covenant of trust between the citizens and the state."

Like soldiers of the Bundeswehr, young German police officers want to be in style and to wear their hair long. Older officers and officialdom object. In the Ruhr basin town of Bochum not long ago, the police chief decreed that hair must be cut when it reaches the officer's overcoat collar and starts to cover his ears, that beards must not be worn, and that sideburns must not be grown lower than the earlobes. Some forty-nine of his officers, all between the ages of nineteen and twenty, objected to the haircut edict, which had been prominently posted on the bulletin boards of precinct stations. Charging that it was "reminiscent of Kaiser Wilhelm's days" and an invasion of their privacy, they challenged the chief's order in court where—as last reported—the case was still pending.

Dissatisfaction with the job, their pay, their status, and their role in the society is widespread. According to one survey conducted in Lower Saxony, nearly one-third of all officers would not choose a police career again were they given a second chance to decide, and more than 60 percent said they would advise their own sons not to go into police work. A similar survey of Frankfurt's police force in the autumn of 1973 disclosed that two-thirds of the officers believed their colleagues on the force were dissatisfied and disgruntled with their jobs. An overwhelming 63 percent felt they were not accepted by the public.

Equally pervasive is the feeling among the police that the laws they are required to enforce are not necessarily just. They face a conflict between social conscience and their sense of duty. Among the Frankfurt policemen, nearly 60 percent expressed the opinion that justice is not equal for rich and poor alike. Even more astonishing was the observation that 51 percent of those queried approved of squatters occupying empty houses in Frankfurt's West End to prevent these being torn down by real estate speculators to make room for high-rise office blocks. This, despite the fact that the police are repeatedly called out to evict the squatters by force. Nearly 28 percent of the officers indicated they would personally take part in such squatting demonstrations.

To deal with such attitudes and problems on their forces, a growing number of West German police executives are turning to industrial and social psychologists for professional help and advice. The first to do so was Munich's Manfred Schreiber, who hired a staff psychologist as long ago as 1964, following five nights of bloody and controversial confrontations between a thousand of his officers and thirty thousand students, artists, and young malcontents in Schwabing, the city's Latin Quarter.

"Traditionally," Schreiber told me, "the task of the police was to support justice and fight injustice. They were expected to make distinctions in the gray area lying between these opposites. This has always been a difficult task, but as the gray area has gotten larger and the demarcation lines have become less distinct, the task has become more difficult. Psychology can help. It can help the officer to find his proper place in society and to distinguish between right and wrong."

Demonstrations such as the ones in Schwabing, are in fact generally cited as the beginning of the crisis of confidence in which Germany's police now finds itself. They provided the impetus for the reassessment, which is still in progress, of the cop's role in society. And it was one demonstration in particular—in June 1967 in West Berlin—which provided the turning point.

Until that tragic day the position of the police in the West German social order had been clearly defined. Though no longer regarded as the unchallengeable incarnation of state authority which it had been during the monarchy and certainly no longer the instrument of terror and tyranny which it had been in the Third Reich, the police, nevertheless represented the law. A robber was a robber and a cop a cop. There was no equivocation regarding the law and the police enforced it in an authoritarian—frequently very high-handed—fashion. Though the cop inspired fear, he was also respected in that deferential manner once regarded as an ingrained German character trait. Almost nobody seemed to mind. The exceptions were those who detected in the behavior of the German police and the attitude of the public toward them disquieting symptoms of Germany's totalitarian past. But they never voiced their concerns very loudly.

But then came June 2, 1967, when several thousand West Berlin university students staged a perfectly peaceful and orderly demonstration against the official visit of the Shah of Iran and his autocratic regime. With clubs raised and pistols drawn, eight hundred Berlin policemen marched in to break up the demonstration. Shots were fired, and when the demonstrators and passersby had been dispersed, a student, Benno Ohnesorg, lay dying on the street, hit by police bullets.

The police action had been entirely unjustified and unprovoked. It touched off a wave of protest which soon flooded West Germany with student demonstrations—demonstrations against just about everything: the outmoded and ossified educational system, consumerism, social hypocrisy, and political sterility. Increasingly the public mood swung in favor of the students. The more repressive the police measures became, the greater was the crisis of confidence between public and police, not to mention the crisis of self-confidence among the police themselves. For they, too, had begun to recognize the innate justice of the student cause and many recognized their own sons and daughters facing them across the barricades.

Nearly two years of continual demonstrations might have served the purpose of eventually transforming and reforming the police had the student revolt not also given rise to a new menace—a real one—calling for even sharper repressive measures: political terrorism.

"All attempts at reform," says Dr. Kurt Gintzel, vice-chairman of the German Police Union, "all efforts to create a police that would identify itself with the citizenry and with which the citizens could identify themselves, were endangered and thwarted by the rise of the Baader-Meinhof anarchist gang."

Andreas Baader, thirty-two, and Ulrike Meinhof, forty, are the living symbols of a wave of terrorism that has gripped West Germany since 1970 and tilted the mood of the country from benign liberalism to law-and-order hysteria.

Baader, the son of a Munich municipal archivist, is a high school dropout, who has held two jobs in his life: a three-week tryout as a newspaper reporter and a brief stint as a construction worker. He first made news in April 1968 when he and his girlfriend, Gudrun Ensslin, now thirty-four, the daughter of a prominent and widely respected Protestant minister, and a graduate student working on her doctoral dissertation in literature, were arrested for setting fire to two Frankfurt department stores. They described the arson attack as a "political act of protest against the tyranny of property" and "the Vietnam war." Tried and convicted, they were sentenced to three years' imprisonment, but were released in June 1969 pending appeal. Both disappeared from sight, but in April 1970 Baader was caught and rearrested.

Six weeks later Ulrike Meinhof entered the scenario. A divorced mother of twin girls, she was known largely as the managing editor and chief columnist of *Konkret*, West Germany's leading left-wing magazine, which she published together with her ex-husband. At that time she was regarded as one of the sharpest political thinkers in the country and was the darling of Europe's "new left." In June 1970 she masterminded Baader's armed escape from custody, a feat for which she has meanwhile received an eight-year prison term and which she herself described as "an exemplary metropolitan guerilla action involving the entire strategy of armed anti-imperialist struggle."

Then Baader and Meinhof dropped from sight, allegedly went with Gudrun Ensslin and other friends to Lebanon for combat training by Palestinian guerillas, formed a group they called the "Red Army Faction," and launched, so the prosecution in their trial charges, a two-year terrorist campaign that ended—temporarily at least—with the arrest of Baader, Gudrun Ensslin, Ulrike Meinhof, and two others—Jan-Carl Raspe and Holger Meins—in the spring of 1972.

On May 21, 1975, after three years of investigative custody in solitary confinement, during which Meins died from the effects of a hunger strike, Baader, Raspe, Ulrike Meinhof, and Gudrun Ensslin went on trial in a specially built fortresslike courthouse in Stuttgart. They were charged with five counts of murder, fifty-four attempted murders, five bank robberies, six bombings of public buildings including the May 1972 attacks on two U. S. Army installations that took the lives of four American servicemen and seriously wounded fourteen others, and a whole catalogue of lesser charges.

The "trial of the century," as it has been called, is expected to last at least one year, although court and prosecution officials have predicted that it may run two, possibly even two and a half years. Some 1,000 witnesses and experts are on call to testify. To support its case, the prosecution has amassed 18,000 pieces of evidence and an entire library of scientific analyses, statements, and depositions. The indictment alone ran to 354 pages. To hold it, a courthouse costing $5 million and providing for the most elaborate security precautions imaginable, was built adjacent to the Stuttgart prison. It features every conceivable safeguard against armed attempts to free the defendants, including wire netting over the concrete, bombproof roof to protect it from aerial and rocket attack.

The prosecution's aim is to emphasize the purely criminal nature of the acts. The four defendants have been seeking to underscore their political motivation and to try to turn the courtroom into a platform for their political views.

Those views, which have preoccupied intellectuals of such international stature as Jean-Paul Sartre and Nobel Prize-winning novelist Heinrich Boell, can best be summed up as "revolution for the sake of revolution."

Baader and his co-defendants are not alone. They were merely the leaders of a terrorist wave that attracted activists, sympathizers, and supporters from the radical fringes of the student protest movement and the youth rebellion of the 1960s. At the time of this writing, eighty-eight members of the Baader-Meinhof "Red Army Faction" and an allied group that called itself the "June Second Movement" (in commemoration of the June 2, 1967 student-police battle that took the life of Benno Ohnesorg) had already been convicted and sentenced to terms ranging from a few years to life imprisonment for crimes ranging from document theft to murder. Two dozen more were awaiting trial and another twelve were on the German police "most wanted" list. Federal Interior Minister Prof. Werner Maihofer estimated in the spring of 1975 that a "hard core" of a hundred more may still be on the loose.

Among them are but a handful of professional criminals. The majority are students, teachers, lawyers, doctors, psychologists, social workers, and even a business executive. Polarized politically and emotionally in the late 1960s, theirs can best be described as a private guerilla war against society in general. To label them either leftist or anarchist would probably be elevating their cause, for their aims seem to be a fuzzy melange of Leninism, Maoism, Bakuninism, and Guevaraism with a strong hint of Fascist tactics.

As a movement they are blamed for the November 1974 assassination of West Berlin's chief justice, Guenther von Drenkmann; the March 1975 kidnapping of West Berlin's CDU mayoral candidate, Peter Lorenz, which led to the release of five other convicted terrorists and their flight to asylum in South Yemen; and the hostage-taking bomb attack on the German embassy in Stockholm a month later which ended in a bloodbath that left two diplomats and two terrorists dead. A whole series of other killings, attempted murders, dynamitings, robberies, automobile heists, weapons thefts, and burglaries of government offices are ascribed to these political extremists and self-styled revolutionaries.

The hunt for them has at one time or another mobilized up to 40,000 policemen and taken the lives of a half dozen. Six terrorists have been killed in shoot-outs with the police; two more are known to have been "executed as traitors" by their own comrades.

Whatever their aims may originally have been, the radicals have actually nurtured that very police-state penchant, still latent among Germans, especially the older generation, which they claim to oppose. They unleashed a law-and-order hysteria in the mid-1970s that came to loom as one of the central political themes—an issue on which elections were won and lost, public careers made and broken, for toughness on terrorism became the primary political criterion any hopeful and aspiring politician had to meet.

As the cries for draconian measures became louder, Chancellor Helmut Schmidt's government, under pressure from the opposition and the right-wing sensational press, became ever more ready to listen. To deal with the problem, vast sums were allocated for special police anti-terrorist squads. The law itself was bent. Basic principles of justice were jettisoned, such as passage of a law that enabled the court to exclude all three of Andreas Baader's chosen attorneys on the grounds that they allegedly served as channels of communication between him and the underground network. At the time of this writing, a whole packet of additional measures was in the Bundestag hopper, including one that would prescribe physical surveillance "by an independent judge" of correspondence and meetings between "suspect" defense lawyers and their imprisoned clients awaiting trial.

In the wake of a reign of terror unleashed by no more than two hundred political desperados, hope for a long-overdue reform of Germany's nineteenth-century judicial and penal code has been abandoned. Principles of justice and practices of law, dating to the darkest epochs of German history and crying for abolition, have instead been reinforced. Most tragic of all, perhaps, is the deep—though one can only hope not permanent—impact which it has had on West Germany's police. It taught them to shoot first and ask questions later.

The Baader-Meinhof era imbued West German police with a callousness, aggressiveness, and militancy it had never had before. The cases of innocent burghers who have been shot to death by itchy-fingered cops, the incidents of beatings in precinct stations, and the scandals about jail and prison inmates virtually tortured to death by their guards, are too numerous to recount. Suffice it to say the chasm between citizen and cop, once narrowing, appears to be widening again.

Surveying these developments, Erhard Denninger, a Frankfurt University law professor, asked a question loaded with political and historical import for Germany's future: "We have passed through the stages of enlightened absolutism, constitutional monarchy, bourgeoisie republicanism, totalitarian dictatorship, and are now in a democratic, social state based on the rule of law. Will we always have one and the same police?"

4

Revolution
in Germany

ANKE Riedel-Martiny, thirty-six, is tall, blond, blue-eyed, shapely, and modishly dressed. Her husband Frank, thirty-eight, is dark-haired and striking, with a neatly trimmed full beard. They have three children—Kai, aged ten; Katja, eight; and Tim, who is six. They live in a cozy, two-story, six-room duplex house, surrounded by a patch of lawn and garden, in Eching, a middle-class suburb north of Munich.

Anke, Frank, and their children might almost be a clichéd picture of the modern West German family whose father, as Vera Elyashiv, an Israeli journalist and author, once phrased it, "now looks and dresses more like a handsome Italian, whose mother looks like a fashion-conscious Parisian and whose kids appear and act like little Americans."

Anke and Frank belong to that generation which is too young to have more than vague childhood recollections of Germany under Hitler or during the war. Raised in bourgeois families able to provide them with solid educations, they met and married while still in the university. Frank was studying engineering, Anke was preparing her dissertation for a doctorate in musicology. Between bearing and raising her children, she worked intermittently as a music critic for local papers and wrote commentaries for classical record jackets. Frank became a sales executive and consulting engineer for a Munich firm which manufactures and exports ceramic building materials.

Their tastes and lifestyle are typical of millions of couples of their age, education, and family background. Their living room is crammed with a wall of books, records, and a comfortable mixture of modern and traditional furniture that shows the wear and tear of three alert and active children raised in a more or less anti-authoritarian manner. They have two beetle-shaped Volkswagens, one more slightly used than the other. Both have seen a bit of the world—Frank more than Anke, because his job has taken him to Eastern Europe, the Balkans, and Africa.

On weekends, and whenever else he has time or the mood moves him, Frank putters around their rented house, cutting the lawn and repairing what needs to be repaired. Anke is said to have a secret recipe for baking spice cookies and makes her own marmalade and preserves. She is renowned among friends and relatives for the rum punch which she starts with fresh fruit each summer, nurses to potency through the fall, and ultimately serves to appreciative guests at Christmastime.

The Riedels (Martiny is Anke's maiden name which, like many educated professional women in Germany she continues to use in hyphenated form along with her husband's) would be typical of their generation and social class were they not also nationally famous. They have been in the news, gossip, and editorial columns ever since Anke was elected to the Bundestag in November 1972 and Frank told his employers that he would need three afternoons off each week to mind the house and look after the children while his wife sat in parliament in Bonn.

Dr. Anke Riedel-Martiny, a Social Democrat, is by no means the only woman serving in the Bundestag. There are twenty-nine others, including another female deputy from Bavaria and two who are even younger than Anke. But she was the only one to be greeted upon her arrival in Bonn's parliament building by an elderly floor guard who asked rather testily: "Aren't you the new lady whose husband now does the cooking?"

Anke is a typical product, so to speak, of the frustrations and boredom nagging at well-educated, intelligent, and reasonably affluent West German women who find the suburban life of being "just a housewife" too restrictive. Though she would write occasional texts for record jackets, it was not enough to satisfy her.

"I didn't just want to sit around at home," she told me. "I felt I had to do something."

One of the first things she did was start a night school for adult education in Eching. Then she became increasingly active in local Social Democratic politics, having joined the party itself as long ago as 1965.

That she ended up in parliament was largely accidental. The district party organization nominated her the first time in 1969 because they thought a woman candidate would be given a better position on the state ticket than a male. They reasoned correctly. The position was good, but not good enough. She didn't make it. For the next three years she worked hard at cultivating grass-roots support and was nominated again in November 1972, when Willy Brandt called a special election because his majority in the Bundestag had dwindled to a stalemate with the opposition. And this time she made it.

What makes her case so unusual, even among the other women deputies and female politicians in Germany, is the switch she and Frank have made in their traditional roles. To enable his wife to spend from Tuesday through Friday representing the 209th parliamentary district during the nearly seven months each year when the Bundestag is in regular session, Frank has become a part-time "houseman." Anke takes the Pullman from Munich to Bonn on Monday evenings, returns by night train Friday evenings, arriving in Munich early enough on Saturday mornings to make breakfast for her still-sleeping family. On their joint income—Anke receives more than DM 6,000 a month in salary and expenses; Frank, who took a pay cut in order to have three afternoons off to be with the children, earns a gross of 3,000—they can afford a housekeeper and frequent baby-sitters. But when he is home, Frank does most of the cooking and housekeeping, and assumes the dual role of father and mother. In a traditionally patriarchal country, in a society where stern, strong men were expected to rule autocratically while the domain of women was restricted to the "three K's" of *Kinder, Kirche, Kueche*— children, church, and cooking—the switch of roles in the Riedel family borders on the revolutionary.

Even more revolutionary, perhaps, is Anke's outspoken justification for it and Frank's rather enthusiastic acceptance of her point of view. "For the first seven years," she says, "he was able to develop and build his career. Now it's my turn." And they have an agreement, which Anke doesn't broadcast to her constituents, that her turn will be limited to eight years. She plans to run for reelection again in 1976 but has already decided that her second four-year term in parliament will also be the last. "The children," she explains, "will then be in their adolescence. And while the last thing any teenager would want is a hovering-bird mother, I do think they should have a full-time mother around."

Anke Riedel-Martiny's "liberation" represents the second emancipation of German women since the war. It was the war itself which accounted for the first. More than twenty million German males were called to arms between 1939 and 1945. By the time the war ended, nearly half of them had been killed, wounded, maimed, or taken prisoner. Millions of women became the sole breadwinners of their families, and when the guns stopped shooting it was the women of Germany who cleared the wrecked cities of rubble and began the country's reconstruction.

In effect, the war changed the traditional role of German women. It left them clearly in the majority. And they are still in the majority, accounting for more than 52 percent of West Germany's and 54 percent of East Germany's population. Moreover, it started their liberation process. From the outset that process was faster and more advanced in East than in West Germany. But despite considerable disparities between the two, the women of both Germanys are more emancipated than ever before in their history and have gained more rights and exert more influence on society as a whole than women anywhere. The constitutions of both Germanys state specifically that men and women have equal rights, East Germany's going so far as to say that the "advancement of women, in particular professionally, is an obligation of society and the state."

That first emancipatory movement, however, dictated largely by economic circumstances rather than a new female consciousness, was only partially successful and quite uneven in its impact and achievements. It drew vast numbers of women into the economy so that females now account for nearly 36 percent of the total labor force in West Germany and almost 50 percent in East Germany. But despite laws guaranteeing equal pay for equal work, women on the whole earn less than men, with the discrepancy between the sexes being considerably greater in West than in East Germany. In the Federal Republic it has been estimated that although women account for more than one-third of the total labor force, they earn only one-fourth of the national payroll. Conversely speaking, the average man earns 50 percent more than the average woman.

The reasons for this discrimination are varied and complex, being deeply rooted in woman's traditional role in society and the male view of that role. She has been more restricted and disadvantaged in acquiring the education, training, and on-the-job experience that would qualify her for the better-paying jobs and positions. And even when she is equally qualified for a job or a promotion for which a man is also competing, the man is more likely to get the nod. A variety of subjective and objective factors account for this. They may range from simple prejudice on the part of a male personnel manager to his feeling that a woman is less likely to devote and commit herself as totally to the job as a man because of present or future family obligations. This particular aspect was dealt with succinctly in an East German cartoon a number of years ago. "I'll have to give the job to Paul," said a factory executive pointing to a somewhat stupid-looking man while smiling apologetically at a bright woman applicant with a big diploma in her hand. "He may not have a degree but he'll never have a baby."

According to a recent West German survey, women working in industry are invariably relegated to lower pay groups than men, though both may actually do the same work. For example, in one factory making kitchen furniture, both men and women are employed on the assembly line to drill holes into cabinet doors. But the women have been categorized in pay groups I and II while the men are paid according to the scales of groups IV and V, where the pay is up to 30 percent higher. The reason, according to Herta Lischke-Arbert, a woman trade union official: "The men drill holes into heavier and bigger doors." A similar discriminatory policy at a plant making radios and television receivers was justified by a male shop steward on grounds that "men are usually the breadwinners in their families while the women are merely supplementing the family incomes." One company official justified his discriminatory pay for women on grounds that men are physically stronger. "Women," he said, "have only sixty to seventy percent of the physical strength of men." The argument that both were doing the same work which required men to expend 20 percent, and women 30 percent, of their strength reserves, failed to sway him.

Postwar developments did open unprecedented educational opportunities to women who now account for more than 30 percent of the total university and college enrollment in West Germany. But this female invasion of the cobwebbed hallowed halls of higher education seems not to have changed the traditional attitudes of the ossified, hierarchical, professorial caste. Taken as a group, they hold the view that coeds really have no place in their lecture halls. They frankly regard women as less capable, occasionally referring to Dr. Paul Mobius, a turn-of-the-century

German male chauvinist, whose 1902 book expressed the pseudoscientific view that "females are physically and mentally weaker than males," and recommended closing all girls' secondary schools in the Kaiser Reich. Though the average elderly Herr Professor (and a lot of his younger colleagues, too) does not consider woman totally devoid of mind and ability, he ascribes to her aptitudes which are considered of secondary importance for qualifying as a full-blooded German academic, which in Germany means being a member of any profession that requires a higher degree. According to one survey of professorial attitudes, the majority of German university educators will admit that women may be more diligent, eager to learn, meticulous, conscientious, receptive, and equipped with better memories than male students. But those attributes they regard as less important than logic, intelligence, critical observation, ability to think independently and to take the initiative—in all of which they consider men superior. They deliberately make it tougher on female students and when, as a consequence, the female dropout and failure rate is higher, they point to the rate as proof that women are less qualified for and less suited to a higher education. Moreover, the pervasive attitude among professors seems to be that women enter universities primarily to obtain "Mrs." degrees, only to drop out upon marriage.

"Shortly after my engagement to Frank," Anke Riedel-Martiny told me, "one of my professors happened to notice the ring on my finger and asked: 'Oh, I see you're engaged. Why do you keep on studying then?' "

Such attitudes and obstacles notwithstanding, West German women do play a proportionately larger role in the professions and business than women in most other West European countries and in the United States. And in some fields, notably medicine and journalism, they have scored a dramatic breakthrough.

Although only 3 percent of the tenured judges and prosecutors and a mere 4 percent of the university-level instructors in West Germany are women, one-fifth of all West German and one-third of all East German physicians are female. Women account for 15 percent of the West German and 25 percent of the East German dentists. They represent more than half of the university-educated and registered pharmacists in both countries. Some 40 percent of the schoolteachers in both Germanys are women.

The editor-in-chief of *Die Zeit,* West Germany's largest and most influential political, economic, and cultural weekly newspaper, is Countess Marion Doenhoff. Julia Dingwort-Nusseck is chief editor of West-deutscher Rundfunk, largest of the nine publicly owned West German radio and television networks. The only reason she had not yet been appointed program director of Norddeutscher Rundfunk as these lines were being written was because she is a member of the Christian Democratic party and the slot really calls for a Social Democrat. The chief economic and financial correspondent for Second Channel Television is a woman.

Women represent a number of the major German dailies in Bonn. Angela Nacken is the prestigious *Frankfurter Allgemeine Zeitung*'s bureau chief in Prague, having previously held down the same position in Warsaw. Women are the correspondents for First Channel Television in Rome, Geneva, and at United Nations headquarters in New York. Women also play a growing role in management, and according to one 1972 survey, 60 percent of adult West Germans now regard women to be as qualified as men for top positions. But the breakthrough into corporate boardrooms and managerial jobs has been fraught with obstacles and appears to be limited to smaller and medium-sized firms.

More than 12 percent of West German company presidents are women. Some 1,350 of them belong to the Association of Female Entrepreneurs, headed since 1954 by Dr. Lily Joens, herself the chief executive of a company manufacturing thermoelectric measuring instruments with a payroll of 850. On the other hand, only 6 percent of the gainfully employed women—compared to 25 percent of the men—are in the top two salary brackets and a miniscule 2 percent of all corporate executives are women.

Dr. Joens ascribes the contradiction between female success in small and medium-sized business and failure to break into big business to an ingrained bias against women that prevails in the larger corporations. She tells of the proprietor of one large company who refused to hire a highly qualified woman as his general manager on the grounds that "I've got one woman at home and two in my outer office. Three's enough." The chairman of a very large brewery blocked the addition of a woman to the board of directors with the argument that "women do not drink very much beer."

According to Annegret Kruse, thirty-six-year-old head of a small furniture-manufacturing plant in Osnabrueck and mother of three very young children, the real problem is the traditional view that woman's place, no matter what she does professionally or how much she earns, is by the stove and crib. Her duties as housewife and mother are expected to take precedence.

"A family," she says, "places far fewer demands on a working father than a working mother."

Statistics prove her right. According to one 1972 Allensbach survey, some 35 percent of West German husbands of working wives do not even help with the dishes and 25 percent do not help in the house at all. The same ratio seems to be true in East Germany as well. There, 84 percent of the cooking, 78 percent of the cleaning, 90 percent of the laundering, and 76 percent of the shopping is left for the women to do. Male reluctance to help in the home is mentioned as a factor in more than half of the divorce cases in East Germany, and considering that the GDR's divorce rate is half as high again as West Germany's, East German women must really have something to complain about.

Until a few years ago, however, they would have had no legal right to complain at all, for the law required them to do all the housework. Family and marriage codes, changed in 1966 in East Germany and still in force in West Germany, place upon the husband the principal burden of financial support for the family, and upon the wife primary responsibility for maintaining the household. As recently as sixteen years ago the West German supreme court, interpreting that law, ruled that a woman may pursue a profession only when it can be "reconciled with her duties in marriage and to the family."

Although women have made great strides toward emancipation and remain in the majority, they do not rule, and their political influence and power in both Germanys, at least until the early 1970s, remain negligible. East German propagandists, for example, rarely fail to boast that 13 percent of the GDR's mayors and 34 percent of its judges are women or that the female representation in the Volkskammer has increased steadily since 1949 to the point where 159 of its 500 members are now women. But they conveniently forget that there is only one woman in the cabinet—party chief Erich Honecker's own wife, Margot, who serves as minister of education. Moreover, women have almost no influence where the real power in the GDR lies—the leadership bodies of the ruling Socialist Unity party. Although women account for 29 percent of the party's total membership, their representation on its central committee is but 13 percent. Two women, Margarete Mueller and Inge Lange, are non-voting "candidate members" of the party's politburo; but its sixteen full members are all men. There is only one woman, Inge Lange, in the all-powerful party secretariat, and she did not join it until October 1973—the first woman in twenty-seven years of the SED's existence to do so.

In West Germany there are 3.5 million more registered female than male voters. Yet only 6 out of 1,000 women, compared to 40 out of 1,000 men, are dues-paying members of political parties. Although a number of women do play important roles in government, the impression of tokenism is hard to dispel. The president of the Bundestag, a position equal to that of speaker of the U. S. House of Representatives, is Annemarie Renger. A member of parliament since 1953, twice widowed, and until his death in 1952, private secretary to the SPD's first postwar leader, Kurt Schumacher, she is the first woman to hold this office which ranks in protocol right behind that of the federal president and above the chancellor. But her election to the post in 1972 was generally regarded as a sop to female power and a play to keep her out of Willy Brandt's cabinet. The "traditional" female cabinet post—minister of health, family, and youth affairs—went instead to a fast-rising SPD star, Dr. Katharina Focke, a wealthy fifty-three-year-old Cologne widow and a University of Oklahoma graduate, who from 1969 through 1972 had served as parliamentary state secretary and deputy chief of staff to Willy Brandt in the chancellory. It was not until Helmut Schmidt succeeded Brandt in May 1974 that this position was again filled with a woman—Marie Schlei, fifty-five, a war widow, mother of three, former school principal and second-term Bundestag deputy from West Berlin. In addition to these three ranking women in Bonn, three more women serve in the state cabinets—all of them ministers of family, health, and social affairs. One woman justice, Wiltraut Rupp von Bruenneck, sits on the West German supreme court. Yet, despite all this appearance of woman-power, the number of female deputies in the Bundestag has actually decreased steadily since 1949, so that following the last election in November 1972 there were only thirty. Of that group three are nonelected appointees from West Berlin, with limited voting powers.

One explanation for this apparent decline in female political participation—and a prediction of change in the future—has been offered by Dr. Hildegard Hamm-Bruecher, a deputy national leader of the Free Democratic party and that party's floor leader in the Bavarian state legislature. Married to a physician who is chief administrator of all Munich hospitals, the mother of a twenty-year-old son and a fifteen-year-old daughter, she has been active on the political scene longer than any woman in Germany. At fifty-four, she is by far the country's best-known, most influential, and most respected female politician. A member of the "White Rose" anti-Nazi student resistance group while a chemistry major at the University of Munich during the war, she holds a doctorate in chemical science and spent the early postwar years working as a science reporter for the U. S. military government's daily *Neue Zeitung*. Her political career began at age twenty-seven in 1948, when she was elected to the Munich city council on the Free Democratic ticket. Two years later she entered the Bavarian state legislature—of which she has been a member ever since—and launched a singular campaign to reform, first Bavaria's, then all of West Germany's, educational system. On eleven fact-finding missions to the Soviet Union, the United States, East Germany, Scandinavia, and Western Europe, she gathered evidence to support her argument that the Federal Republic is "an educational hinterland." Her merciless criticism and proposals for sweeping reform, which I shall discuss at length in a succeeding chapter, led to her appointment in 1967 as state secretary (deputy minister) of Hesse's ministry of culture and education. In 1969 she was named to a similar position in the federal ministry of science and education in Bonn, a post she resigned in 1973 to return to Bavaria as the FDP's floor leader and to shape up her party's organization there.

"The political emancipation of women," Dr. Hamm-Bruecher told me, "has come in two big waves here, and each one was influenced largely by external forces. The reverses it has suffered can be blamed largely on the women themselves and their relapse into traditional female roles. Only the women themselves are at fault for the tokenism in politics. They simply haven't pushed hard enough in the caucus rooms. They expected the powerful political plums to fall in their laps. But they never do—neither into the women's nor the men's laps. You have to reach for them. When I became state secretary for education in Hesse, I was amazed at the near-total absence of women in executive positions in the school systems. I was told that none had applied and refused to believe it. But then I checked the records and, indeed, almost none had.

"I am the first woman, and thus far the only one, to serve as floor leader of any party in any parliament or legislature in this country," she said.

"But whenever I urge some of my female colleagues in other states or in Bonn to campaign for similar positions, or at least for deputy leader or party whip, they wave me off with excuses. They tell me it'll cause intraparty troubles and, if not that, troubles at home with their families for taking on an even heavier load.

"There you have a partial explanation for what happened to the first female breakthrough right after the war. And it was a breakthrough. Women had to carry virtually all the burdens of the nation's defeat and logically demanded, and got, a voice in the decision-making process. But it was a one-time shot. There was no second string, no second generation of women politicians, to follow in the footsteps of those who had made the postwar breakthrough. In the 1950s and 1960s the potentially eligible women were all too busy getting married, starting families, partaking of the economic miracle, and falling back into their traditional place as subordinates in a hierarchical system.

"You know, in the late 1940s, when I started in politics, people called me one of the youngest women politicians on the scene. Two decades later, in the 1960s, they were still calling me one of the youngest women in politics and, unfortunately, I still was. But then things began to happen—the second emancipatory movement started. It expressed itself in a massive new awareness among women. It was an outgrowth of the student and youth rebellion of the late 1960s, of the spreading political consciousness in the country, of a pervasive desire to participate, of the need for change.

"This phenomenon is no more than three or four years old, but it has a relatively broad foundation at the grass-roots level. Women are taking active roles in parent-teacher associations and showing an unprecedented interest in the education of their children. They are starting and joining citizens' action groups of every conceivable kind with a variety of local, regional, and even national goals. You have the rise of the women's liberation groups, which demand not only more rights but sweeping changes in the relationship between the sexes. We have witnessed the demand for reform of the divorce laws and the code on abortion. You see more women in leading positions. Why, a decade ago no one would even have dreamed of a woman Bundestag president or a woman state secretary in the chancellor's office. And the women who are now entering parliament and the state legislatures are not only younger—representatives of the postwar generation—but more self-confident.

"There is always the danger," Dr. Hamm-Bruecher cautions, "that the two steps forward will lead to three backwards—when women realize that making the jump is the easiest part, sticking it out the hardest, most time-consuming, and painstaking. But thus far, the changes since the early 1970s have been dramatic."

Indeed they have. Women are stating their demands and making their presence felt on a broad front. A woman, thirty-two-year-old Heide Wieczorek-Zeul, has become national chairman of the powerful and influential Young Socialists. Rita Waschbuesch, thirty-five, a mother of four, has been named minister of health, family, and social affairs in the Saarland. Through their political parties, women's groups such as the SPD's Council of Social Democratic Women, women voters are forming intraparty blocs and pressure groups that ultimately may prove as powerful as the youth organizations.

The female revolution is even more evident on the social and economic front, where the big issues continue to be equal rights and equal opportunities. In the spring of 1974, for example, Rita Maiburg, a twenty-two-year-old licensed pilot, shocked the dowdy, all-male board of Lufthansa by filing suit to force the airline to hire her as its first female flying officer trainee. In Munich, Ninon Colneric, twenty-five, a law student, has initiated court action against the state-supported Maximilianeum Foundation, charging that its century-old policy of admitting and giving fellowships only to deserving male students is in violation of both the Bavarian and West German constitutions. In small towns all over West Germany women have already invaded that most hallowed of all male preserves (next to the bowling club): the country's 22,106 volunteer fire departments.

In Stuttgart, grandmotherly-looking Irmgard Sauer has launched a national Society of Widows, whose aim is to abolish what may well be the most discriminatory policy against women in West Germany today. When an old-age pensioner's wife dies, he continues to receive the full pension previously paid to both of them as a couple. But if the husband dies first, his surviving widow receives only 60 percent. Frau Sauer, who insists her husband left her well enough off so that she does not need a pension at all, has started a nationwide pressure campaign and has filed a test suit to force the social security administrations to pay widows the same 100 percent benefits to which widowers are entitled.

In Hamburg a group of 2,000 women has organized a nationally active

Association of Single Mothers, whose aim is to pressure parliament into passing sweeping legislation that would improve the economic situation and reduce the tax burden of West Germany's 360,000 widowed, divorced, and unmarried mothers of minor children. The group contends that existing laws, discriminatory employment policies, and social attitudes place single mothers (and single fathers, of which there are 30,000) into an especially disadvantageous situation. Although they earn, on the average, 40 to 50 percent less than households with two parents, they pay proportionately more taxes because they are disallowed the standard deductions. Only half as many families with one parent live in their own home or condominium as families with two parents. Moreover single mothers are discriminated against when seeking access to government-subsidized low-rental housing because old-age pensioners, low-income families with many children, and newlyweds—in that order—are entitled to preferential placement on waiting lists.

The nation's secretaries and female office workers are also on the march. According to one survey, 70 percent of them are dissatisfied with their work. Their complaint is not about the pay, but about their professional and social standing and the way their bosses treat them. Those queried demanded more information about what is going on in their business or department, greater responsibility, more recognition, and more teamwork. Three-quarters of those questioned saw no or little chance for professional advancement, and 88 percent said they would dissuade their own daughters from becoming secretaries.

Above all, West Germany in the mid-1970s is pregnant with talk, proposals, and experiments intended to improve the lot of women who have to work, and to enlarge the opportunities for those who want to work or to free themselves from slavery to the kitchen sink. The Bundestag, for example, has enacted legislation to assist women returning to the labor market after a prolonged homemaking and child-rearing absence. The law provides them with cash grants and tuition to attend training and retraining courses that will refresh their previous professional expertise or enable them to qualify for better jobs than they had before stopping work.

The ministry of health, family, and youth affairs has also launched a controversial "day mother" project designed to help the parents of 800,000 infants and preschool children for whom there is no space in day-care centers, and nursery schools. "Day mothers" are those with small children of their own who, having no outside job, are willing to care for up to four other small children of working mothers. They will be paid, not by the mothers of the children they care for, but out of social security funds at a rate of from 320 to 630 marks per month, depending on the number of youngsters they take in. In addition, they will be entitled to expenses for food and enjoy full social security and health insurance coverage themselves. To qualify as salaried day mothers they will have to attend brief medical and pedagogical training courses.

The program, which got underway on a test basis in the summer of 1974 in the Stuttgart area, has drawn vehement criticism from women's liberationists on the one side, and on the other, from traditionalists, the conservative Christian Democratic opposition, and the churches. Women's lib advocates have opposed it on grounds that it is demeaning to the day mothers who are relegated to the role of "glorified nannies and wet nurses." Prominent psychologists and educators have opposed it with the argument that even a temporary, daytime separation of children under the age of three from their mothers is likely to cause permanent psychic damage.

The professional argument, curiously enough, may have been inspired by the experiences in East Germany, where the working mother of infant and preschool children is the rule rather than the exception. The high rate of female employment in the GDR, though sugar-coated by the regime as a manifestation of woman's emancipation and equal opportunity, is primarily the child of macroeconomic necessity. Faced since the early 1950s by a critical labor shortage due primarily to the exodus of 3.5 million refugees, the GDR would simply grind to a halt if nearly three-fourths of its adult women did not work. To persuade and enable them to work, the government has offered a variety of inducements, including a widespread network of inexpensive, scientifically run child-care centers. The GDR now has enough day-care centers and nurseries to accommodate 30 percent of all children up to age three, and enough preschools to take care of 70 percent of those between three and six. (The rate in West Germany is less than 2 percent in both groups.)

Although all these centers are models of child care where toddlers are supervised by trained teachers, fed perfectly balanced meals, are examined monthly by dentists and pediatricians, and taught group living in clean and modern surroundings, East German experts have raised serious doubts whether it is all such a good idea. The effect may well be an entire generation of neurotics raised without parental love. The doubts have not been raised publicly, for that would run counter to official policy of the regime. But they are voiced in meetings with Westerners.

As one doctor in the GDR once told me in private conversation: "Kids, no matter how young, are subconsciously aware of the love they receive or don't receive. Children dumped with strangers each day must sense they are in someone's way. Moreover, being raised in such surroundings has a retarding effect. We can recognize immediately which ones have been brought up in day nurseries, which ones have grown up at home. Comparatively speaking, the ones from preschools are retarded. They have been systematically deprived of the impulses they receive in adult surroundings. No matter how good the teachers and supervisors, they cannot devote time to influencing each child as intensively as its mother. With no adults around them for most of the day, they do not learn and merely tend to copy each other."

Actually, the West German day-mother program, borrowed from Scandinavia, would seem to counteract these negative effects of nursery schools, for a woman taking care of a maximum of four children over a long period of time is bound to give them the attention and love they need. But psychologists and child behavioral scientists such as Cologne's Dr. Emil Schmalohr and Freiburg University's Bernhard Hassenstein remain opposed. Hassenstein contends that the shock of daily separation and the existence of several "persons of reference" would have the most serious effects on infants under the age of two. These objections notwithstanding, the program has found widespread popular response and full government support. When finally implemented it will free hundreds of thousands of young mothers to work, and it will be infinitely cheaper than using public funds to build the thousands of preschools West Germany lacks.

Preschool children are not the only ones, however, who restrict West German mothers to traditional roles. The school-age child actually serves the same function, for the vast majority of schools operate on a mornings-only, six-days-a-week basis. Classes generally begin at 8:00 A.M. and are over by noon or 1:00 P.M. when, traditionally, German families have the main meal of the day, supper usually being cold or similar to what the English call "high tea." All day schools have been started on an experimental basis in nearly all the states, but the demand for more of them has grown along with the women's emancipation movement.

The liberating and emancipatory phenomenon, now so prevalent and the focus of so much attention, is, of course, not exclusive to Germany. On the contrary, it is far more widespread and advanced in the United States. And whatever events may have triggered it—such as the youth and student rebellion or perhaps the transfer of power away from the conservative, restorative, church-oriented Christian Democrats—there can be no question that it is largely an import from America. Even the methods and the goals are similar, often identical, to those in the United States. But be that as it may. For Germany, viewed in its historical context as the archetype of the patriarchal, hierarchic, and regimented society, the meaning is special and the impact unique.

Three years ago Anke and Frank Riedel-Martiny might have been regarded as singular exceptions, even in the highly educated, affluent, cosmopolitan, and progressive class of which they are members. But today there are hundreds of thousands of Ankes and Franks who in turn are setting examples, hopefully soon to be emulated, for the millions of German couples—the overwhelming mass—who did not have high-school-equivalent, let alone college-level educations, and who do not have, as yet, the economic and social freedom to choose their style of life and relationships.

But even among them the changes wrought in the last few years are perceptible. Attitudes are changing. Burdens, authority, and responsibility are being spread more evenly between men and women, especially those of the postwar generation. Relations between the sexes are becoming more harmonious; and family life, healthier. With the drift away from male orientation, the family no longer focusses and revolves around the autocratic father figure—the root cause of so much of Germany's emotional and political instability, pent-up aggressiveness, and emphasis on false martial values. Even the traditional family unit—just as in the United States—has been placed in question, and young people are experimenting freely and enthusiastically with new models for living together.

Views on marriage, childbearing, and divorce have undergone far-reaching transformations in recent years. Some 67 percent of all adults and an amazing 84 percent of women and 91 percent of men under thirty years of age favor, or at least have no objections to, men and women living together without being married. A quarter of the adult population and more than one-third of those between ages sixteen and twenty-nine would favor a marriage contract limited in time and renewable with the consent of both partners. Nearly 30 percent either raise no objections or actually approve of the idea of communal families.

Abortion on demand during the first three months of pregnancy became legal in East Germany in March 1972, and after a protracted battle that preoccupied the press, public, and politicians for years, was finally enacted in West Germany in the spring of 1974, though only to be declared unconstitutional by the supreme court in February 1975 because it violates the "right to life" principle. A modified version of the measure will probably be enacted. After years of debate, a new divorce law has also been proposed. For Germany it will represent a dramatic departure from legal codes, practices, and attitudes that dated back nearly two centuries.

Under the existing code, divorce is based solely on the principle of "guilt and fault" on the part of either, or possibly both, partners. To grant a divorce, a court is obligated to establish and assign a measure of guilt. A man, for example, could be held wholly guilty for committing adultery, though the number of incidents or the duration of his infidelity might be considered a contributory factor to the "degree of guilt." Conversely, a wife who had failed to keep house or to prepare the meals properly, could be divorced by her husband as "guilty" of not meeting her marital duties. In a hypothetical situation of a husband committing adultery and wife not preparing meals, the court might divide the guilt between the two. The judges would investigate to determine which violation of the marital covenant had come first—infidelity or the absence of supper on the table. If the husband could prove that he took a mistress because his wife wasn't feeding him, the court might hold him only one-fourth and her three-fourths guilty. Conversely, if the wife could demonstrate that she had stopped cooking when she found out about his philandering, he would end up being more guilty than she. The degree of guilt and fault established by the court subsequently determines the property settlement, custody of the children, and the assessment of alimony and support payments.

The new law will recognize "irreconcilability" as the *only* ground for divorce and treat marriage not as a holy or state-ordained covenant but as a private contract between two partners. Divorce will be granted automatically if the couple have been separated for one year and neither desires the marriage to continue. Three years' separation will result in divorce even if one partner objects. But most importantly, there no longer being a question of guilt or fault, the burden of alimony and support will be assigned to the economically and financially stronger partner. Theoretically, a wife earning far more than her husband might be ordered to pay him alimony, even if he had been committing adultery every night while they were married. Custody of children will be awarded to the parent considered most qualified and suited to raise them, as well as on the basis of where, in the opinion of the court and juvenile welfare officials, they will be happiest.

Whether the new law will result in more divorces—already running at a rate of nearly 25 percent of marriages and twice as high as it was in 1960—remains to be seen. But the majority of West Germans agree that it will represent a more sensible approach to modern relations between men and women. For years, public opinion polls have shown that most people regarded the "guilt" principle out of step with the times and an unjustified interference on the part of the state in private relationships.

East Germany, it should be mentioned, caught up with the times more than a decade ago, abolishing the "guilt" principle in 1965.

By far the most significant development of the emancipatory movement, and closely linked to the mood of the youth rebellion of the 1960s, is the strong anti-authoritarian current one finds among West German parents today. Traditional views on education and on the relationship between parents and children have been challenged, especially by the postwar generation, now parents themselves. Hansel and Gretel, those bowing, curtsying German children who were seen but not heard, have become relics of the past. Although three-fourths of all parents, when asked what qualities they would like to instill in their children, continue to mention "politeness and good behavior," two-thirds also mention "tolerance and respect for the beliefs of others" and "the ability to stand up for themselves, to not allow themselves to be subordinated and suppressed."

More than 75 percent of all West German parents today are either categorically opposed to physical punishment or regard it as a last resort to be used rarely. A majority of those under thirty approve of the anti-authoritarian principles of raising children.

Concomitantly with a freer attitude toward marriage, divorce, abortion, and child-raising, Germany's postwar generation has developed an almost totally casual attitude toward sex itself. Sexual freedom, of course, is not new to the Germans. For a while in the 1920s, Berlin ranked as the sex and decadence capital of the world. But the orthodox winds of the 1930s and the Third Reich completely eliminated sex—officially at least—except as a means of reproduction.

Since the late 1960s, however, there has been a veritable sexplosion. National magazines, intended for family reading, such as *Stern* and *Quick*, attract readers nearly every week with nude females on the covers and, not infrequently, seminude males inside. Even daily newspapers such as Munich's *Abendzeitung* are not above publishing photos of bare-bosomed beauties between the news columns. Topless and bottomless females are used to advertise almost everything from champagne to wristwatches, and deodorants to detergents, while hairy-chested males grace full-color ads for everything from beer to shaving cream. Nudist sun clubs are a national rage, and finding a sauna bath where the sexes are not mixed can prove to be quite a problem. There is no West German city, not even a medium-sized one, without an assortment of "sex boutiques" and so-called marital hygiene shops, offering such varied merchandise as 8mm. skin flicks, pornographic books and magazines, potency salves, exotic con-doms, penis-shaped vibrators, and see-through underwear for both men and women. Partner-switching seems to be a national game, prostitution is legal and rampant in every city with more than a twenty thousand population, and in some cities the municipal governments have even built and own the brothels, leasing the premises to experienced madames. Call girls *and* boys openly advertise their services, attributes, and phone numbers in the classified sections of daily newspapers under the catch-all heading of "models, hostesses, cavaliers, body care, massage." Movie marquees seem to advertise nothing but "facts of life" films, how-to-do-it-better flicks, and pseudosexological documentaries such as the *Schoolgirl Report, Housewives' Report, Stewardesses' Report, Secretaries' Report*, and *Your Wife, the Unknown Creature.*

One "creature" that is definitely no longer unknown, thanks to extensive sociological and sexological research, is the German teenager. By age fifteen, according to a survey conducted by Frankfurt sexologist Prof. Volkmar Sigush, 10 percent have experienced sexual intercourse; by the time they are sixteen, some 30 percent are experienced; among the seventeen-year-olds, half are copulating more or less regularly—although, as Sigush tried to reassure the older generation, generally with a regular partner: a steady boy or girlfriend.

Leaving aside its seedier overcommercialization which may arouse the sensibilities of even the most liberal, and ignoring, if one can, the exploitation of the female body for advertising and marketing purposes, there is a healthiness and wholesomeness to this new sex consciousness which was long overdue. In their rediscovery of sex, the West Germans have also discovered that it is normal and that, above all, the state has no right to control or regulate sexual behavior and attitudes.

Even the East Germans, long held in a vice of Marxist and Lutheran prudery, seem to have rediscovered sex and to be viewing it as a normal function of human life.

For decades, "morality" was something on which East German officialdom doted—often to a degree that bordered on priggish stuffiness. That was a fact of life which many professional anti-Communists in the West refused to believe. They regarded communism as intrinsically amoral because it is atheistic or because some of its wilder exponents once advocated free love. But the days of the "red sex bombs," such as Ruth Fischer and other women who treated Marx like an aphrodisiac, went out with the Roaring Twenties. And by the time Walter Ulbricht took over in East Germany, communism in general—and East German communism in particular—had become as straitlaced as a Victorian corset. Those who doubt me, need merely look up the "ten commandments of socialist morality," which Ulbricht coined in 1958. Commandment 9, for example, said unequivocally: "Thou shalt live cleanly and decently and respect thy family."

Clean living meant that the GDR had virtually no night life, except for a few sleazy Leipzig dives that catered predominantly to Western businessmen attending the city's semiannual trade fair. Prostitution was outlawed and became virtually (though not completely) extinct. Sex became a word that made most East German girls blush as red as communism's banners. East German movies and books generally expunged love scenes after the first brotherly peck on the forehead.

Overt sexuality—except for a brief period of liberalization in 1964 and 1965, which quickly turned into libertinage and opened a dam of pent-up emotions—was taboo. Public discussion or display tended to generate mass embarrassment. Young East Germans, though actually quite normal and free of inhibitions in their private relationships, gave the impression of living in a world more restricted and protected than that of their grandparents. Sex, the party's ideologues maintained, prevents clear political thinking. One East German magazine once warned that the "sex wave in the West" had been instigated by "vengeful capitalist-imperialists to keep the peoples of their countries from discussing and thinking about vital questions such as the battle against nuclear annihilation."

For years the ideal magazine cover girl in the GDR sported baggy overalls and carried a wrench in her hand. And during the short period in the mid-1960s when the taboos were lifted, East Germany went wild. Woman became as much a sex object as in Western countries. Usually sober party newspapers, given to dull, lengthy reports about economic plan fulfillment, began publishing pictures of attractive nymphs in fishnet stockings. The military journals entertained soldier-readers with photos of bikini beauties. Youth magazines published art that bordered on pornography. And as the mold caught on, women started to display a measure of sexual liberation of their own. There were reports of female students in Dresden going out for their annual harvest and potato-digging duties with bared breasts.

But as quickly as it had flared, that East German "sex wave" was snuffed out in what developed into a general repression of all Western influences, especially on literature, art, and music. And the clamps remained on tightly until the early 1970s—following Ulbricht's fall from power—when the current rediscovery began.

To justify the latest policy of liberalization—in many respects more wholesome and constructive than West Germany's—the regime's ideologists have even called upon the founding fathers of communism. Thus they now frequently quote Friedrich Engels, who reputedly once said: "It is high time that the German working masses learn to speak without inhibition about the things they do daily—and nightly: very enjoyable things."

East German women's magazines such as *Fuer Dich* have published supplements that are filled with photographs of female and male nudes and devoted to the themes of love and sex. *Junge Welt*, the official weekly of the party's Free German Youth movement, has been telling its readers that there is nothing wrong with sex or its public discussion. "Sexual relations," it pronounced not long ago, "are clean relations." Young East Germans are now encouraged to write in for answers to their sexual questions and advice about their sexual fears. *Fuer Dich* has even retained a panel of respected physicians who conduct a regular "Marriage Forum" in the magazine's columns.

The most significant development, however, has been the lifting of traditional restrictions and taboos in the GDR's film and television industry. Three recent films in particular, *The Third One*, *Paul and Paula*, and *The Naked Man on the Athletic Field*, are noteworthy. Actually, "the naked man" is a nude male statue, and the film deals largely with the antics and troubles of its sculptor. But right beneath the surface of the main story there is an unmistakable attack on the stuffy hypocrisy in which the GDR was mired for so long.

Paul and Paula, unanimously regarded as the best East German film in more than two decades, is the story of a tragic triangle. Paula is a single mother of two children. Paul, her lover, is locked into an unhappy marriage with a beautiful but domineering and unfaithful wife, and is himself the father of one child; but he is reluctant to obtain a divorce because he fears it will hurt his career. Paula wants clarity: either he breaks with his wife or they sever their relationship. Before a decision can be reached, one of Paula's children is killed on the street by a car. She wants another child and wants it from Paul, though doctors have warned her that she would not survive another childbirth. She becomes pregnant nonetheless and, as predicted, dies in labor, although the baby lives. The final scene shows Paul, apparently free of his wife, playing with all three children: the one from his broken marriage, Paula's first, and the baby they had together. The film is not only thematically daring but has bedroom scenes more frank than any previously shown on GDR screens.

The Third One touches on aspects of the male-female relationship which even Western cinéastes have been reluctant to broach. Who is entitled to be the more aggressive partner? In the film a successful woman computer analyst, mother of two fatherless daughters, takes a liking to a man she has seen, though never met, but feels too inhibited to make the first move toward him. "Here I am," she says in the crucial scene, "supposedly emancipated, and yet social custom dictates that I'd be making a fool of myself if I told a man I want him." Ultimately, of course, she does precisely that, winning a husband and lover and a father for her two children.

Shortly after *The Third One* became a box-office sensation in East Germany, GDR youth and women's magazines began discussing its theme in letters-to-the-editors columns. "We've been talking about a similar problem in class," one teenager wrote. "The question is why only boys should ask girls to dance, and not the other way around."

There may be no answer to that until children are imbued from the cradle with the idea that relationships between men and women should be those of two equal partners. Both Germanys, it seems, have a long way to go before that goal is reached. In the GDR, for example, a recent survey among first-grade pupils revealed that, emancipation notwithstanding, they ascribed very traditional roles to their parents. They were asked to describe what their mothers and fathers do. Mother, according to most of the youngsters, "cooks the meals, does the shopping, mops the floor, washes the clothes, and sews on buttons." Father, they explained, "reads books and newspapers, watches television, drinks beer, and smokes cigarettes."

In West Germany the most widely used reading books for primary schoolchildren still contain such phrases as the following: "A girl is almost as good as a boy." "If you are a little lady there is nothing wrong with being a little fraidy-cat." "The man wears the pants in the house."

Even in a house as apparently emancipated as Anke and Frank Riedel's, the children seemed to be rooted in traditional role assignments. "Katja," Dr. Riedel-Martiny told me, "came to me one day and said: 'You know what I want to be when I grow up?' I shook my head and played the usual guessing game, replying: "A pilot?" 'Oh, no,' she shot back, 'only boys can be pilots. I think I want to be a nurse.'"

"The question of emancipation," says Katharina Focke, Bonn's minister of health, family, and youth affairs, "is first and foremost one of education."

5

A Land of
Poets and
Thinkers?

ONCE upon a time, in the late 1960s, West Germany was described as "an economic giant but a diplomatic and political midget." Since then its role in the world has changed dramatically. Not only has it remained one of the major economic powers, but by maturing and proving itself, it has become a diplomatic one as well.

Curiously, however, even more than in the 1960s, it ranks as an "educational dwarf." Dr. Hildegard Hamm-Bruecher once mercilessly called it an "educational Appalachia"—a sad assessment in which the majority of international experts readily concur.

"In spirit and structure," says a 1971 report by the OECD, the European Organization for Economic Cooperation and Development, "schooling in the Federal Republic remains old-fashioned. In an age when secondary and higher education are being rapidly developed in the other advanced states, the FRG has made do with a system that until now has effectively shut off some 90 percent of the children from the possibility of entering universities. . . . There is not a single area of science in which the Federal Republic can today be considered a leader."

The statistics are shocking. Since the end of the war West Germany has persistently spent less of its gross national product for education than any of its European neighbors and only half as much as Sweden, the Netherlands, and East Germany. France, Italy, and Belgium in 1970 were spending a percentage which West Germany does not intend to spend until *after* 1975, and it will not be until 1985 that the Federal

Republic intends to devote the same proportion of its GNP which East Germany allocated to education in 1974.

At present, it has a shortage of 250,000 elementary and secondary school teachers. More than 65 percent of West German classrooms have more than 30 children and in certain areas of the country, classes of 50 and 60 children are the rule rather than the exception. Universities and other institutions of higher learning are hopelessly overcrowded and in the fall of 1974 were able to accommodate only about 17,000 of the 65,000 eligible secondary school graduates who applied for admission. In some fields, such as pharmacy, dentistry, veterinary, and general medicine, there were up to 15 applicants for each university space. The outlook over the next decade is even more bleak. By 1980, according to most prognoses, a half-million eligible youth may be locked out of colleges and universities simply because the institutions lack the physical facilities and faculty to accommodate them. Berthold Martin, a CDU Bundestag deputy, has likened this phenomenon to the "unemployment problem of the Weimar Republic" and has warned that it may have the same "political and sociological consequences."

Yet, despite this massive crowd of applicants, West Germany has proportionately fewer college and university-level students and youth eligible for admissions to institutions of higher learning than any other industrialized country—West or East. Per 1,000 population, the Federal Republic today has but one-fourth as many college-level students as the United States, one-third as many as the Soviet Union or East Germany, and only half as many as the Netherlands, Great Britain, France, or Japan. Although the percentage of those eligible for university admission has more than doubled since 1962, it is still substantially below that of all other industrialized countries. In 1974 the proportion of those qualified for college was 15 percent, and by 1980 it is expected to be 22 percent—compared with 25 percent throughout Western Europe, 30 percent in the Communist countries, and 60 percent in the United States.

But even those youths—the vast majority of young West Germans—who neither plan nor are academically qualified for higher education now find their futures blocked. Of 400,000 "graduates" of general schools applying for apprenticeships in industry and trade in the spring of 1974, only 350,000 could be accommodated. The remaining 50,000 teenagers were condemned to futures as unskilled laborers and in a year or two their annual number is expected to top 100,000.

West Germany's is a cobwebbed nineteenth-century educational system that is totally unsuited for a twentieth-century world. It is hierarchical, elitist, class-oriented, authoritarian, and is obsessed with imparting and acquiring prodigious amounts of encyclopaedic knowledge. It is oblivious to the requirements of a modern industrial society and to the need to educate young people to participate and accept responsibility in a democracy.

Among the first to warn about and draw attention to these failings was Georg Picht, professor of religious philosophy at the University of Heidelberg. In the early 1960s his book *The German Educational Catastrophe* became an immediate best seller and touched off a nationwide discussion about the needs for reform. But those reforms, as Picht says today, were all superficial. They were hampered by the decentralized administration of the educational system, the traditions and sacred-cow ideologies of nearly two centuries, and amounted to little more than patchwork.

"What we have now," says Picht, "are young people graduating from schools where they really haven't learned anything and in which every gesture of independence and initiative is suppressed. From there we are encouraging them to apply for universities that cannot accommodate them and where they cannot learn what they need, for the curricula do not meet the real requirements of the students or contemporary society. . . . The situation has been very bad, and it is going to get even worse."

Picht's analysis of West Germany's educational predicament, says Dr. Hamm-Bruecher, "triggered a decade of talk and proposals that has produced virtually nothing. Of course, we could go on for a while pretending that matters will eventually improve. We can stick our heads in the sand for another few years and delude ourselves into thinking that a few partial improvements are tantamount to reform, just as you can hang the laundry on the line and pretend that the motion caused by the wind is forward movement. But one of these days, in the not too distant future, our procrastination in educational policy is going to catch up with us the same way our procrastination in policy toward East Germany, Eastern Europe, and the Soviet Union did. Just as we had to face reality in our relations with the East, so we shall have to face reality in education. The public will have to be told the truth. The truth is going to be hard and the price—political, social, and monetary—of finding our way out of an increasingly desolate situation is going to be very high."

Like most progressive observers and critics of West German education, Dr. Hamm-Bruecher sees its problems as dating back to the time of Wilhelm von Humboldt, the Prussian minister of education from 1809 to 1810, who reformed the German university system and was the architect of the Gymnasium, the German high school.

For his world and his epoch, Humboldt was indeed a reformer whose concepts of a classical, humanistic education, with strong Christian and authoritarian overtones, led to a widely emulated model.

The essence of the Humboldtian Gymnasium, graduation from which, after passing the *Abitur* examination (called *Matura* in Austria), implied automatic acceptance of the "mature" youth by the university, was education for a small elite of the moneyed bourgeoisie and the titled aristocracy. His system laid the foundation both for Germany's eighteenth- and nineteenth-century glory and tragedy: for the great intellectual and scientific achievements of the Germans, on the one hand; and on the other hand, for the political ignorance that culminated in nazism. But besides a monopoly of education for a small elite, Humboldt also created an inferior system of education for the masses. The *Volksschule*, meaning literally "people's school," but being in essence a general elementary school, depended on second-rate teachers with mediocre intellects and third-rate training who taught the four R's of reading, 'riting, 'rithmetic, and religion—just enough to make the masses diligent, conscientious, and obedient subordinates.

For all practical purposes—various reforms and democratization notwithstanding—the Humboldtian system has survived in the Federal Republic to the present day. The first attempts to liberalize and democratize it were undertaken after World War I and the collapse of the Kaiser Reich. Standards of training and qualification for Volksschule teachers were raised to the point where they had to have some college-level education and certificates from teacher-training academies before they were licensed to enter a classroom. The first four years of Volksschule became mandatory for all, regardless of parental caste and standing. A system of nationwide testing of ten-year-olds was introduced to determine which of the fourth-graders were intellectually equipped to transfer to Gymnasium, at age eleven, and which ones were to remain in the Volksschule, where inferior courses of instruction ended with the eighth grade at age fourteen, whereupon these youths would embark on three years of apprentice training in some trade.

Although this represented a significant step forward, in practice little changed. The educated and wealthy—those being one were invariably also the other—were intellectually, socially and politically in a sufficiently advantageous position to assure that their children passed the exams for admission to Gymnasium. They were also able to assist their children—personally or by hiring tutors—in mastering the grueling intellectual work load, heavy with Greek, Latin, German literature, and higher mathematics, which the *Gymnasien* imposed on their pupils.

The vast majority of young Germans—around 95 percent—were barred from these elite schools that represented the only avenue to higher education, even when they were able to pass the fourth-grade admissions exams: Attendance required tuition which their parents could not afford to pay. Moreover, most working and lower-middle-class parents, steeped in nineteenth-century tradition, preferred their children to learn trades, feared that they would not be able to help with the homework, and were afraid that Gymnasium attendance on the part of their offspring would lead to class and caste alienation within the family.

Whatever further efforts may have been underway to reform German education in the late 1920s and early 1930s, they came to naught after Hitler took power and turned the entire educational system into an instrument of Nazi ideology and indoctrination.

After 1945 one of the first measures of the Allied administrations was to reform German education. "Look at the various military government edicts, ordinances, and proposals," Hildegard Hamm-Bruecher once advised me, "and you will see the same ideas, concepts, and recommendations which have been advanced since the mid-1960s and for which progressive educators and reformers are striving and fighting today. They have merely been refurbished, repolished and repackaged, and are being offered as the newest of all new ideas. But it is just as hard to sell and implement them today as in the late 1940s."

To embark on a detailed exploration and analysis of the reasons why they were not introduced and implemented during the Allied occupation would go beyond the province of this book. Suffice it to say that Allied, especially American, plans and proposals for German educational reform went much the same way as judicial reform, reform of the police, and reform of the entrenched, hierarchical civil service system. They became victims of the incipient cold war whose real and imagined exigencies called for the speediest end to Allied administration of postwar Germany.

But whereas the judiciary, police, and civil service were eventually subjected to varying and more or less successful measures of reform by the West Germans themselves, education—both qualitatively and quantitatively—became a stepchild of reconstruction, the "economic miracle," consumerism, and the West German preoccupation with the "good life." By the time educational reformers such as Georg Picht, Hildegard Hamm-Bruecher or Rolf Dahrendorff, the professor-politician who now heads London's School of Economics, won the public ear with their warnings and pleas, and by the time West German students took to the streets to demonstrate for educational and social reform in 1967 and 1968, it was in large measure already too late.

"Our children," says Frau Hamm-Bruecher, "have turned out to be the real losers of the war."

Virtually the only change in West Germany's educational system after the war—a change equal to retrogressing to the Reformation and Counter Reformation of the sixteenth and seventeenth centuries—was the sharp division of *public* schools along *denominational* lines: Protestant and Catholic. Religious instruction being mandatory in the West German schools because of various agreements between the states and the Lutheran churches and the 1934 Concordat between the Vatican and Berlin, nothing seemed easier than packing Protestant children into Protestant schools, Catholic kids into Catholic schools.

In areas too small to justify the maintenance of two schools, religious apartheid was imposed on the existing institution. In one village in the Rhineland, not far from Bonn, a school was equipped with four lavatories: one each for Catholic girls, Protestant girls, Catholic boys, and Protestant boys. The weekly news magazine *Der Spiegel* once published a photograph of a "separate but equal" bicycle rack installed for children at one country school. It was, in fact, through Hildegard Hamm-Bruecher's protests and campaigns against the denominational school system that she first gained national prominence as an educational reformer.

For all practical purposes, if one disregards a few backwoods areas of Bavaria, the system has been abandoned. Religious instruction, however, is still mandatory in West German schools and it has been estimated that in all the years they spend in class, children receive six times as many hours of religious instruction as they do civics, and four times as many as they spend learning physics or chemistry.

Leaving aside reform experiments, pilot projects, or special and technical schools, the West German educational system, over which the federal government exercises virtually no control and the state governments almost total control, is, from the fifth grade on, a three-avenued system. It has no real equivalents in any other country. Those three avenues lead not only to totally different opportunities in life, they actually categorize youth and, in the case of two of them, virtually entitle people to professions, civil service ranks, and executive positions in industry and commerce to which the other educational road, travelled by the majority, does not.

At age six the West German child enters an elementary school, the *Grundschule,* which lasts, as it always did, for four years. Although tests are no longer given and reforms since the late 1960s have been designed to widen the opportunities for working-class children, fourth grade remains a crucial time in the life of any West German child. For it is in that year that the sum of performance, ability, and aptitudes are assessed to determine and recommend along which of the three avenues of secondary education the child should continue.

The overwhelming majority—nearly 65 percent—enter the *Hauptschule,* which is but a new name for the old Volksschule, usually located in the same building in which the children spent the first four grades. It offers a course of instruction that lasts another five years, which used to be only four years until the late 1960s and in a few states is now being expanded to six years. At age fifteen, Hauptschule "graduates" are expected to take apprentice training in industry, the trades, or commerce. Most apprentice courses last three years and apprentices may be trained wherever there is a *Meister,* that is, a master craftsman. That may be in the "master shop" of the garage mechanic, the mason, the baker, or the candlestick-maker around the corner; it can also be at the excellently organized, beautifully equipped, and professionally staffed apprentice-training division of a large industrial enterprise such as the Volkswagen Corporation. Until age eighteen, apprentices are also required to attend vocational schools, where they are taught general subjects, as well as trade-related courses, for two schooldays weekly.

The three distinguishing features of the Hauptschule system are, besides its brevity, its relatively low academic level, the lower qualifications of its teaching staff, and the fact that its graduates are barred from higher education and virtually all but blue-collar and inferior white-collar jobs. While instructors in the other two types of schools must be full university graduates with degrees equalling at least the American master's if not actually a doctorate, teachers in the Hauptschulen are usually graduates of pedagogical training colleges which grant diplomas roughly equivalent to an American baccalaureate. Higher mathematics, physics, and chemistry are not taught, and the foreign language instruction is very limited. Graduates of the Hauptschule are automatically barred from the middle- and upper-level civil service, from becoming military officers, from all the professions, and from most managerial and executive jobs. They cannot enter universities or colleges unless they take the long hard "third road" of adult evening education to qualify for admission.

The second avenue open to the fifth-grader is the *Realschule*. Though dating back to the early decades of this century, this type of school has become increasingly popular in recent years. It offers a six-year course of instruction and graduation at sixteen with a diploma called a *Mittlere Reifezeugniss*, which is roughly translatable as "a certificate of median maturity." Currently attended by approximately 17 percent of any year's crop of fifth-graders, the Realschule's course of instruction approximates the first six years of the Gymnasium. Its teachers must have the same qualifications as Gymnasium instructors, the books and educational materials are often the same, and the courses as tough. The basic difference is that it does not last as long, that no grueling examination need be passed to graduate, and that graduation from a Realschule does not entitle a student to college or university admission. Thus, Realschulen graduates cannot enter the professions and are barred from military commissions, but they are eligible for middle-level service posts and junior managerial jobs.

Finally there is the Gymnasium itself, once open to less than 10 percent of any annual group of fifth-graders, now attended by approximately 17 percent. It is a nine-year school whose graduates, at age nineteen, have a level of education that most American universities equate with two to three years of college. The Abitur diploma conferred by the Gymnasium depends on successfully passing stiff written and oral examinations, usually lasting several weeks and administered on a statewide basis. The exams are so tough and standards in these schools so high (five to six years of Latin and in some cases Greek, five years of English, and four or five of French being par for the course), that only three-fourths of those who enter the Gymnasium at age eleven graduate from it at nineteen. One can debate whether the Gymnasium curriculum, steeped in the nineteenth-century Humboldtian tradition of humanistic education of an intellectual elite, still has any relevance to modern times. But there can be no question that it is probably the toughest and most demanding type of school in the world today. Graduation from the Gymnasium is an open sesame to the professions, top managerial positions, military commissions, and senior civil service jobs.

And in theory, the Abitur, also called a "certificate of maturity for higher education," is the ticket to the German university, which has no entrance examinations. And that, in part, is the German educational dilemma today, for as more and more young West Germans obtain an Abitur they are discovering that it is a ticket to a bus so overcrowded that it cannot move. The Abitur explosion of recent years has a number of causes. There was first of all the baby boom of the 1950s and 1960s, which produced the millions of young Germans now in their teens. Secondly, reform attempts in the educational system have opened the Gymnasium doors to almost twice as many youths as a decade ago. Abolition of the fourth-grade exams, of tuition and textbook fees, and widespread encouragement of the intellectually able, has doubled the proportion of working-class children now entering the Gymnasium system and obtaining Abitur degrees. The universities have simply not been able to keep pace with the growing number of eligible applicants at their gates. Despite substantial infusions of federal and state money, older institutions have not really been expanded and too few new ones—a total of nineteen since 1960—have been built. At present, in addition to sixty-nine teachers' colleges which churn out instructors for the elementary schools and the Hauptschulen, the Federal Republic has only fifty-six universities and equivalent institutes of higher learning. Of these, seventeen are theological seminaries.

Moreover, the very nature of the West German university system— under sharp attack from reformers—contributes to the expanding crowd of applicants. Steeped in traditions that go back centuries, the German university is dedicated to scholarship, knowledge, and wisdom for their own sake. Until very recently it rejected all notions that it should be an institution that prepares young people for professional life. The suggestion that it transform itself from a "university of education" to a "university of instruction" has met stiff resistance from most of those connected with it—professors and students alike.

Because of its ivory-tower traditions, the method of study is highly unorganized. There are no classes in the American sense and no attendance requirements. Nor is there any limit to the number of years a student may spend before he has acquired the sufficient quantity of subject certificates, passed the required exams, and written the necessary dissertations to obtain his degree. The object, after all, is the acquisition of wisdom in an atmosphere of scholarship. And with that object in mind, German students have traditionally spent more years attending university than British or French, not to mention Americans.

In recent years this period of enrollment has become even longer—by an average of 40 percent—so the average West German now spends more than six years studying for the majority of degrees and as long as nine years for doctorates in medicine and the sciences. Ironically, one reason for this increase has been a reform program designed to open opportunities of higher education to a broader cross-section of the population. Tuition and lecture fees have been virtually eliminated. But since the income of assistant professors and lecturers depended in part on a share of those fees, they have been delivering fewer lectures and turning increasingly to more lucrative above-salary projects such as writing and research on contract. Students, as a consequence, must wait even longer before acquiring the necessary "knowledge" that entitles them to subject certificates and enables them to pass the exams. And the longer the average student remains enrolled, the fewer spaces there are for newcomers and the greater the number of those who cannot be accepted.

To tabulate and analyze all the proposals of the past ten years for partial and total reform of West German education, from preschool to the university system, is almost a science unto itself. To discuss more than a fraction of them would require another book. Even leading reformers themselves now speak candidly and with dismay of "a carrousel of recommendations, suggestions, proposals, studies, pilot projects, experiments, committees, commissions, councils and boards of inquiry that has left the public at large dizzy, disgusted and confused." To cite but one example, a "framework law" for university reform, first drafted and introduced in 1969, has been revised so often that more than a dozen versions of the bill now exist. And despite the government's firm resolve to push it through parliament in the spring of 1974, the Bundestag was no closer to passing it in the spring of 1975 than it had been six years earlier.

By far the most sweeping and, according to Hildegard Hamm-Bruecher, the most essential reform proposal is to transfer basic authority and responsibility for education from the various states to the federal government, somewhat along the lines on which educational policies have been centralized in the United States. This would require not only an amendment to the constitution, but entail overcoming an entire obstacle course of local and regional objections, jealousies, suspicions, prerogatives, and carefully protected interests and privileges. To many West Germans for whom Prussian attempts at hegemony over educational policies and centralized Nazi control of all schools remain nightmares, any and all moves in this direction are anathema. Yet without greater centralization of the system, no other reform is possible because the current federal structure means that while Bonn may propose, ultimately the states dispose.

Proposals for reform of the primary and secondary school system are all aimed at "democratizing" both its content and structure. The goal is to make high-quality education available to the broadest possible spectrum, to offer an educational program that is responsive to the needs of society, and simultaneously to imbue the parent-teacher-pupil relationship with a spirit of genuine partnership.

"For without optimal education for all," says Carl-Heinz Evers, West Berlin's former education minister, "without an enormous potential of highly qualified labor reserves, a highly industrialized democracy cannot function."

One of the most important steps in this direction would be abolition of the three-avenued secondary school system. To replace it, reformers recommend a *Gesamtschule*—a comprehensive school—more or less patterned along American lines and free of both social and intellectual class distinctions. Though it could be divided by age groups, much as it is in the United States, it would be an "all-through" system of at least ten years' duration, providing eleventh- and twelfth-grade courses for those willing and qualified to go on to higher education. The plan foresees eventual abolition of the Abitur and its exams, substituting for them a school-leaving diploma and university entrance examinations.

The first such Gesamtschule opened in West Berlin under Evers' aegis in 1968. Since then 129 others, with a total enrollment of seventy thousand pupils, have been started in all the other states, though the overwhelming majority are in those states governed by the Social Democratic party or by SPD/FDP coalitions. There are only twelve such schools in the five states—Bavaria, Baden-Wuerttemberg, Saarland,

Rhineland-Palatinate, and Schleswig-Holstein—where the CDU, the more conservative and tradition-minded party, is in power.

Along with the "comprehensive school," reformers are also calling for introduction of the *Ganztagsschule*—the "all-day" school—as the optimal pedagogial solution to what ails West Germany. The all-day school, like that in the United States, would have a period of instruction from approximately 9:00 A.M. to 3:30 P.M., instead of the current 8:00 A.M. to noon schedule, with children, in most cases, eating their lunches at school. It would reduce the school week from the current six to five days, presumably open opportunities for more extracurricular activities such as school clubs, and hopefully cut down the massive load of homework with which children are presently burdened and with which, by tradition, parents are expected to help but in practice often end up doing themselves.

It is, in fact, the "homework syndrome" which in the view of many reformers has posed such a bar to breaking down social and class barriers in German education. Because of the traditional brevity of the schoolday there are prodigious amounts of homework to do. And it has always been regarded axiomatic that parents would help. But working-class parents, lacking the educational background needed to help children attending Gymnasien and Realschulen, are reluctant to have their children go to such schools. Hyperconscious of their own "ignorance," they fear that if they were unable to help their children with homework, the children would be disadvantaged. Some have prevented their children from entering secondary schools because "when the homework has to be done the kids would discover how little we know."

The all-day school, presumably with scheduled study halls and a sufficient number of teachers to help the pupils, would reduce the German "homework catastrophe," as it has been called. But introduction of the all-day school also implies a sweeping change in ingrained family traditions and lifestyles, and would entail a vast outlay in educational infrastructure. Facilities for lunchrooms, cafeterias, and kitchens would have to be built. Additional help would have to be hired. Families in which mothers do not work, and fathers either come home for the noon meal or eat it at work, would have to change their schedules, for the noon meal in a large proportion of families is still the main meal. The all-day school concept has also met with considerable opposition from teachers, who feel it would burden them with longer working hours.

At present there are no more than a few score all-day schools in the Federal Republic, forty of them being comprehensive *Gesamtschulen*.

Compared to 28,000 Gymnasien, Realschulen, and Hauptschulen having a total enrollment of nearly six million pupils, the 130 comprehensive schools now operating with seventy thousand youngsters in attendance do not, of course, represent much more than an experimental drop in the educational bucket. But it is a most important drop and the experiment thus far has proven successful. Sooner or later the Gesamtschule is expected to become the rule rather than the exception of West German secondary education.

Educators associated with the program insist that these schools have raised the educational niveau of all the children attending them and that they have contributed to breaking down social distinctions and tension. The climate in them has been described as "a vast improvement" over that in the other types of secondary schools. Enthusiasm and the feeling that "school can be fun" are replacing the traditional spirit of drudgery and boredom. The percentage of pupils participating in school activities and in pupil self-management and self-government is markedly higher than in the other schools.

Above all, it is said, the Gesamtschule is breaking down old hierarchical structures and a partner-relationship between pupils, teachers, and parents is developing. Fear—for many decades the German pupil's primary emotion toward his teachers—is giving way to genuine respect and friendship.

It is, in fact, the pupil-teacher-parent relationship that has been most needful of reform in German education.

"Many of Germany's problems in history," a Bonn Gymnasium teacher once said to me, "were due to an exaggerated emphasis on respect for authority, which began right in the schools where the dominant elements were authority and fear. The teachers—in their dual capacity as instructors imparting knowledge and demanding its absorption by the children, and in their role as tenured civil servants representing the power of the state—were the embodiment of authority. Both parents and pupils had been raised in an atmosphere of fear of that authority. But that sort of relationship does not serve as a basis either for real education or for democracy."

No one was more acutely aware of this than the late German-American social philosopher Professor Max Horkheimer who, upon returning to

Germany in 1949 after spending fifteen years in emigration in the United States, reopened his famous Frankfurt University Institute for Social Research. Under the auspices of the American Jewish Committee, whose chief consultant for German affairs he was, Horkheimer in 1960 launched an important program to "educate the educators." Funded by the Ford, Volkswagen, and Thyssen foundations and the U. S. and West German governments, it provided for sending small groups of teachers to the United States each year to study civics, history, and social science instruction and the practice of democracy in American classrooms.

The program was launched under the impact of the wave of swastika smearings and antisemitic incidents that rocked Germany and shocked the world in late 1959 and early 1960, and the initial motivation was to induce German educators to teach more, and more accurately, about the Nazi past. But from the outset Horkheimer stressed that "teaching children about Hitler is in itself not enough."

"To develop Germany into a viable democracy," he said, "it will be essential to educate its educators. A fundamental change in method and approach is needed."

As a reporter in Germany in the 1960s, frequently covering the education scene, I had numerous opportunities to talk to the teachers who had gone to the United States under the auspices of the Horkheimer program and to record their reactions and impressions.

"Education toward responsible citizenship in America," Dr. Hans Graaf, a Gymnasium teacher from the town of Laasphe, said shortly after his return from the United States, "is due more to the school atmosphere than any curriculum or lesson plan. For us, it will be essential to do away with the autocratic attitude teachers take toward pupils as well as the autocratic stance of school administrators toward teachers. I was amazed to see how relaxed both teachers and pupils were in a Baltimore school when a couple of senior officials from the city school administration paid a visit, and even more amazed to see the officials stand in line, waiting their turn along with pupils and teachers, during lunch in the school cafeteria."

One school superintendent who participated in the program came back from the United States determined never again to let a teacher or principal address him by his title, *Herr Schulrat*—Mr. Superintendent. "The impact of this is potentially revolutionary," one of Horkheimer's associates told me. "All the titles in our school system, you know, are formal civil service ranks as well. The lowest rating for a tenured

Gymnasium teacher is that of *Studienrat*. It is his formal title but also a rank, equivalent in pay to that of major. An *Oberstudienrat* would be equivalent to a lieutenant colonel, and so on. A Schulrat, which is a title, position, and rank, equals a brigadier general. An entirely new relationship will evolve when teachers are no longer called *Herr Studienrat*, the teachers no longer call the principal *Herr Studiendirektor,* and the principals no longer address the superintendent as *Herr Schulrat.* Everybody will have to come off his pedestal, stop being a demigod, and democratic principles, not to mention real education, will have a chance."

"The real learning process," said Erhard Dornberg (no relation of mine), a Duesseldorf Gymnasium instructor, "begins with decision-making. In the United States pupils are taught to decide, to judge for themselves, and to reach conclusions after sifting through a mass of conflicting information. This is real learning.

"We in Germany," he told me emphatically upon his return, "always believed that we had reached the zenith of civilization and culture by acquiring knowledge. But knowledge in itself is not what we should seek. We must teach young people to convert their knowledge into action and to apply it to daily problems. If it cannot serve that purpose, it is useless knowledge.

"Our schools must not be isolated from the rest of the world," he said. "The purpose of education should be to prepare youngsters for the world and for life. You cannot do this by isolating them in an academic atmosphere which is geared primarily to funneling information into their heads without teaching them to think. It was this practice, and the German intellectual's traditional abhorrence of political action, that enabled a Hitler to come to power."

Another German educator, Dr. Martin Greiffenhagen of Muenster, came back from the United States convinced that a key solution to the problems in Germany was more parent-teacher cooperation. And the only way to achieve this, he said, is for greater integration of schools into the local communities.

"In the United States," he stressed, "the schools *are* community institutions, financially dependent on the neighborhoods and towns in which they are located. Here the school is merely one more element of the state administration and, as such, leaves little action room for community initiatives."

One of the participants in the program was Dr. Reinhard Tausch, a "psychologist of teaching" who, together with his wife, used the time in the United States to compare behavioral patterns between American and German educators. Armed with tape recorders and stopwatches the Tausches had first invaded classrooms in the Federal Republic, then the United States, to measure how often teachers said "Thank you" or "Please," how many words were uttered by pupils, how many by teachers, how many commands were given and how many questions asked.

They determined that in the average forty-minute school period, German teachers ask 56.3 questions, Americans 41.3. Whereas 44 percent of the American teachers' questions were directed to individual students, only 29 percent of those asked by German teachers were directed to individuals, the rest to the class as a whole which was then expected to reply in unison. The Tausches felt that German children were intimidated by their teachers, asking only a fourth as many questions as American youngsters. The German teachers, moreover, rarely used the words "please" or "thank you" and tended to spend most of the instructional period declaiming. More than 90 percent of the time, the classroom behavior of German teachers, according to Tausch, was "autocratic in nature."

The Tausches subsequently published their findings in a book that triggered protests from traditionalists and a running controversy in pedagogical circles. Although a decade has passed since its publication, older teachers still work up a foam of rage whenever it is mentioned. But in that decade a new generation of younger teachers has come of age and represents the majority in the classrooms. The consensus among them is that much is to be learned from the Tausch findings.

Indeed, over the years, the seeds sown by the Horkheimer program have begun to bear fruit. Slowly, but surely, West German education is being liberalized, modernized, and democratized. In 1973, for example, the city-state of Hamburg passed a revolutionary law establishing "school councils" in which parents, teachers, and pupils have an equal voice. The councils are even authorized to elect school principals. According to the law, principals will be chosen and hired for two-year trial periods by the councils and after the probationary time will be given ten-year contracts subject to approval by the councils.

By 1976 the whole approach to teaching and learning in the upper two

Gymnasium grades is expected to change in most German schools. A pilot program, testing the new method, has been operative in the town of Opladen, near Cologne, since 1972 and has won the approval of the majority of state ministers of education. It is designed to encourage independent study and research. The number of mandatory courses will be reduced to the barest minimum, and Gymnasium juniors and seniors will be offered a wide range of electives. The program, if indeed it is implemented, marks a dramatic break with the traditionally restrictive, stuffy, rote-learning, and declamatory atmosphere in the elite schools. And from what I have been able to determine, it will create an educational atmosphere similar to that found in most American colleges.

Older teachers, naturally, continue to regard themselves as representatives of an "institution of learning." But the younger ones—many of them bearded, long-maned veterans of the student and youth rebellion of 1967 and 1968 and decried by conservatives as "wild-eyed Marxists and revolutionaries"—view themselves as "leaders of a group willing to learn."

One of the most remarkable phenomena in this context is the spreading use of the familiar second-person singular pronoun *Du* on the part of pupils when addressing their teachers. Perhaps it was inevitable that the fearful, awe-inspired titles of *Herr Lehrer, Frau Studienraetin,* or *Herr Oberstudienrat* would eventually be supplanted by a more relaxed *Herr Schmidt* or *Frau Schultz.* But the fact that pupils are now addressing their teachers by first name and, instead of the more respectful *Sie* are calling them *Du,* is surely causing old Wilhelm von Humboldt to whirl in his grave. In a country where some university rectors still demand that they be addressed as "His Magnificence," and lifelong friends still address each other in the second-person plural *Sie,* calling a teacher *Du* is nothing short of revolutionary.

And to judge from what young people say about it, the practice is not only widespread but is having a most beneficial effect on education. "The pupils feel freer," a fifteen-year-old girl wrote the editors of *Die Zeit* which runs a weekly "open forum" column for teenagers. "It has enabled them to study more independently. The teacher has become less a 'personage of authority' and more of a comrade. That has not reduced our respect for him. After all, I say *Du* to all my friends and classmates and I respect them too."

"If a teacher works *with* the pupils and they regard him as a partner in the learning process," said a sixteen-year-old boy, "addressing him with *Du* is the most natural thing in the world."

"This practice," said another fifteen-year-old girl, "has improved the working atmosphere tremendously. Classes are more relaxed and the kids are losing their fear of speaking up, giving their views, and asking and answering questions."

Parents, too, are adopting new attitudes toward teachers, the schools, and education in general. They are demanding a say in the running of schools, in the selection of faculty, and in decisions on curricula. A decade ago no West German parent would even have entertained the thought of attending classes with a child or going to school unless called by the principal or teacher because of disciplinary problems. Today all but two of the states literally invite parents to come and watch what goes on in class and parents do so.

And unthinkable as recently as five years ago are the parent and pupil strikes that have taken place in numerous areas since the first one made headlines in Bremen in the spring of 1973. The issues are varied. There have been strikes against teachers considered too leftist and against those regarded as too autocratic and disciplinarian. Parents have struck because they felt teachers' sex education "bordered on the pornographic." They have struck against overcrowded classrooms, too much homework, lesson plans that are too inflexible and those that are not tight enough. The problems are generally local, and in the overall picture of a school system crying for reform, not too important. What is significant, however, is the new participatory mood of both parents and pupils, a manifestation, as Hildegard Hamm-Bruecher put it, of the dawning awareness that "the time for lip service to reform is over."

That awareness is, more than most West Germans realize or admit, an outgrowth of the student rebellion of the late 1960s. What began as leftwing demonstrations against the Shah of Iran, the Vietnam war, the right-wing Springer Press chain, and police terror tactics, soon developed into a pervasive revolt among West German youth against virtually all the old values and what youth regarded as the Establishment's manipulation and exploitation of the new. Short-lived as the rebellion may have been, it accomplished far more than is generally known: It set in motion a process of societal change, the ultimate impact and dimensions of which cannot yet be measured. Moreover, being a rebellion primarily of students, it has left its most indelible mark on the German universities themselves. The universities, on the other hand, being preserves of conservatism and tradition, have reacted with a degree of nervousness that borders on hysteria.

There are a number of misconceptions about the West German universities today which, I believe, need urgently to be dispelled. Old Heidelberg, for all its meticulous preservation of idyllic romanticism and appeal as a tourist attraction, is no longer a place to find a student prince. The last time it made significant news was in December 1972 when it was a bubbling cauldron because Baden-Wuerttemberg's minister of education had called out twelve hundred helmeted, club-wielding state troopers for a showdown with four thousand unarmed students who were demonstrating peacefully against a ban on a left-wing, "anarchist" professor's use of university property for a political lecture.

Although there are still dueling and drinking fraternities at German universities, dueling (let's leave drinking out of it) is no longer a prerequisite for belonging. But historically speaking, the "corporations," as the fraternities are called, have about as much relevance as the dinosaur. Once the vanguard of progress and reform when they were conceived as movements for German unity in the early nineteenth century, the fraternities today, dueling and nondueling, have a declining membership of approximately forty thousand out of a total student body of more than six hundred thousand.

Tightly disciplined, highly organized left-wing extremists *are* a factor in West German universities today. They have penetrated the student bodies. Some of them are lecturers and assistant professors. A few are even life-tenured *Ordinarien*, that is, department heads and chair-holders. They have organized violent demonstrations, disrupted lectures, pelted some professors with rotten eggs, physically assaulted others, and terrorized a few into resigning their positions. *But* they are nowhere near the menace to intellectual freedom nor the threat to the democratic order they have been alleged to be by conservatives in West Germany and alarmists abroad. The number of lectures they disrupted in Frankfurt, the most dissension-torn of all universities, during the "hot winter" of 1974, amounted to no more than one percent. They are not about to subvert all of the country's pedagogical institutions and there is no danger that the next generation of elementary and secondary school teachers will all be a bunch of radical Maoists or Marxists. Indeed, at last count, the most militant of all the groups, the Maoist-oriented Communist Student League, had only 18 seats of the 1,016 on all the student councils all over the Federal Republic. True, Spartakus, the youth organization of the infinitely more conservative, Moscow-oriented German Communist party, has done better than that. Half of all students regard Spartakus as a "decisive, effective, reform-minded group." But that infatuation with Spartakus does not benefit its parent organization, the Communist party, for whom a scant 5 percent of students would vote at the next election.

Finally, although some university reforms have been enacted, they have barely begun to scratch the moss and crust of centuries of tradition from this most conservative of all West German institutions.

The most important changes that have taken place—and they have not been enacted at all universities, for the universities, though institutions of the states, are autonomous and self-governing—involved their administration and the rights of students and subprofessorial lecturers.

Traditionally, German universities had been headed by "rectors," who were elected for one- or two-year periods by the academic "senates"—assemblages of full professors and chair-holders. The rectors were themselves full professors who served in the top administrative office more or less on an honorary, part-time basis. Since 1969, however, more and more universities have been going over to a U. S.-style "presidential system," that is, a university head who, presumably, has some administrative and managerial qualifications, serves full time, and is elected to the post for a longer period, in some instances for as long as ten years. The objective is twofold: to make the universities more efficient and responsive to the needs of society and to break the near-autocratic hold of the chair-holders, the Ordinarien.

The German *Ordinarius* has no equal in any university system elsewhere in the world. Although he can be equated with the American type of department head or chair-holder, his position, in fact, is far more exalted and powerful, for he is the only one at a German university who has tenure, and it is life tenure at that, and his authority over his department is tantamount to that of a dictator. Everyone under him—the assistant professors and lecturers—having no tenure or job protection at all, are more or less dependent on him and his good graces, even in terms of scholarship and research. That this system lends itself to abuse is obvious, and over the decades it has been badly abused. One check on it is to give the other two "castes" at the university, the students and the "middle-class" lecturers and assistant professors, a greater voice. This has and is being done by giving all three groups one-third parity in codetermining university operations. As originally conceived and enacted in the state of Lower Saxony, it would give all three groups equal voice over everything, from curriculum to staff appointments. Early in 1973, however, a group of Ordinarien challenged the constitutionality of the Lower Saxon reform law before the federal supreme court, and the court ruled that on the question of determining research and appointing new full professors, that is other Ordinarien, the chair-holders cannot be overruled by students and assistant professors and lecturers.

Beyond these two measures—introduction of the presidential system and one-third parity—there are many other proposals for university reform in various stages of discussion and legislative approval.

The most important, obviously, is to provide more spaces by building new, and enlarging old, university facilities. A federal government plan, introduced in the summer of 1974, calls for the investment of DM 12.6 billion in federal and state funds so as to provide facilities for a student body of 800,000 by 1978. That would entail making room for about 200,000 more students than are currently enrolled. But the proposal has been widely criticized as falling far short of requirements. It has been estimated that by 1978, if all eligible applicants are to be accepted, the universities must provide space for 930,000 students.

The other proposals all seem to have more or less the same goals in mind: a more democratic university, a more efficient university, a university more responsive to the needs of society, and a university more geared to the realities of life. In the opinion of most reformers, this would entail new personnel structures and the replacement of the Ordinarius system by something akin to the American department heads, giving students and assistant professors an even greater voice than they presently have, redetermining student goals and adjusting programs of study to correspond to those goals, limiting the number of years students may stay at the university before obtaining degrees, reorienting university programs so as to make them more "scientific and technical-minded," and, finally, abolishing the Gymnasium Abitur and introducing university admissions exams.

"Our trouble thus far," says Georg Picht, "is that the reforms introduced to date have all been on the surface and have all failed to take into account that a modern university is a highly complex enterprise which cannot be changed by shouting a few slogans. Another basic mistake is that until now we have approached educational reform on two tracks—the schools and the universities—failing to see and treat them as a system, as a whole."

Hildegard Hamm-Bruecher would take even that idea a step further. "Reform of our educational system," she says, "must be reform from top to bottom and bottom to top to create a vertical, integrated structure, starting with preschools and leading right through to adult education."

That, in essence, is what East Germany did years ago.

A comparison of East and West German education once prompted the weekly *Die Zeit* to say: "It is inconceivable that the two systems had a common origin." Quantitatively, East Germany is the best educated country in Europe today, and as most West German educators reluctantly admit, educationally it is an entire epoch ahead of the Federal Republic.

Proportionately it has 70 percent more teachers than West Germany and its classrooms are only two-thirds as full. Some 85 percent of all pupils receive at least ten years of formal schooling, compared to only 35 percent in West Germany. Some 99 percent of all secondary school graduates, including those going on to higher education, learn a trade and obtain journeyman's papers. The GDR has fifty-four universities and institutes of higher education—almost as many as the Federal Republic—and although it has less than one-third of West Germany's population, it has more than half as many enrolled students. For the past two decades it has consistently spent a greater proportion of its gross national product on education than the Federal Republic, and currently this outlay is almost 50 percent higher than West Germany's. Above all, despite reforms and drives to open the opportunities of higher education to a greater number of working-class and lower-middle-class children, university education in West Germany has remained more or less a privilege of the upper- and upper-middle classes, whereas in the GDR the majority of university students are the children of blue-collar workers and farmers.

One of the reasons for this East German educational explosion is the old Marxist slogan that "knowledge is power." This was the principle on which the nineteenth-century "workers' education societies" were founded, and it was from these societies that first the Social Democratic and subsequently the Communist parties evolved. And when they came to power in the Soviet occupation zone after World War II, they wasted little time before applying that principle to the reform of East German education. Their aim was to raise the general level of education, erase class and social distinctions, and equip as many children as possible with both theoretical and practical knowledge. The end product is a vertical, highly disciplined, intensely competitive and achievement-oriented system of education that begins with the infant nurseries, and preschools and leads right through the universities to a diversified and widely propagated program of adult education. East Germans, it seems, are learning or studying at all ages and at all times—in the kindergartens, schools, universities, through correspondence courses, and in their factories and collective farms.

Indeed, they are so education-conscious and so obsessed with obtaining certificates, diplomas, and degrees of one kind or another that the GDR's officialdom has expressed concern as to where it will all eventually lead. For as more and more people acquire professional and semiprofessional standing, less and less of them are satisfied with being "just workers." Thirty years after the end of the war, the GDR is on the verge of becoming a country of more chiefs than Indians, "a nation," as one critical observer wrote in the daily (East) *Berliner Zeitung*, "made up entirely of professors."

The trunk of this system is the comprehensive "unified ten-year polytechnical upper school," patterned after that of the Soviet Union. Except for a greater emphasis on manual training and the fact that older and younger children are generally not segregated in separate buildings, it is also a school system that is very similar to America's. With the rare exception of artistically and scientifically very gifted children or those who are retarded or physically disabled, it is attended by every East German child. Its basic course of instruction is designed for ten years, and 85 percent of all children complete it. The minority of 15 percent who do not are those who lack native ability and generally leave school after completing the eighth grade to learn trades. Of the remaining majority, approximately half continue for another two years in the eleventh and twelfth grades to obtain the East German equivalent of an Abitur, which entitles them to enter a university. But there are other avenues to higher education as well, including the extensive adult education program and, most important, a system of four-year trade and technical schools, graduation from which also leads to university admission. Obviously the East German tenth-grade diploma requires more scholastic achievement than the ninth-year certificate from West German Hauptschulen, being approximate to the *Mittlere Reife* degree of the Federal Republic's Realschulen. Whether it is equivalent to an American high school diploma is probably open to debate, but there is no question that the East German Abitur, obtained after twelve years, is on a par with the one received in West Germany after thirteen years of formal schooling and which is equal to approximately two years of college in the United States.

One important aspect of East German education is the emphasis on practical and manual training at a relatively early age. Manual training of sorts begins in first grade and continues throughout the entire period of schooling, becoming increasingly technical and specialized as the child grows older. Starting in the seventh grade there is the equivalent of at least one hour's shop and technical training daily, conducted in the school if it is large enough and has the facilities, or in nearby industrial plants, especially if these happen to have good training divisions and foremen with pedagogical aptitudes. While all this may not seem unusual to Americans, in Germany, where there was traditionally a sharp demarcation between education and practical training, it represents a radical innovation. Those youngsters who leave school with a tenth-grade diploma then become apprentices for another two or three years, completing their training with a journeyman's or skilled-worker certificate. Those who continue through eleventh and twelfth grade to prepare for the university, receive their apprentice training in school, and upon graduation have not only the Abitur but a skilled-worker certificate.

The universities themselves have little in common with those of West Germany and nothing whatsoever in common with the idyllic, ivory-tower alma mater of Wilhelm von Humboldt's days, even though, in veneration, East Berlin's university on Unter-den-Linden is named after him. They are tightly disciplined, highly organized learning factories with tough standards of performance. The objective is not to acquire knowledge and wisdom at one's leisure and perhaps with no specific purpose, but to prepare students for professions and to turn them out as quickly and efficiently as possible. Classes begin sharply at eight o'clock each morning and continue in a highly regimented form each day with mandatory attendance. There is little room for independent study, and in every course, tests and quizzes—unknown in West Germany—are given frequently during the semester. An American student would find the operation more or less familiar; a West German one, totally alien.

Undeniably, the East German reform of education is admirable. It is providing youth with greater opportunities and more education than Germans have ever had before. But the quality of that education is another matter. The GDR's schools, even more than West Germany's, dispense knowledge, but even less than the Federal Republic's they are not teaching young people to think and to challenge. The spirit of East German education is a pernicious mixture of Prussian pedantry and Communist indoctrination. Unable to free themselves from their own heritage, East German educators are using traditional and antiquated teaching methods in the service of official state dogma and ideology. In effect, they are raising a new generation whose heads are crammed with facts, but a generation that is highly uncritical and all too obedient.

Moreover, as in the Soviet Union itself, educational opportunities in East Germany are closely linked to total loyalty to the state. Young people who fail to toe the political line, who do not learn their Marxist-Leninist catechisms, or are insufficiently enthusiastic about or active in the Free German Youth (FDJ) organization, may find themselves as barred from educational opportunities and advancement as those who fail to perform scholastically. Those in the universities who do not receive passing marks in courses on dialectical materialism and political economy, may be expelled or deprived of their generous government scholarships. Unquestionably, East German youth learns a lot, learns it early, and learns it well. But, unfortunately, one of the things it learns is to *act* enthusiastically and to repeat the political phrases verbatim. And that, in essence, is learning hypocrisy.

Although it had West Germany in mind, *Der Spiegel* could well have spoken of East Germany, too, when it said not long ago: "The sociopolitical future of the country is so closely related to its educational system, that what is happening or not happening in the schools and universities now will determine the political and economic course in decades to come."

More education, as West Germans are learning from the East German example, is not necessarily better education. But they have also come to realize that better education is a matter of the highest national priority and urgency.

"If you accept the historical principle that revolutions result from suppressed reforms or those never undertaken," says Frau Hamm-Bruecher, "then you must realize that inability to reform our educational system will ultimately lead to a loss of our freedoms to extremist enemies of freedom on both the left and the right. Educational reform is part of societal reform and in both we have no time left to squander."

6

Germany for Germans?

As THE story goes, a man was taking a stroll along the Main River embankment in Frankfurt when suddenly he tripped, stumbled, and plunged headlong into the water. Flailing his arms and trying desperately to keep afloat, he yelled: "Down with the Jews! Down with the Jews!" Passersby and police ran to the scene and he was pulled out just moments before drowning. Instead of being rushed to the hospital, he was sped to the nearest precinct station. There cops grilled him mercilessly as to why he had shouted a phrase clearly violating the federal law that forbids defamation and inciting hatred of national, racial, or religious groups. "I knew," he replied, "that if I just called 'help' I wouldn't get anywhere near the attention I would by shouting about the Jews."

Told to me by a German Jew who miraculously escaped the holocaust by remaining in hiding from 1940 until the end of the war and has lived in Frankfurt ever since, that facetious and apocryphal anecdote reveals much about the ambiguous status of the Jews in Germany today and the ambivalent German attitude toward them.

To speak of Germany's Jews today—thirty-two thousand in the Federal Republic, a scant one thousand in the GDR—is to speak of a minority that has much in common with the whooping crane. Reduced from its pre-Hitler figure of half a million, it is miniscule and enjoys full official protection. Periodically faced with total extinction over the past three decades—either through emigration or attrition or both—it has in recent years experienced a moderate renaissance and a slight numerical increase. That a Jewish minority exists at all in Germany is remarkable and in many respects anomalous. To the Germans, the overwhelming majority of whom have never met or seen a Jew, it serves as a constant reminder of shared guilt and evokes shame.

Overtly there is no antisemitism and one might well ask how there could be, when Jews are so few in number and so concentrated in the major cities that they barely count in a West German population of sixty million and an East German one of seventeen million. But it goes beyond that simple issue, for the Germans today propagate what can best be described as overt philo-semitism of which the story of the drowning man shouting "Down with the Jews!" is representative.

In West Germany (the GDR being a case by itself because of its official anti-Israeli and anti-Zionist stance) no act is more likely to provoke the full wrath of the law than any public expression of anti-Jewish attitudes. Not only is pro-Jewish sentiment cultivated, but matters have reached the point in recent years where the West Germans practice flagrant discrimination toward the *other* semites of the world—the Arabs.

Although they outnumber Jews two to one, the Arabs in the Federal Republic are also a tiny, almost invisible, minority. Of the sixty thousand living and working there as laborers, businessmen, and students, more than half are Moroccans, Algerians, or Tunisians; some nine thousand came from Jordan; the remainder are from Egypt, Lebanon, Syria, and Iraq. Many of them have been resident in Germany ten years and longer, are married to Germans, and are legally entitled to German citizenship, were they to apply for it.

Following the Palestinian terrorist attack on the Israeli team at the 1972 Olympic Games in Munich, the Arabs became the focus of mass hatred and hysteria by a nation and its officialdom that believed its meticulously constructed image of a "new, different and better Germany" had been shattered by the tragic massacre at the Olympic Village and Fuerstenfeld-bruck air base. Subsequently hundreds of Arabs—more than two thousand in Bavaria alone—were brusquely deported as "undesirable aliens," and hundreds more were turned away at borders and airports.

Officially, the arrests, expulsions and deportations were explained as "preventive measures" against "politically suspect" Arabs to forestall further acts of terrorism, thwart Palestinian political activity, and to decimate potentially dangerous and subversive Palestinian refugee organizations operating on West German territory. But the actions were conducted in an emotional atmosphere of blind hostility which, fanned by the popular press, especially the Axel Springer-owned, multimillion circulation *Bild Zeitung*, had not fully abated more than two years later.

The "preventive measures" were carried out in an illegal and semilegal manner ominously reminiscent of Gestapo tactics. Police staged predawn raids on the rooms and apartments of scores of Arab residents, yanked them out of their beds, and forced them aboard airplanes bound for the Middle East before they could even say good-bye to their families and wives, many of them German, obtain legal help, or settle their affairs.

Tough new regulations led to arbitrary and supercilious behavior by immigration and passport control officers at points of entry which one Lebanese businessman, a frequent visitor to the Federal Republic, described as "nothing short of arrogant racism." Among those subjected to the peremptory imperiousness of immigration officers, for example, was the septuagenarian speaker of Lebanon's parliament. In the spring of 1974 he was kept waiting for four hours on a drafty railway station platform at Freilassing in Bavaria while passport controllers telephoned back and forth to Munich and Bonn to check on him before allowing him into the country. The only reason for the delay, it turned out, was that he was an Arab.

The scope and style of the anti-Arab campaign, the German Students' League charged, "are reminiscent of the antisemitic pogroms of the 1930s. The sublimated antisemitism of the Germans now appears to be reasserting itself in the form of anti-Arab racism."

How sublimated is that antisemitism? Despite propagated philo-semitism and notwithstanding its being officially proscribed, even severely punishable by the courts, antisemitism has not, of course, been entirely obliterated. Although swastika smearings and cemetery desecrations of the type that swept the country in the late 1950s and early 1960s are rare these days, it would be naive to ascribe all those which do occur to "innocent apolitical youthful vandalism." And although in nearly twenty years of living in and covering news of Germany I personally heard or overheard only two or three unmistakably antisemitic remarks, I know Jews who claim to have been victims of discrimination and any number of Jews as well as non-Jews who speak of a "lingering antisemitic mood" that manifests itself "periodically, here and there."

Disregarding the incorrigible old and new Nazis—the former an aging, disappearing species, the latter a political fringe group as the decline of the National Democratic and other far-right parties since 1969 has shown—antisemitism in Germany today expresses itself in a strange mixture of old biases and prejudices with new social fears, based partially on ignorance, indelible religious bias, and the inexcusable gap in historic education during the crucial period from 1945 to 1962. It is this sort of antisemitism:

"With all that reparations money they received, the Jews went back into business and again are charging outrageous prices. They put up the prices so high that everyone else has to raise theirs to keep up with them."

"Everything the Jews own today they got through reparations money and we had to pay for that. But I've heard they don't have to pay taxes at all."

"Of course they suffered as a group. But all those who are back here now, how can you really prove they suffered anything at all? It's impossible to check and anyone who dares to try is immediately branded as antisemitic."

"I have nothing against them individually, but as a group, well. . . ."

"You can't say anything about the Jews today because that would be regarded as racist and antisemitic."

"We suffered, too. Think about Dresden and the deportation of the Germans from Silesia and Pomerania."

"Of course, everyone has competition but with us it's especially bad. You know, so many Jews have come back from abroad and they are all getting right back into the textile business. They seem to be coming from all over."

"I asked my mother why all those terrible things were done to the Jews under Hitler, and she explained that they had always been persecuted because they put Jesus on the cross."

"A peddler came to the door one day and wanted to sell something. My father made him go away and when I asked him what it had been about, he said: 'Oh, just a Jew trying to sell something.' I was disappointed, because I had never seen a Jew before and I asked whether he was sure it had been a Jew. And he said, 'Oh, yes, I can tell. I've had my experiences. They have different eyes and noses and they talk in a strange way.' "

"Isn't it terrible—all those bars and honky-tonk places downtown, and the prostitution? You know most of them are owned by Jews."

"I was standing and looking at a 'wanted' poster in the hallway of the city hall in this little town. A policeman, standing next to me, commented on the crime—the murder of a prostitute. And he said: 'You know, we have all these Jews and other foreigners now.' "

It is the sort of antisemitism that can be registered by opinion surveys. Thus when the Allensbach Institute in 1971 asked a cross-section of West Germans which organizations on a multiple-choice list they thought had too much political influence in the Federal Republic today, 46 percent said "the unions," 29 percent listed "big business," 28 percent mentioned "the Springer press concern," and 6 percent cited "the Central Council of Jews in Germany."

More than one-fourth of adult West Germans tend to think that Jews "never help anyone unless they can gain something out of it themselves," that Jews "exploit and live off the labor of others," that Jews "don't keep their promises," and more than 15 percent regard Jews as "miserly." As recently as the spring of 1965, nearly 19 percent of those questioned still believed that West Germany would be better off if it had no Jews at all.

And in August 1973, when a four-alarm, six-hour fire broke out on the top two floors of an unfinished, forty-story Frankfurt office building, the city's highest and most controversial, thousands of people watched the pyrotechnical display and hundreds of them jeered its owner, mumbling, "It serves the Jew right." The skyscraper is one of those erected on the site of deliberately run-down residential structures in Frankfurt's West End and, because of its height, a symbol of the real estate speculation being practiced there and under sharp attack by left-wing student groups. The "Jew" who owns and built it, however, is no Jew at all, but an Istanbul-born Persian, Ali Selmi, who arrived in Frankfurt twenty years ago with a few dollars in his pocket which he parlayed into one of the largest fortunes in Germany.

In most respects, West Germany's is a form of antisemitism which is really no different from what one finds in most industrialized societies today—much less pronounced and vehement in its expression than, for example, the antisemitism one encounters in the Soviet Union or Austria, which claims to be one of the "victims of Nazi aggression," or France, or for that matter, the United States. But antisemitism in Germany, where antisemitism found expression in acts of genocide unprecedented in human history, has a special meaning. It reopens wounds still not healed in anyone thirty years or older and touches nerves still raw from suffering.

In the summer of 1966 I covered the fifth plenary assembly of the World Jewish Congress in Brussels, at which one of the points on the agenda was a special panel discussion about relations between Germans and Jews. The participants were—on the German side—Eugen Gerstenmaier, then president of the Bundestag, and Thomas Mann's son Golo, a professor and historian; and on the Jewish side—Professor Gershon Sholem of Hebrew University in Jerusalem and Salo Baron, Austrian-born professor at Columbia University in New York, with Nahum Goldmann, president of the WJC, as moderator.

Staged barely a year after the Bonn government had recognized Israel diplomatically, at the expense of ruptured relations with nearly all the Arab countries, it was a memorable meeting. Tempestuous and emotional, it was delayed at the start by a succession of impassioned speakers who marched to the lectern in Brussel's Palais de Congrès to argue emphatically why a dialogue between Germans and Jews should not take place at all and why they intended to march out in a body to avoid hearing it.

The dialogue itself lasted until well past midnight and centered on the question that has plagued Jews and Germans alike since the war's end. Was the Nazi liquidation of a third of world Jewry a singular catastrophe, perpetrated by a handful of racist madmen who had usurped power, or was it, as many contend, an inevitable consequence of German history? The question came no closer to being resolved that night than it may ever be. But going through my notes on the debate and my dispatch about the meeting eight years later, I found a statement by the American rabbi, Dr.

Joachim Prinz, who entered the discussion with a statement that I find highly pertinent today:

"The Bible tells us that it took the Israelites forty years of wandering in the desert before they could discard their Egyptian experience and start afresh. Similarly it may take forty years—or a generation—before the Jews will submerge in their consciousness the tragic experience of the Nazi era. And it may also take forty years before the last vestiges of Nazi ideology and methods have been relegated into a corner of the German national consciousness.

"Many Germans have said that they miss the Jews because we were the 'pepper and salt' of German life which the Germans themselves lack. To them I say: 'It is too bad the Germans cannot produce the spices of life they need, but my people refuse to serve as the condiments of the German nation.' "

Biblical generations lasted longer than those of the twentieth century. The Bible's and Rabbi Prinz's forty years may well be the thirty-year turning point in German history to which this book is devoted. Surveying the relationship between Germans and Jews today there is little doubt that the horror and tragedy of the past are already being submerged and relegated to a corner of the mutual consciousness. One need merely look at the "special relationship" between Israel and the Federal Republic for evidence of that. But more importantly, Jews are again becoming a certain spice of German life. They may represent an infinitesimal minority in Germany, and among the fourteen million Jews throughout the world, they are a minority too. But they are there and flourishing. Thirty years after the holocaust, Jewry in Germany is alive and well.

"Many Jews," says Dr. Hans Lamm, sixty-one, a returnee from emigration who is now one of the leaders of Munich's four-thousand-strong Jewish community, "were for a long time schizophrenic about their situation here. Victims of Nazi persecution or the children of such victims, they were traumatized by suffering and so hurt that they regarded society as hostile. They would have felt that way even outside Germany. But here they felt that the land was 'drenched with Jewish blood.' For years, although they remained here, they 'sat on suitcases,' ready to leave on a moment's notice. But gradually, the suitcases have been transformed into swimming pools."

Unlike the pre-Hitler Jewish community in Germany, whose 500,000 members could trace its origins not only to the Dark Ages but in western and southern Germany to the days of Roman rule, it is anything but a cohesive community and is disparate in its composition. It is made up partly of German Jews who managed to survive the Nazi terror by staying hidden and underground, often enjoying the protection of their Christian friends; German Jews, mostly elderly, who have returned from periods of emigration in the United States and Israel for reasons of money, nostalgia, homesickness, and, in the case of intellectuals, affinity for the German language and culture; East European Jews—the majority —who survived the death camps and were stranded in postwar Germany as displaced persons; and, finally, the children of all three groups who now represent almost one-third of West Germany's total Jewish population. Together they account for the 32,000 who "officially" comprise West German Jewry—a figure that is based on the number who pay the government levied "church" tax or, in the case of Jews, the synagogue tax. To these must be added an estimated 10,000 Jews who, like a growing number of Protestants and Catholics, refuse to identify their religion to internal revenue and residency registration offices, thereby escaping the tax levy which for German Jews, Christians, Moslems, and Buddhists alike amounts to 10 percent of a person's assessed income tax and is passed on by the internal revenue administration to the churches, synagogues, and mosques. In addition there is an undetermined number of half-Jews.

Of the four main groups comprising German Jewry today, the Jews of East European origin are, for reasons of language, cultural background, and the gravity of their wartime experience, the least assimilated. The odyssey that led them into West Germany is also the most tragic. When the war ended, some 200,000 East European Jews—survivors of the death camps and refugees from the new antisemitism taking root in the Soviet-controlled countries of Eastern Europe—streamed into the U. S. and British occupation zones of Germany. These were the DPs—the displaced persons—who lingered for years in refugee camps, mostly in Bavaria, waiting for an opportunity to emigrate either to Israel or to the United States. By the time the mass emigration effort was considered "completed" in 1952, some 12,000 were left in the Federal Republic. They formed the nucleus of West Germany's Jewish community as small tradesmen, exporters, importers, and—a source for some of the postwar antisemitism—as owners of the bars and nightclubs that catered to

American soldiers in the garrison towns of the U. S. zone. Their tragic past, their painful relationship to the Germans, and their linguistic and cultural heritage drove them into a self-imposed spiritual and intellectual ghetto existence that to this day still sets them far apart from the mainstream of German life and, to a greater degree than anyone would like to admit, from their fellow Jews of German origin.

By contrast, the most integrated and assimilated—as they always were—are the German Jews themselves. And although tempered by the experience of their ordeal, they regard themselves, as they always did, first as Germans and then as Jews.

For those among them who survived the war and the deportations by hiding in cellars, attics, backyard sheds, or occasionally by passing as non-Jews, the relationship to their fellow Germans was bound to be different than that of any other Jew. For them the contours of Third Reich society were never as clearly delimited between good and evil as for those outside the Reich or those who experienced the camps and the machinery of genocide. Protected by German friends who more often than not were activists or sympathizers of anti-Nazi resistance groups, often in close communication with Socialists and Communists who themselves were operating underground, or, in the case of some, Communists and Socialists themselves, they understood at an early period that German society under Hitler was not as monolithic as it appeared outside. When the Nazi tyranny was broken and the war was over, they emerged from their cellars and attics to join forces with their Christian, Democratic, Socialist, and Communist friends to rebuild a different Germany—as Germans.

Then there are those German Jews who returned from abroad. The degree of their assimilation depends on the motivations and the time of their return. The elderly who could not cope with social customs or physical climate in their lands of refuge and came back to live out their lives on pensions, obviously play a different role in postwar Germany than those who, due to restitution and compensation payments, reentered German commercial and professional life in their forties and fifties— young enough to rebuild their careers and to reassimilate in the society of their youth and formative years.

The most integrated of all are the intellectuals—the writers, artists, actors, directors, philosophers, sociologists, and historians—for whom the German language and culture were the juice of life itself. Leavened and broadened in their outlook, and their gifts enriched by their experiences in England, the United States, Israel, and Switzerland, they contributed immeasurably to the postwar rebirth of Germany, and in numbers represent a larger group than most Germans realize. Quite a few of them went to East Germany out of political persuasion: Arnold Zweig, the novelist; Hanns Eisler, the composer; Lea Grundig, the artist; Alfred Kantorowicz, the literary historian and critic; Ernst Bloch, the Marxist social philosopher; to name a few. Some of them, such as Kantorowicz and Bloch, disillusioned with the Ulbricht regime, left the GDR to settle in West Germany, where they joined a growing Jewish intellectual and artistic community that included such towering figures of the stage as the actors Ernst Deutsch, Fritz Kortner, Therese Giehse, and Ida Ehre; writers such as Robert Neumann and Willy Haas; sociologists and philosophers such as Max Horkheimer and Theodor Adorno. Some of them are now dead, others retired or in semiretirement. But their impact on postwar Germany survives them.

Although these disparate elements still comprise the majority of the Jewish community in Germany today, they will not be a majority for long. In another five years they will be displaced by that generation born since the war. These Jews under thirty experience the same generational conflict with their parents and elders as Germany's non-Jews, and like young Jews around the world, they suffer the same identity crisis. But their generation gap and their crisis of identity are exacerbated by the specific experience of being Jews in Germany. They find themselves in a constant field of tension between their German environment and the world of their parents. To escape, they look toward a variety of solutions. Some have set emigration to Israel as their goal; others are developing a strong consciousness of German Jewishness predicated on the theme that "Jewish is beautiful." Not a few have identified themselves with far-left student movements in Frankfurt, Berlin, and Munich, and a surprisingly large number are assimilating into a middle-class professional life, where their Jewishness takes second place to being German.

The choices they make—insofar as there is choice—their attitudes, the width of the gap with their elders, and the depth of their identity crisis all depend in large measure on the backgrounds and experiences of their parents.

Those who are the children of the postwar DPs find themselves in the most critical situation. They were raised in the spiritual and intellectual ghetto of their parents—a ghetto of self-isolation—that imposed on these youths an attitude of fear and distrust of the society which their parents had reluctantly adopted and in which they themselves were born. Though educated in German schools, they remained immersed in a cultural and linguistic environment that was not German. Now driven by a youthful urge for emancipation, they discover that their only avenue of emancipation is away from the Jewish community. But not being "German" in their orientation, they cannot hope to integrate or assimilate. More than the others, they look either toward Israel or, if students, toward acceptance by the far left in German universities.

Micha Kochen, a twenty-three-year-old medical student at the University of Munich, is in many ways a typical example. The son of parents who survived the concentration camp, his childhood was largely influenced by the emotional experience of his parents from whose world he did not free himself until he joined Marxist student groups. "Marxist ideology," he told a young Israeli reporter, "is what emancipated me from the Jewish ghetto." But it is merely a partial emancipation, for the central theme of Micha Kochen's ideology appears to be that the threat of fascism and the far right, which he views as an outgrowth of capitalism-imperialism, is every bit as great in Germany as it always was. And that, of course, more emotionally than ideologically grounded, is what his parents and their peers believed ever since circumstances forced them to settle in the land of their erstwhile tormentors.

Those who are products of German culture have it far easier. They can cultivate a new German-Jewish consciousness or assimilate, and be reasonably at peace doing either. Two-thirds of all the young Jews in Germany getting married today, marry non-Jewish partners. On the other side of the coin, however, one of Munich's most popular hangouts for young Jews is the Shalom Bar in Schwabing, the city's student and artist quarter. Except for a few Israeli and Jewish specialties on the menu, it is, if one is looking for Jewish tradition, about as Jewish as a ham sandwich on Yom Kippur. Its clientele, Jewish and non-Jewish, is vibrant, alive, long-haired, blue-jeaned, and, judging from the stares I've gotten whenever I have penetrated the inner sanctum, dedicated to the belief that anyone over thirty is not to be trusted. I find it representative of the "Jewish is beautiful" theme to which many of the young are committed.

One exponent of that is Michael Wolfsohn, twenty-six, an Israeli army and Six-Day War veteran who returned to his native West Berlin in

1971, dedicated to his conviction that he is "a German Jew." He teaches religion and Jewish history to the children at the Jewish Community Center, with emphasis on the content and meaning of prayers in contrast to their ritual recitation and reading. As a German Jew, Wolfsohn flexes both his Judaism and his Germanism, determined to further politically the "strong democratic, pluralistic currents" in contemporary West German society which he senses and supports.

Perhaps the most successful of the young Jews in Germany today is Marek Lieberberg, an aggressive pop-music promoter who arranged the first Woodstock-style festival in the Federal Republic and learned the ropes of publicity while working as an Associated Press staffer. Although the son of Polish Jews and born in a refugee center, he was raised in Frankfurt, and regards himself as a German—nationally, culturally, and politically.

"I feel completely at home here," Lieberberg says. "It is my home and I understand German culture. I feel quite comfortable. Certainly I've been to Israel—many times—and I have great sympathy for the Zionist movement. But when I return to Germany I feel love for this country. It is truly a splendid land, with a higher standard of real justice than any other Western nation. Certain changes must be made. The situation in education is catastrophic. We need more schools, more teachers. Worker codetermination in industry is a move toward true socialism. It must grow and be nurtured. And abortion reform was absolutely essential."

If young Lieberberg has any deep concerns about Germany's future course, it is that the shift to the political left could be halted and swing back in the other direction. He regards Franz-Josef Strauss, the CDU's Bavarian powerhorse, as a clear and present menace to democracy. But it is a fear of and aversion to Strauss which has nothing to do with Lieberberg's Jewishness: it is an expression of concern for the future of a country that he regards as his own and which he shares with millions of Germans of his generation.

"What I regard as a menace," he says, "is the popularity of a man like Strauss. . . . That he continues to be attractive to people—not the ones in the cities, of course, but those who for whatever vague reasons desire a bigger, stronger Germany—is what I consider a threat to democracy in this country."

But Lieberberg is also confident that his generation will not permit such threats to become imminent. "The new, young voters responded

strongly to a humane and progressive socialist program the last time, and
with any luck—and more new voters the next time—the response will be
even stronger."

Antisemitism? For young German Jews such as Lieberberg it is no
issue.

"The problem of tolerance toward minorities is common to all
societies," says Robert Morris, a Jewish law student and one of
Lieberberg's age peers, who regards himself as a "Jewish German" with
all the "rights and duties" which that entails, including service in the
Bundeswehr from which, as a Jew, he could legally claim exemption.
"There was a time when intolerance focused on Jews. Today it focuses
on the *Gastarbeiter*—the foreign workers."

Young Robert Morris, who is sharply critical of the "Jewish-German
establishment" for being "primarily preoccupied with Jewish-Israeli issues
rather than general German questions," has a valid point. In many more
ways than Germans—Jewish or non-Jewish—realize or even care to
know, the Gastarbeiter—the foreign "guest workers"—may well turn out
to be the "Jews of tomorrow." Today they are already West Germany's
single largest social problem. Often ostracized and exploited, despite
legislation that entitles them to the same social rights and privileges as
Germans, they congregate and are forced into urban ghettos, with every
social consequence which that term implies. As a result, the face of
German cities is changing. Slum housing is spreading rapidly. Crime, due
to ghetto-living pressures, is rising at such a pace that pessimistic
criminologists predict that by the end of the decade it will equal that of
today's American megalopolises. Illiteracy among the underprivileged
foreigners' children is spreading like a fungus. And among the German
lower-middle and middle classes—both blue collar and white collar—
some of the old, long-forgotten xenophobic attitudes and new fears and
resentments, focussing largely on the question of their job security, are
being rekindled.

The pattern is almost a mirror image of the problems created by
immigration to the United States at the turn of the century and the more
recent shifts of population by the black, rural southern poor to the
industrial urban centers of the North. What makes it such a uniquely
German problem, however, is that for Germany, discounting a similar
but much less numerous wave of immigrants from Poland to the
coal-mining Ruhr basin before World War I, it is a new phenomenon.

And a phenomenon, moreover, that is complicated by the fact that the foreign workers are considered—and consider themselves—transient and temporary rather than immigrants to be integrated into German society. Although 80 percent of the foreign workers express a desire to return to their homelands "eventually," more than half of those presently employed have been in the Federal Republic at least four years and nearly one-fourth for seven and more years.

The sheer statistics of this foreign-labor invasion are staggering. Their number has tripled since 1963, doubled since 1968, until now there are 2.4 million foreign workers, accompanied by 1.5 million dependents, accounting for 11 percent of West Germany's total labor force and nearly 7 percent of the country's total population. Turks, with 530,000 employed and an estimated 450,000 women, children, and other relatives to make a round million, represent the largest working contingent, followed by some 460,000 Greeks, 270,000 Yugoslavs, 250,000 Italians, 180,000 Spaniards, and scores of thousands of Portuguese, Moroccans, and Tunisians. In some industries, especially construction, they make up 25 to 30 percent of the total payroll; to list but one example, at the Ford Motor Company plant in Cologne, foreign workers, predominantly Turkish, account for more than 12,000 of the 32,000 employed.

The old hallmark, Made in Germany, may still be imprinted on the goods which the Federal Republic exports around the world and, legally speaking, the merchandise was made there. But the notion that it was made by Germans is largely a fiction, for much of that German car, camera, or hi-fi equipment one buys has been produced and assembled by non-Germans.

In some cities, notably Munich, Stuttgart, Frankfurt, and Cologne in that order, foreign laborers and members of their families make up more than 15 percent of the total population, and in certain ghetto districts of those towns—such as Munich's Schwanthaler Heights and Haidhausen— they represent 50 percent. Of seventy-seven corner taverns, cafes, and restaurants in the Schwanthaler Heights area of Munich, twenty-five are now operated by foreign lessees. The venerable old "Ried-Wirt," "Wiesn' Stueberl," "Westend Bierstueberl," and "Bierklinik"—all inns in the German *Gasthaus* tradition where ruddy-faced burghers used to wash down mountains of dumplings with rivers of beer—are now operated, respectively, by a Jordanian, an Egyptian, a Yugoslav, and a Greek. Right beneath the quaint signs advertising Augustinerbraeu,

Loewenbraeu, and Hofbraeu beers, there are those advertising Eteki—
The Best Greek Wines and Liquors. Instead of pigs' knuckles and
sauerkraut, the kitchens now turn out kebab, shashlik, and dishes made of
hominy and eggplant. Where once one heard the bells of baroque
churches calling Bavarians to mass, one now hears the cry of the muezzin
summoning the faithful to prayer. Alien sounds of Oriental rhythms and
instruments emanate from open windows. Dark-haired, flashing-eyed
women—pantalooned and their faces half-veiled by kerchiefs—dash
silently from shabby apartment house entrances to nearby grocery stores
to shop for exotic fruits and vegetables the likes of which Germans have
never seen before. Mustachioed men, invariably in jackets too short, too
tight, and too garish—the uniform of the peasant poor—stand in little
knots on street corners, gesticulating wildly, fingering strings of beads,
and discussing, no German knows what, in a language most Germans
cannot understand. And wherever you look there are children, children,
children.

In the fall of 1973 the Bonn government imposed a ban on further
hiring abroad and by the spring of 1974 the Federal Labor Office was
predicting that the downturn in the economy and an expected rise in the
unemployment rate would reduce the number of foreign workers by
nearly half a million within a few months. Ten months after that
prediction, unemployment had, indeed, risen disturbingly by another half
million to more than 5 percent of the labor force, but the contingent of
foreigners was virtually just as large. Not only are they entitled to the
same rights of job protection and unemployment benefits as Germans but,
as people soon realized, the foreigners perform the dirty, heavy, and
menial tasks which no German, no matter how desperate for work or how
long on the jobless dole, is now willing to do.

Having originally recruited and infused foreigners into the economy in
the late 1950s and early 1960s and become dependent on them, West
Germans are now discovering that, short of a major recession or
depression, economic life would simply grind to a halt without the army
of Turks, Greeks, Yugoslavs, Italians, and Spaniards who fill every fourth
job in the construction business, every fifth in the catering trade, and
every sixth in the metalworking, plastics-processing, and textile industries.

Not only will they continue to be needed, but more foreigners want to
come to Germany despite the disadvantages and hardships they face.

Largely of peasant origin, with minimal educations and minimal industrial skills, they cannot speak the language, cannot compete for the better jobs, and cannot hope to integrate. As a result, despite equal employment opportunities, equal protection under German health and joblessness insurance, and the principle of equal pay for equal work, they invariably are relegated to lower-paying jobs and the average take-home pay of foreign blue-collar workers is 30 percent less than that of Germans. The housing available to foreigners is substandard at best, although they pay 40 to 50 percent more for it than Germans would. They face separations from wives and families, and even when the families arrive, find themselves isolated in an alien and often hostile environment.

And yet, compared to home, it is utopia—a place to make dreams come true, to buy the tinsel of the consumer society, and to save for a better future. Foreign workers who salt away as much as DM 1,000 monthly and have accumulated small fortunes of DM 50 to 100,000 are not unusual. Of a total DM 30 billion paid out to foreign workers in 1973, after withholding tax, health, unemployment, and old-age insurance deductions, an estimated DM 7.6 billion was sent to families back home, DM 10 billion was spent for current needs and consumer durables such as cars and appliances in West Germany, and more than one-third—DM 13 billion—was put away in savings accounts. If ever they do return to their homelands some day, the foreign workers will use these savings to buy more farmland, start small businesses, and educate their children.

But even if the German economy could function without them, increasingly there will be fewer legal means to prevent certain categories of foreigners from coming to the Federal Republic to compete for jobs and seek their fortunes. Italians, as citizens of a Common Market country, are already entitled to complete freedom of movement within the European Economic Community and require neither residence nor labor permits to settle and work in West Germany. Except for suffrage and the right to be elected to political office, they enjoy the same rights as Germans. Virtually identical rights and privileges will accrue to the Turks starting in 1976, when Turkey becomes an associate member of the EEC. Today some 1.2 million Turks are already inscribed on application lists waiting for work and residence permits in West Germany. How many will there be a year or two from now when such permits are no longer necessary? Greece has also applied for associate status, and full membership for Spain is regarded as a distinct possibility before the end of the decade.

Regardless of future developments, however, the problem of foreign workers already looms as the largest single sociological dilemma in the Federal Republic today. The infrastructure of the cities—short of satisfactory housing, schools, teachers, and hospitals—cannot absorb them, leading to the creation of slums and substandard districts with the typical urban ghetto problems which Germany has never had in modern times. Animosities on both sides—incited and exacerbated by the sensational, popular press and radical political fringe groups on the left and right—are growing.

Unskilled, untrained, uneducated, and underprivileged on arrival, the majority of the foreigners invariably end up sweeping the streets, collecting garbage, hauling bricks, digging ditches, washing dishes, doing domestic services, and performing mindless, stultifying assembly-line work that requires few qualifications. This is turning them into a new subproletariat precisely at a time in history when West Germany seems bent upon reducing and eventually eradicating class distinctions. But at the same time, the longer they remain and the more exposed they become to German ways and standards, the higher their level of social consciousness will be. They already are expressing justified demands for better treatment and a voice in the social-economic decision-making processes, such as the right to be represented on union shop councils and the establishment of municipal "foreign worker parliaments." Pressures of social and political disorder are virtually a certainty in the years ahead. A series of wildcat strikes, organized by Turkish workers in the West German metal and auto industry in the summer of 1973, was but an adumbration of things to come.

Politically disenfranchised in Germany, the foreigners remain keenly aware of political developments in their homelands and are not above conducting their own political battles on West German territory. Conversely, their own governments do not shy from attempting to pressure Bonn into suppressing political activity among guest workers which may be embarrassing or inimical to whomever happens to be in power in Ankara, Athens, Belgrade, or Madrid. But not infrequently such suppressive action turns out to be a violation of German civil rights. In 1972, for example, the Greek and Spanish governments intervened repeatedly, and successfully, to censor the Bavarian Regional Network's daily Greek- and Spanish-language broadcasts for foreign workers in the Federal Republic. The programs in Greek, directed by Pavlos Bakojannis, a Greek employee of Bavarian network, were cited by the Athens junta as an act of "German interference in the internal affairs of Greece." But as Bakojannis countercharged, "Actually the colonels' intervention is an act of interference in the internal affairs of Germany." The programs, he stressed, are beamed solely to listeners within the Federal Republic. Any attempt on the part of Bonn to suppress or censor them would be a violation of the West German constitution.

Finally, there is the tragic schizophrenia of the foreigners' status and of their own attitudes. Unlike immigrants to the United States or, to name a more comparable European example, the Commonwealth immigrants to Great Britain during the past decade, they are looked upon as, and consider themselves, transients. But their "transience" has become increasingly a form of "semipermanence" which lasts for years and is interrupted only by annual vacation trips to their homelands, usually around Christmastime. Both the workers and those who hire and recruit them seem to encourage this "semipermanent" status: industry because constant turnover is costly and the retention of laborers who have acquired experience and on-the-job skills is more efficient and economical; the workers because they have long-range monetary goals which they cannot achieve on short-term bases. But as a result the workers, psychologically and emotionally, have become wanderers between two worlds from both of which they are alienated.

The German public attitude toward the "guest workers" are ambivalent and have changed for both better *and* worse during the past decade. Compared to ten years ago, nearly twice as many Germans today regard Gastarbeiter as "thrifty, hardworking, conscientious, good-hearted, helpful, and polite"; however, almost twice as many also consider them loud and inclined toward violence, and the percentage of those describing them as "not very clean" increased from 30 to 41 percent.

Nearly half of all West Germans would have some objections to having a foreign-worker family as neighbors (the number who would object to living near drug addicts is almost twice as high), yet when asked in an Allensbach opinion survey what they think "other people complain about the most," only 21 percent mentioned Gastarbeiter. Such issues as rising prices, long-haired teenagers, the rising crime rate, and high rents, ranged far up on the list at 42 to 71 percent.

While an increasing number of Germans regard the foreign workers as "a difficult problem," the number of those who favor hiring and recruiting more of them has also gone up.

Obviously, no meaningful sociological conclusions can be drawn from surveys that present such patently contradictory results. Nor are surveys among the foreigners themselves any more revealing. The Yugoslavs seem to be the most satisfied with their situation; the Turks, the least so. Nevertheless, statistics show that proportionately far more Turks than Yugoslavs want to go to West Germany. Although nearly three-quarters of the foreigners rate their living conditions as "good" or "very good," some 40 percent express dissatisfaction with housing conditions. They admire the punctuality, orderliness, quietness, and conscientiousness of the Germans, but see themselves as thriftier, friendlier, more tolerant, and more capable of enjoying life. And almost all of them consider the Germans "too haughty and aloof."

Social intercourse between the two is minimal. A scant 15 percent of Germans and foreign workers say they have ever had social contacts with each other outside of work. Linguistic and cultural barriers obviously make it difficult for them to know and assess each other, though when the barriers are breached the picture that emerges is not always a pretty one.

"The Germans just don't want us here," said a Greek grocery dealer in West Berlin who is fluent in the language and who has sharp ears. Among his customers are a few Germans with a liking for Greek specialties and produce. "But you can't imagine what they go through to buy from me," he said. "They are insulted and derided by the majority of Germans in the neighborhood who see them shopping here."

"Let's put it this way," said a young Spaniard whose parents have been in Germany so long that he went through Gymnasium, got his Abitur, and is now studying at a German university. "They are unfriendly and impatient with us. You run into attitudes of vexation mixed with rancor wherever you go. When I first started in school here, the class teacher called the roll and when he came to my name, stopped and asked whether I was a foreigner. I told him I was Spanish and he said: 'I don't like foreigners. I'm going to make it tough on you.' And let me tell you, he did. But a lot of this also has to do with your social standing. The poorer you look and the further down on the social ladder you are, the worse your German or the more foreign you appear to be, the greater the aloofness and vexations which the Germans will show."

A handful of foreign workers do not encounter such attitudes at all. They are the fortunate ones who have made it big in Germany, climbing from subproletarian status into the ranks of the moneyed bourgeoisie. Some have become millionaires. One such is Burhan Öngören, who arrived in Stuttgart with less than twenty dollars in his pocket fifteen years ago. He got a job in a ball-bearing factory, had a Turkish butcher teach him how to make Sucuk sausage, and subsequently became the largest purveyor of sausages to Turks in Germany; annual sales in his plant top DM 7 million. Then there's Franco Corsi, who started as a docker in Hamburg in the early 1960s and is now Germany's largest importer of Italian wines and cheeses; he has a fleet of his own delivery trucks and his annual sales top DM 3 million.

No West German would think of referring to *them* in such widely used pejorative terms as "mustafa" or "spaghetti gobbler."

Whatever the reasons, the Germans seem to want to conceal their prejudices and they appear to be good at doing so. But the prejudices are there, and apparently no group is more conscious of them than the estimated 100,000 German women who have married Gastarbeiter. Their status is that of second-class citizens, not to mention that they are living proof of how far women in Germany still have to go before they can call themselves emancipated.

These women's problems did not really become known until scores of their husbands were deported following the Munich Olympic massacre in 1972 and one of them, Rosi Wolf-Almanaresh, the thirty-three-year-old wife of a Jordanian and mother of two children, organized the League of German Wives of Foreigners.

One of her first discoveries was that women married to foreigners have but a fraction of the rights enjoyed by German men with foreign wives. The attitude of immigration officials and the courts is that a wife has the duty to follow her husband, the breadwinner, wherever he goes, and upon the foreign husband's expulsion, his German wife is expected to accompany him. But conversely, no official or court would expect a German husband to follow his deported foreign wife abroad. While a German husband can easily post surety for his alien wife and get her permanent-resident status, no German wife of a foreign husband, regardless of her financial status, is allowed to post an affidavit for him, and his residence is subject to the whims and interpretations of police, judicial, and immigration authorities. There are two disparate standards of justice based entirely on sex. German women who marry foreigners are exposed to de facto and de jure discrimination, and the more southern, exotic, and alien the husband, the greater the de facto discrimination. The wives become "semiforeigners" themselves and their children are not automatically entitled to German citizenship. Conversely, the foreign wife of a German man becomes a quasi-German, needs no residence permission or work permit, and her children are automatically German citizens.

But beyond the legal discrimination, the attitude of officials toward foreigners' wives reveal what they really think of the foreigners. "Why do you go with types like that?" one official asked one of the league's members. "If you have an affair with a guy like that it's not our responsibility," another women was told.

"The way officials speak to us," one woman complained, "leaves no doubt that they regard us as prostitutes, especially if our husbands are Arabs, Turks, or Africans."

There is a pervasive fear among many, if not the majority of West Germans, that the country's spiralling crime rate is attributable to the foreign workers. The crime statistics show that this is not true. Although criminal incidence among the Gastarbeiter population runs at 11.5 percent, compared to only 7 percent for the country as a whole, this is due solely to the fact that foreign workers fall into a more crime-prone group. Demographically, they are much younger than the cross-section of West Germany's population. Some 77 percent are between the ages of twenty and thirty-nine. Compared to similar age and social groups among the German populace, the foreigners' crime rate is actually lower. But the attitude that Gastarbeiter commit most of the crimes persists nonetheless, and it is a feeling that has been irresponsibly nurtured by the sensational boulevard papers and tabloids which seem to make a special point of always identifying foreign criminals by nationality. Thus, hardly a day passes without such headlines as BERSERK SPANIARD KNIFES GIRLFRIEND, DRUNKEN GREEK DEMOLISHES TAVERN, or LOVESICK TURK ATTACKS HOUSEWIFE ON STREET.

But even if the crime rate among the foreigners is not yet higher than among socially comparable Germans, the potential for a dramatic rise certainly exists. By 1980, says the police chief of Cologne, there will be more than 600,000 teenage children of foreign worker families, most of them concentrated in the urban centers. Marginally educated, raised in slums, alienated from their homelands and from the environment in which they have been raised and live, minimally employable because of their lack of skills and qualifications, barely conversant in German—they will all be, he predicts, potential juvenile delinquents and criminals. About half of them will have been born in Germany, the remainder will have been living in the Federal Republic since their infant years.

Dismal as the prediction sounds, German officials are not alone in making it. They are seconded by any number of educated foreign workers themselves.

"In a few years," says Sener Sarguth, a thirty-one-year-old Turk who teaches in a Frankfurt elementary school, "a whole army of uneducated, barely employable adolescents from Anatolia, Sicily, and Greece will threaten the cities of Germany."

The children, unquestionably, pose the greatest problem and are the most tragic victims. Isolated in a cultural, linguistic, and intellectual no-man's-land, they are surrounded, foglike, by a language they do not really understand and are given no real opportunity to learn. They have no chance to develop or preserve any identity. "They are simply lost," says Ekrem Ozelik, forty-two, another Turk teaching in Frankfurt. "No one takes them seriously, no one really cares about them. In Germany they are becoming rebellious and attempt to compensate for their fears and inferiority complexes by mounting aggressiveness. If they go home, they will be laughed at. They aren't Turks any more, since they no longer speak their mother tongue, and they are not Germans because they speak no German."

"Illiterates in two languages," is the way Sener Sarguth describes them. And Michailo Elec, a forty-one-year-old mechanic from Sarajevo, says sadly: "It is the price we are paying for our good life here. One day our children will end up being half-German, half-Yugoslav." Or neither.

By law, of course, the foreigners' children are entitled and required to have the same education as German children. In practice, however, it does not work that way. Of the estimated 850,000 foreigners' children between preschool age and fifteen, the minimum school-leaving age, some 100,000 are attending preschools and 300,000 are in regular German schools. The remainder, as far as one can estimate, are simply truant. The younger ones are spending their time on the streets. The older girls, whose educations are considered of secondary importance by their parents anyway, are probably minding little brothers and sisters and keeping house so their mothers can work. And the older boys, in all likelihood, are working illegally and without permits.

But even when they are enrolled and do attend school, the educations they receive are minimal and substandard. Those who arrive speaking no German cannot be integrated into German schools. They are placed in one-year preparatory classes where, theoretically, they are to be taught German, and foreign teachers are supposed to instruct them in other subjects in their native Turkish, Greek, Serbo-Croatian, Italian, or Spanish. After a year they are expected to join German children of their own age groups in regular classes. But the German-language instructors, as experience shows, are inadequately trained and equipped for the job, and in a country faced with an overall shortage of 250,000 teachers, there are simply not enough of them. Moreover, a year in a preparatory class is not long enough. It could, were there enough instructors and appropriate educational materials that relate to the subproletarian Gastarbeiter environment, provide them with a basis in conversational German; but not with a command of the language which enables them to cope with the theoretical and abstract mental processes required of the average school-child. Consequently, when they transfer from the preparatory to regular classes either they cannot keep up or the teachers lower the standards in order to pull them along. This brings vehement protests either from foreign parents who accuse the teachers of moving too fast and demanding too much, or from German parents who complain that their children are being held back. When the proportion of foreign children reaches 40 to 50 percent, as it does in many urban schools, neither the German nor the Gastarbeiter pupils can be taught properly.

"Our school has an enrollment of two hundred and twenty," said the principal of an elementary school in the coal-mining town of Gelsenkirchen. "Of these, fifty are foreigners. That high a percentage of pupils who either have no, or merely a limited, command of German has a deleterious effect on instruction. They cannot follow the lessons and they cannot communicate with the teachers and the other children."

Such situations are aggravated when the foreign children are of several nationalities. In one Ruhr basin elementary school, with a total enrollment of three hundred, there are sixty foreign children from nine different countries, not one of whom speaks sufficient German to know what is going on in class.

Moreover, tens of thousands of foreign children never even leave the preparatory classes because their parents don't want them to. In some cases the parents come from such underdeveloped areas and from such backward peasant origins that they are suspicious of any alien education. In the majority of cases, however, it is the fear that if their children become integrated in a German school, they will be raised as Germans, not Turks, Yugoslavs, or Greeks. Although a large percentage of these parents have been in Germany longer than five years and may remain a decade, they are emotionally committed to the idea of eventually going back home, and the legal and economic uncertainties of their "guest" status in Germany persuades them that they may have to do so even sooner than they intend. And they then want their children to fit in back in Turkey, Greece, or Yugoslavia. Many more are afraid they will no longer be able to communicate with their own children. As one Greek worker told a Munich principal through a translator: "I don't want Basil to learn your language. If he does, he will no longer speak mine." A Yugoslav, speaking to a Frankfurt principal in a West End school where 394 out of 800 pupils are foreigners, expressed his view precisely: "German good," he said, "but Serbo-Croatian better."

As a consequence, and in violation of the edicts of all the state ministries of culture, these children spend five, six, and more years in the preparatory classes claiming, on orders of their parents, and perhaps really not being able, to speak, understand, write, and read German. They are taught little more than the three Rs by teachers in their own language, many of whom are amateurs or exchange students at German universities who do the best they can with a dearth of pedagogical training and educational materials.

"It violates our instructions which specify that no child should spend longer than one year in a preparatory class, but it's better than no education," said one Frankfurt principal. "I don't even dare to ask anymore what's better or what's worse for these children. All I can say is that no one has recognized the seriousness of the situation."

A number of proposals have been made and some pilot projects started. In Hesse there are now a few programs to train both German-language instructors and foreign teachers. Munich, the city with the largest actual and proportional number of foreigners, began an experiment in the fall of

1974 with eight hundred Gastarbeiter children who are receiving instruction in both German and their mother tongues simultaneously. They attend music, art, physical education, and manual training classes together with German children. But in the view of most educators, all such programs are too little and too late.

"By no stretch of the imagination," said one teacher, "are these children getting what one might call an education. And I'm convinced the primary reason why they show up in the schools each day is because the classrooms are nicer and warmer than the holes they are supposed to call home."

Those holes, whether they are barracks or dormitories for the approximately 60 percent of foreign workers who are single or unaccompanied by their families, or rooms and apartments which they share with their wives and children and other relatives, are, in a single word, scandalous.

On an average, across the country, three male foreign workers share 17 square yards of living space, equipped with three beds, three chairs, three lockers, and one table between them at prices that range from 40 to 300 percent more per square foot than the German norm. Many of these dormitory rooms are supplied by the companies the men work for and provide their employers with lucrative additional profits. When the workers change jobs, or tire of barracks-style living, they must hunt for places of their own in a housing market where doors are slammed in their faces by angry landlords shouting *"Nix Gastarbeiter!"* ("No foreigners!") Hence the workers fall victim to extortion and usury. In Munich recently there was a case of a landlord who had converted a three-room apartment, for which the regular rent was only DM 280, into a dormitory for eighteen foreigners, each of whom he charged DM 100 for a bed—a neat profit of more than 600 percent. Cases of eighteen and twenty men being forced to share two-room apartments are not uncommon. In one building on Frankfurt's once-posh Westend Strasse, forty-three Turks—families and singles—share three bathrooms and toilets.

When the foreign workers' families arrive, the real problems start. The only living quarters with manageable rents are in decrepit buildings in working-class districts from which Germans move out as soon as foreigners start to move in. When the proportion of foreigners in a building reaches 30 percent, a veritable German exodus begins. The more turnover there is in the house, the lower its value, and the more inclined the owner becomes to let it deteriorate. Some landlords deliberately allow them to run down so that they can be condemned and demolished and replaced by lucrative high-rise office and commercial blocks.

A survey in the state of Northrhine-Westphalia revealed that 40 percent of Gastarbeiter apartments have no kitchens, 64 percent have communally shared toilets in the hallways, and 13 percent have no running water, hot or cold.

Foreigners converge on such districts not only because the living is cheaper or because landlords elsewhere refuse to rent to them, but because others of their countrymen are already there. In these developing ghettos they feel more at home, especially when foreign merchants, often using Germans as legal fronts, open shops selling the food and merchandise the foreigners are accustomed to, and take over taverns and cafes in which they create atmospheres reminiscent of home. The ghetto becomes a place where the guest worker can isolate himself from the alien and hostile culture of his "hosts." There is hardly a German city today which does not have its Klein Istanbul, Little Sarajevo, or Miniature Madrid. And each and everyone of these enclaves is on the way to becoming a German Harlem or Watts.

Whether or not the Gastarbeiter will indeed become the "new Jews" of Germany, that is to say, the scapegoats of society, no one can say. What worries many Germans, however, including most members of Helmut Schmidt's government, is that they are already well along the path toward becoming the "Blacks" of Germany.

And what of Germany's real Blacks today? As the Gastarbeiter have come to dominate the center of Germany's minorities stage, the Blacks seem almost to have been forgotten. But they are still there and so are their problems. As a minority they must be divided into three distinct categories with different status and different problems: the more than ten thousand illegitimate children of black American servicemen born since the end of World War II, who are German citizens, consider German their mother tongue and were raised in a German milieu; the five thousand or more African students and workers; the approximately twenty thousand black U. S. soldiers currently stationed in the Federal Republic.

Whatever progress Blacks may have made toward breaking down the barriers of segregation and discrimination in the U. S. military since President Harry S. Truman officially integrated the services in 1947, their status outside the barracks gates in Germany has hardly changed in thirty years. "Discrimination," high-ranking U. S. Seventh Army officers in Heidelberg admit, "remains a serious problem."

"It can be subtle discrimination," Gen. Michael S. Davison, Seventh Army commander, once said, "taking the form of delayed service in restaurants, cold food, and so on. But it can also be quite explicit. Black soldiers are barred from certain restaurants, taverns, and bars. Those living off post are refused apartments by certain landlords."

And the general might have added that black GIs pay premium rents for the flats to which they do have access and that racial fights are often the result when they are denied entry or refused service in public places.

For nearly seven years, from 1956 to 1963, first as a reporter and then as the editor, I covered the U. S. military scene in Germany for *The Overseas Weekly*, a privately owned paper for American servicemen in Europe. I cannot begin to count the number of stories we published about racial strife and discriminatory practices against black GIs. In the dozen or more years since I left the paper, the situation has remained static. German officials still claim they are powerless to do anything about it: The law allows landlords, restaurant owners, and bar proprietors to decide which clientele they wish to serve. The U. S. Army's authority still does not go beyond placing such establishments off-limits to all soldiers. And the off-limits ban generally lasts only a few weeks. New arrivals are still subjected to orientation sessions during which they are instructed on how to order a German meal or a beer, how to pay for a taxi, and, if the orientation officer is savvy, how and where to find a girl. Both the U. S. military and German officialdom are still dedicated to "reducing friction," which, in practice, reduces to issuing pontifical appeals.

What has changed is the proportional increase of black officers in the army who are less likely to acquiesce to discriminatory practices than enlisted men and the increase in black militants who hammer at the theme that black soldiers should not be subjected to slights at the hands of Germans whom Americans a generation ago fought and defeated. The result: more friction than ever before.

The position of the Africans is analogous and yet vastly different. Unlike U. S. soldiers who enjoy quasi-diplomatic and quasi-occupational status, they are subject to the whims and eccentricities of German immigration regulations and the laws applying to foreigners. Being citizens of weak, underdeveloped countries, they do not have the protection of powerful embassies and consulates. Since the waning of the Cold War, which had placed the Third World into the unique position of being a much-courted and sought-after ally, they do not even have the clout of the East-West conflict as a weapon to use against German discrimination and intimidation.

For reasons which no one in Bonn seems able to explain, the majority of these estimated five thousand Africans are concentrated in northern Germany, in and around Hamburg and Lueneburg. Those who are in the Federal Republic legally have the official status of students and trainees. They attend German-language courses; if academically qualified, they attempt to enroll in universities or, as is generally the case, enter subcollegiate technical training institutes. But like those who have entered the country on ninety-day tourist visas and remain illegally for many months, sometimes years, the Africans are not permitted to work. However, unless they happen to have wealthy parents who can send them money periodically, they have to work to survive. And that exposes them to the most blatant exploitation practiced in Germany today.

Scores of these young Nigerians, Ghanaians, Kenyans, and Tanzanians end up washing dishes in the honky-tonk bars of Hamburg's St. Pauli sin streets or shoveling manure for the farmers on the Lueneburg Heath at wage rates 50 percent below the legal hourly minimum. Being black, they find it next to impossible to obtain housing, and often end up with four and five to a cell-sized room which usurious landladies rent out to them at DM 100 per bed. Inevitably they are drawn into the flourishing Hamburg underworld of crime, prostitution, and drug peddling. And when finally they leave the country, they leave embittered at the white man in general and the German in particular.

"I'm going back to Accra," a young Ghanaian told a reporter for the weekly *Die Zeit*, "and I'll be entering politics back home. You'll be hearing about me in a few years. But I can tell you one thing now: I'll never set foot in or have anything to do with your country again."

That is a choice the vast majority of Germany's "brown babies," now numbering well over ten thousand, do not have. The brown babies—the children whom U. S. black servicemen (and a few French soldiers) left behind—are the real German Blacks. Thousands of them are no longer babies. Indeed, many have children themselves. A few, a very few, have made it big. Erwin Kostedde, twenty-eight, son of an American soldier and a German mother, is one of them. Center for the Offenbach Kickers and a member of the national soccer team, Kostedde is one of the country's highest-paid (DM 200,000 per year) and most popular ballplayers. But like the majority of his brethren, he started on the road as a total outcast. Born into a society which had been indoctrinated with the notion of racial superiority and a country which, because of its brief stint as a colonial empire, had no indigenous Blacks, they are the most outside of all outsiders. Raised as Germans in a totally German environment with German as their mother tongue, they represent an anomaly in a country that only thirty years ago was totally white.

Until the early 1960s, when the oldest of them left school, began apprentice training, and entered the adult world, no one had really paid any attention to them. Most of them had been raised in orphanages and foster homes, only a few by their real mothers. Spread over the four states of Bavaria, Baden-Wuerttemberg, Hesse, and Rhineland-Palatinate that had comprised the old U. S. and French occupation zones, they were of insufficient number in any one area to be of more than peripheral concern to youth and welfare agencies, school authorities, or apprentice training boards. Yet the prejudice and animosity against them had always been bubbling. Kate Nissen, a Danish woman who had arranged for the adoption of more than one hundred brown babies into homes in Denmark, said a number of years ago! "You only have to walk one block on a German street with one of those children and you won't only be conscious of the stares but hear the most awful things being said."

The children became, according to Dr. Klaus Eyferth, a Darmstadt Technical University psychology professor, the objects of a multitude of prejudices and biases. Eyferth became interested in the problem in the early 1960s when he attempted to adopt one of the children and was threatened with eviction by his landlord. Unable to find another apartment where he could make a home for the child, he gave up the idea of adoption; but, together with a team of researchers at Hamburg University, where he was then teaching, he conducted a study and made recommendations which subsequently served as guidelines for youth and welfare agencies around the country.

"They were ostracized as 'occupation babies,' " according to Eyferth. "They were regarded as children of mothers with bad reputations who had carried on freely with 'enemy' soldiers. They were illegitimate. The color of their skin and their racial features made them easily recognizable as such—in contrast to the tens of thousands of white 'occupation babies.'

"But consciously and subconsciously, the Nazi racial theories entered the picture too. There was the widespread notion that racially mixed children inherit the worst traits of both parents. This, added to the 'master race' theory, provided fertile ground for prejudice."

In a booklet he published at the time, Eyferth recommended a broad program of public enlightenment, a concerted effort toward more government assistance and attention to the problem, and above-average educational opportunities to make the children better equipped to deal with a hostile environment. He also stressed that because so many had been raised in orphanages and substandard social environments they would be doubly disadvantaged. He suggested that they be given intensified foreign-language training so that, as adults, they could make an easier choice about whether to remain in Germany or emigrate to countries where, as Blacks, "they will not be stared at like monkeys."

One American Black, the late Al Hoosman, who made the plight of the brown babies his personal crusade, flatly rejected the notion of eventual emigration. Hoosman, a professional boxer who had come to Germany for a prizefight in the late 1950s and then settled in Munich where he worked as an actor until his death in 1968, devoted most of his money and time to an organization he called CAUSE—Children Abandoned by U. S. Servicemen in Europe.

"They've been raised in these surroundings and their outlook is essentially German," he once told me. "True, they are looked upon as oddities and freaks. Because of the milieu into which they were born—the economic circumstances and their color—they face lives as third-class citizens. And I won't even venture a prediction of the troubles they'll face once they start looking for places to live or for partners of the opposite sex. But they *are* Germans and think in German categories."

I remembered Hoosman's remark not long ago when I needed to have some touch-up painting and plastering work done in a house I rented in a Munich suburb. The journeyman painter who came to do the job was a twenty-six-year-old German Black. When I opened the door for him I first thought he must be an American—probably a student, or maybe a GI working part time—and proceeded to explain to him in English what needed to be done. His replies soon indicated that he had barely understood what I had said and apologetically he told me in a fractured school English that he had had only a year or two of English instruction.

Didn't I speak *any* German? he asked. "Oh, yes," I answered. And with a sigh of relief we entered into a dialogue in which his Bavarian dialect was as thick as pretzels and beer.

"Of course I run into prejudice," he explained, "but matters could be worse. I'm not a foreigner. I don't live in a ghetto. I don't need a residence permit. I don't need permission to work. I can't be deported. And I can communicate—even with non-Bavarians if they're willing to make a little effort. You see, *I* am a German."

7

Anatomy of
a Miracle

SEVERAL years ago I heard an anecdote that is very revealing about Germany today:

Adolf Hitler was given a week's leave from Hell in order to see Earth again. To the Devil's great surprise and consternation, the erstwhile Fuehrer returned early from his spree, looking very dejected.

"What's the matter," Satan asked him, "didn't you like it?"

Shaking his head vehemently, Hitler replied: "It's disgusting. Who needs a world in which the Jews are the warriors and the Germans are the businessmen?"

Business, industry, and trade—these were always major factors in German life, of course. But the vigor with which they were pursued was nothing compared with today. The Germans—West and East—are now devoting themselves to making money with the same dedicated energy—and, on occasion, the same lack of scruples—with which they previously attempted military conquest.

The story of their recovery from postwar ruin to their preeminence as industrial and trading powers has been told so often it has become tiresome, even to Germans themselves. And the description of that recovery as a *Wirtschaftswunder*—an economic miracle—borders on being a cliché. But cliché or not, it is a miracle based on a spirit of industriousness, matched only by the Japanese, and helped along by massive infusions of outside aid and capital just when they were needed most.

Thirty years ago the pressure gauges of the German economy pointed to zero. The country was a cadaver, flattened by bombardment, ravaged by battle, bled of its youth and sense of purpose. Nearly seven million Germans had been killed, an estimated twelve million men were prisoners of war. Some 20 percent of all housing had been totally destroyed, and in the key urban and industrial areas, destruction ranged between 50 and 75 percent. Although total damage to industrial capacity was only 20 percent, the Western allies, particularly the French, dismantled and demolished about 8 percent of what remained in their zones, while the Soviets carted off more than 45 percent in theirs. Moreover, the infrastructure lay in ruins. The transportation and communications networks were in a state of total chaos. Nearly all road and rail bridges had been bombed out. More than half the railway rolling stock had been wholly destroyed or damaged beyond repair. If the victors had really wanted to implement the plan of U. S. Treasury Secretary Henry J. Morgenthau, which envisaged reducing Germany forever to a land of agricultural toilers, there would have been little reducing left to do.

The country was not only at a standstill, but its people were starving and freezing. In urban areas the average daily food intake in the first two years after the war often dropped to as low as 800 calories per person. To keep alive, city dwellers scavenged the countryside in search of food, offering farmers clothing, chinaware, furniture, and family heirlooms—whatever might be of value—in exchange for a few pounds of flour or potatoes. Coal was so scarce that stealing it wherever it could be found—off railway cars, from track beds, out of storage yards—became a national pastime officially condoned by the churches.

There was only enough cloth to provide every fortieth man with one suit a year, every tenth with a shirt. Only one in seven could be provided with a plate, one in five with a toothbrush, and one in 150 with a washbowl. And wood was so short that there was virtually none for heating and just enough to provide every third body with a coffin in which to be buried. A fellow journalist, Johanna Prym, whom I have known for many years, once told me how, in order to heat her rented room when she worked for the U. S. Army daily, *Stars and Stripes*, in those days, she methodically filched the chucks of wood holding back the rolls of newsprint in the paper's plant in Pfungstadt. The day after she had taken away the last block, the whole supply came thundering through the wall into the editorial offices.

By the end of 1947, industrial production in West Germany still was

barely half of what it had been before the war. The turning point came in
1948. To spell out the history and the reasons for the miraculous recovery
which began that year in West Germany—considerably later, of course,
in the East—would go beyond the purview of this book. Certainly, the
infusion of $3.8 billion in U. S. Marshall Plan aid was a major factor, the
significance and impact of which Germans today are all too inclined to
forget and underrate. So was the June 1948 currency reform. This was
followed by the implementation of Ludwig Erhard's concept of a "social
market economy," which represented a dramatic break with the traditions
of tight control of the economy practiced under Hitler and even before.
Then, too, there was the Korean War, which provided markets abroad
for West German exports.

In East Germany there was, first of all, the gradual change in the Soviet
attitude in the 1950s that prompted Moscow to stop treating the GDR as
an exploitable colony. The building of the Berlin Wall in 1961 enabled
the GDR to halt the mass exodus of its labor force which had brought the
country's economy to the brink of collapse. And finally, there was the
introduction in 1964 of economic reform, the New Economic System as
it was called, which marked a break with the hypercentralized, Stalinist
command economics practiced in East Germany since 1945.

As early as 1950, West German industrial output had already exceeded
the prewar levels, and West Germans were enjoying a higher standard of
living than in 1938, the last full peacetime year. East Germany, with less
than one-third of the population and territory and a fraction of the West's
industrial capacity and resources, was nonetheless by 1964 producing
more than the entire German Reich in 1938.

Today both Germanys are, in their own right, economic giants, the
Federal Republic ranking along with the United States, Soviet Union, and
Japan among the world's top four industrial powers; East Germany is
among the top ten, and second only to the USSR itself in the Communist
bloc.

Nine of Europe's top twenty industrial concerns are West German, as
are five of the world's thirty largest steel companies. The Federal
Republic is the largest, most prosperous industrial power in Europe and
by far the richest member of the Common Market. It produces more
steel, chemical products, automobiles, trucks, electrical and electronic
goods, textiles, and plastics than Great Britain, France, or Italy. With

export surpluses ranging from $5 to $10 billion annually, it is the most successful trading nation in the world—a development which has enabled it to amass the world's largest reserve of foreign exchange, especially dollars, and has made the deutsche mark one of the strongest currencies in international finance today. Where once it required only twenty-four cents to buy one DM, it now takes about forty. Even in 1974, when the Western world faced the threat of recession and economic disorder, the West German economy, though not immune, proved to be the most orderly and viable of all. Compared to inflation rates of 26 percent in Japan, more than 18 percent in Italy, 17 percent in Great Britain, nearly 12 percent in France, and 11.8 percent in the United States, the West German rate hovered under 7 percent. There were, proportionately, only half as many unemployed in West Germany as there were in either the United States or Italy, and less than in France, Great Britain, or Belgium.

East Germany, if one takes into account its unique handicaps such as a dearth of infrastructure and natural resources, years of deliberate Soviet exploitation and even more years of ideologically based economic mismanagement, has fared even more miraculously. With less than a half percent of the world's total population, it produces more than 2 percent of the world's wealth each year. Its gross national product is growing faster annually than Britain's, Italy's, West Germany's, the Soviet Union's, or that of the United States. It ranks among the world's ten leading producers of electric power, artificial gas, chemical fibers, fertilizers, plastics, synthetic rubber, railway rolling stock, radio and television receivers, household appliances, industrial machinery, machine tools, and optical and precision instruments. Since 1945 the GDR, which depends on the Soviet Union and neighboring Poland for anthracite coal, oil, natural gas, and ores, has built a dozen major power plants, fifteen iron and steel mills, ten huge chemical combines, twelve machine-tool factories, seven new electrotechnical and optical plants, eight major cement works, four shipyards, and the world's only plant where soft "brown" lignite can be turned into coke for steelmaking. Its major exports include computers, cameras, automobiles, farm tractors, agricultural machinery, plastics, pharmaceuticals, machine tools, X-ray equipment, typewriters, calculators, television sets, washing machines, refrigerators, as well as ocean-going freighters, tankers, and passenger ships. In fact, the GDR, which started without a port, is now one of the world's major shipbuilding and seafaring nations, with a high-seas fleet of 194 vessels totalling 1.5 million tons. As recently as 1950 the GDR's ship line had consisted of one rusty, leaky coastal freighter.

East Germany today has the highest standard of living of all countries within the Soviet bloc, a living standard, moreover, which is two-thirds to three-fourths as high as West Germany's, depending on which of the paraphernalia of the consumer-oriented society—automobiles, refrigerators, television sets, washing machines, vacuum cleaners, record players, furniture, clothing, and daily calorie intake—one chooses to throw into the equation. And by those same criteria, the Federal Republic today has one of the highest living standards in the world, topped only by such traditionally affluent countries as the United States, Sweden, and Switzerland—all three of which escaped the direct ravages and destruction of war.

With the exception of privately owned single-family houses, the West Germans today need to work fewer hours to acquire automobiles and most consumer durables than the British, French, Swiss, Swedes, and Japanese. Only for the average American are such goods still cheaper than for the average West German. More than 90 percent of all families in the Federal Republic now own washing machines, television sets, refrigerators, vacuum cleaners, and radios. More than half have tape recorders, record players, and electric sewing machines. A third or more homes are equipped with telephones and deep-freeze units.

Even Hitler's promise of "automobiles for the people" has come true. The beetle-shaped Volkswagen, conceived and designed at his behest, was never much more than a propaganda gimmick during the Third Reich, a means to bilk more than a quarter million Germans out of a thousand Reichsmark, each of which was then used to help finance the war. But since then the Volkswagen has become virtually a symbol of economic recovery, aside from the fact that its production, which is now being phased out after thirty years, paved the way to mass motorization. Today there is a privately owned automobile for every fourth West German, one for every tenth East German.

Drawing on traditions and legislation that date back nearly a hundred years to the time of Bismarck, both Germanys today have comprehensive social welfare systems—replete with compulsory health, unemployment, and old-age insurance—which are equalled or surpassed in their totality and benefits only by those of the Scandinavian countries.

Their reputation for industriousness notwithstanding, the Germans today work fewer hours for proportionately more pay than almost any other people in the world. The forty-hour week is almost standard. More than eight thousand firms and government offices in the Federal Republic have instituted systems of staggered, variable working hours that affect nearly three million white-collar workers who are more or less free to decide on their own when to clock in and out each day, provided they put in their eight hours. A thirteenth-month salary, in lieu of or in addition to Christmas bonuses, is virtually the rule throughout West German industry. And considering that the average worker is entitled to twenty-one days of paid vacation in addition to twelve legal religious and secular holidays each year, he is actually putting in less than eleven months on the job for thirteen months' pay. In some industries thirty-five-hour workweeks are being tested, and the hours themselves are becoming shorter with the introduction of eight-minute hourly breaks for assembly-line workers, a system now being tried out in the metalworking plants of Baden-Wuerttemberg. Although many of these benefits do not yet apply in the GDR, East Germany is catching up rapidly. A minimum of eighteen days' paid vacation became the law there in 1974, and the forty-hour workweek is virtually the rule.

A burgeoning economy which, until mid-1974 enjoyed full employment and was so short of labor that it had to import 2.4 million workers from abroad, was unquestionably the primary reason why German workers have fared so well. But be that as it may, the fact is that the Germans—West and East—have never had it so good. It is indeed a "miracle." But nonetheless, the miracle has blemishes which have potentially far-reaching social and political implications.

In East Germany the overriding problems are, as they have been since the 1950s, the basic weaknesses of the centralized, overbureaucratized, entirely state-owned and operated economy; the shortage of certain goods, and the sporadic distribution of most of them. Compared to the neon-lighted superabundance of the West, life in East Germany is still grim and austere and often gives the impression of having stood still since the 1930s. It is a country with only eleven cities that have more than 100,000 population comprising only 22 percent of the people, a land that seems composed largely of small, provincial, grimy manufacturing towns where joys have always been few and hopes even fewer. Dull and shabby, dusty and sooty, they were never really cheerful places. Most of them are products of the nineteenth-century's industrial revolution and monuments to that century's architectural ugliness. Too unimportant to be bombed or fought over during the war, they have persevered through the peace with little change, except that time and neglect have chipped the gray plaster from the brick walls of their old houses and potholed their cobblestoned streets. The exigencies of recovering from the war under the most adverse conditions and the drive to "build socialism" have tended to render them even drearier.

Unquestionably, the GDR has progressed a long way from those days when people went hungry, when shop windows displayed more portraits of Lenin and Marx than merchandise, when there seemed to be nothing but left-footed shoes, right-handed gloves, mops without handles, handles without mops, and nails but no hammers, or hammers but no nails. That was the era—in the 1950s and 1960s—when people shopped not for what they wanted or needed but for whatever was momentarily available. The classic story of those times is about a man walking across a town square with a huge funeral wreath who is asked by a concerned friend: "Who died?" And the man replies cheerfully: "Oh, no one died. But they were selling these wreaths today and I thought I'd better get one to keep until I did need it."

The GDR is no longer like that, of course. Average net family income is merely 20 percent lower than in West Germany, and because of price stability in the GDR and inflation in the FRG, incomes in both countries are now almost equal in purchasing power. The larger cities have all been rebuilt and the smaller ones are being slowly, but surely, renovated. Although East Germans must still pay outrageously high prices for durables and what the regime categorizes as "luxury goods" (coffee, spices, alcohol, synthetic-fiber clothing, and so on), they pay only a fraction of what West Germans are compelled to spend on housing, public transportation, services, and the basics of life.

But shortages still exist, distribution is still haphazard, and plans still go awry. Something is usually missing somewhere, sold out yesterday, or perhaps not available until tomorrow—"provided you come early, Comrade." In August 1973 in Dresden, for example, the list of "unavailable items" included writing paper, toothbrushes, automobile spark plugs, clothespins, and rubberbands. The next week it could easily have been pencils, toothpaste, windshield wipers, clothesline, and paper clips that were in "short supply."

The lack of choice, coupled with periodic shortages of some goods and the sudden oversupply of others, makes shopping a nerve-straining task. One East German woman described her dilemma this way: "A West German or American housewife can sit down in the morning, make up a shopping list, and plan her meals, then go to the supermarket and buy as much as her budget permits. But my meals are dictated by what I happen to find on the shelves. No noodles? I take rice or macaroni. No veal? Try pork. There aren't any real shortages, but I always end up shopping for what is available, not for what I really want or need. You just cannot find everything all of the time and there are some items you find none of the time. I fill my pantry or my refrigerator according to the whims of some invisible planning expert in Berlin."

The smaller the town or the farther it is from the main supply channels, the larger these problems loom, and they are aggravated by the East Germans' expanding opportunities to compare their standard of living with West Germany's. West German television can be and is received by nearly 80 percent of the populace—the exceptions being those viewers who live in the most southeastern corner of the GDR, which is out of range of West German and West Berlin transmitters. They see the advertising—very limited and restricted to brief time blocks—and programs which open windows to an entirely different world. To the television exposure one must now add the personal contact that has resulted from relaxation of travel restrictions between the two Germanys. Although East Germans remain walled-in, leaving only the elderly, the privileged, and the politically reliable free to travel to the West, there has been, since the signing of the basic treaty between the two Germanys and the establishment of quasi-diplomatic relations, a virtual deluge of West Germans visiting the GDR. Invariably they expose their friends and relatives to a higher standard of living which raises aspirations in the GDR that the East German economy cannot yet fulfill.

When discussing those aspirations, most East Germans are also quick to interject that their system has some obvious advantages over West Germany's which have become all the more apparent since stagflationary pressures raised the prospects of recession and unemployment in the Federal Republic. "People value the security of this system," a top executive in the GDR's chemical industry told me. "The state rewards the hard worker, but it also protects those who cannot or do not work so hard. Our pace is slower. We take it easier. That may be one reason why we are behind. But I wouldn't trade." The same attitude was expressed even more firmly to me by an assembly-line worker in a Zwickau automobile plant who said: "I know what I've got here. It may not be as much as in West Germany. But where's the guarantee that in the FRG I wouldn't be selling apples on the street some day. It happened once in Germany; it could happen again."

Yet, despite this attitude, the pressures to achieve a living standard comparable to West Germany's remain, and in the years to come seem likely to be greater. They are not of such magnitude as to induce tens of thousands of East Germans to flee again to the West should the wall come down and restrictions on travel be lifted, but they are pressures which will place continuing strains and demands on an economy that has little flexibility, few reserves, and only a shallow foundation of capital, natural resources, and entrepreneurial efficiency and imagination.

The problems in West Germany, on the other hand, revolve around completely different issues. One that looms larger than it really is, is the incursion of foreign, especially American, economic interests into the Federal Republic. Another is the trend toward monopolistic concentration of industry; the re-creation of the old cartels under different names; and the transfer, despite rising living standards, of an ever-larger share of the national wealth and capital to the hands of a few who represent the elite. The problem looming largest of all is that class warfare, notwithstanding three decades of peace between labor and management, is far from dead. It has given rise to the maximum, radical demand for socialization of the principal means of production, and the minimum, moderate call for a larger worker share of the pie and a larger labor voice in the managerial and decision-making process.

The question of foreign ownership and control of West German industry is a politically loaded issue that has cropped up periodically in recent years, and though relatively quiescent at the present time, could easily rise again. It depends on economic developments and on whether a politician wants to make use of it, as Franz-Josef Strauss once did and the radical right still does.

Some West German industry, it is important to keep in mind, has always been owned by American corporations. The Opel automobile works in Ruesselsheim near Frankfurt, Germany's third largest car-maker and the country's sixteenth largest industrial enterprise, has been a wholly owned General Motors Corporation subsidiary ever since its founder, Adam Opel, one of the pioneers of the automotive industry, sold it in the late 1920s. One of the ironies is that the Opel plant was making trucks for the Wehrmacht during World War II and—though no satisfactory explanation has ever been given—suffered virtually no damage during Allied bombing raids. Like Opel, Ford, the fourth largest automotive plant, is also entirely American-owned—by the Ford Motor Company.

Some of the other large American corporations which play significant roles in the German economy are Exxon, International Business Machines, Sperry Remington Rand, International Telephone and Telegraph, Mobil Oil Company, Texaco, Goodyear Tire and Rubber Company, Firestone, Boeing, General Foods, Swift and Company, Armour Company, National Dairy Products, Proctor and Gamble, North American Rockwell, General Electric, E. I. du Pont de Nemours, and International Harvester, to name but a few. They either hold substantial shares in German firms, operate subsidiaries, or own companies that previously were German and whose proprietors have sold out.

Although American holdings represent only 8 percent of the total nominal capitalization of West German industry, U. S. companies and subsidiaries do play especially large roles in certain key fields, such as automotive manufacturing, petroleum products, electronics, and data processing. This has enabled extremist political groups to make political capital out of German fears of an "American takeover." The ultrarightist weekly, *Deutsche National und Soldaten Zeitung*, rarely passes up an opportunity to charge that the U. S. role in the German economy is "analogous to Soviet domination of East Germany."

Curiously, no cries of "foreign takeover" were raised in the summer of 1974 when the Shah of Iran became a major shareholder in the Krupp steel concern. On the contrary, the Shah's entry into the German economy was hailed as a progressive move that would compensate Germany for the increased price in Iranian oil.

The internationalization of big business is, in fact, a worldwide phenomenon in which West Germany plays more than just a passive role. Big German corporations have shares in plants and own subsidiaries in Africa, Asia, and Latin America. And to remain competitive in the United States, because of rising German labor costs and the relative devaluation of the dollar versus the deutsche mark, the Volkswagen Corporation is planning to open an assembly plant in the United States.

The Siemens electrical conglomerate, second largest of the German corporations, has expanded into nearly every continent and has bought up dozens of plants and subsidiaries abroad during the past twenty years.

The expansion of Siemens abroad, however, is merely a faint shadow of this huge company's expansion through mergers and outright purchases of smaller firms in Germany itself—an expansion that raises the spectre of cartelization, trust-building, and the concentration of wealth and capital in the hands of a few.

One of the first steps undertaken by the Allies after World War II was to break up the huge German cartels, especially in the steel, iron, mining, and chemical industries. Those moves were dictated largely by political considerations based on the fact that the giants of German industry had not only aided Hitler's rise to power but had formed the financial and material foundation for the creation of the German war machine.

In the 1950s, when the Federal Republic became sovereign, laws against cartel-building were enacted and a Federal Cartel Office, based in West Berlin, was established. But the legislation was largely ineffectual. It was predicated on Ludwig Erhard's laissez-faire notions that the free interplay of market forces would suffice to prevent unfair exploitation of strong positions. The Cartel Office became little more than a watchdog agency to guard against price-fixing agreements and had virtually no power to prevent the formation of monopolies and trusts.

In 1974 a tougher law was introduced. It bans fusion of corporations with DM 1 billion or more in annual sales and mergers that would result in one company gaining a 40 percent or larger share of the market. But the consensus among businessmen and economists is that the new legislation lacks teeth and comes too late.

In the past decade, according to the Cartel Office, there have been nearly two thousand "major concentrations" either through takeover or merger. A major concentration is described as one in which the firms involved jointly control 20 percent or more of the market for their product or, in the twelve months preceding the fusion, jointly had a payroll of at least ten thousand or sales in excess of DM 500 million. The majority of these concentrations have been in the banking, chemical, electronic, machinery, iron, and steel businesses.

The most striking example is the Thyssen Steel Group, now the world's fifth largest, nongovernment-owned steel producer. It has an annual output of nearly fifteen million tons of steel and steel products and a nominal capitalization in excess of DM 1 billion. Since 1956 Thyssen has bought up or obtained controlling interest in more than ten other giant steel companies and conglomerates.

During the same period some 200,000 small, medium-sized, and large German firms—manufacturers, wholesalers, and retailers—have sold to, been swallowed by, or merged with, larger competitors. The motivations for selling to or joining with the bigger companies are often personal, mixed with the inexorable pressure for greater economic efficiency. For example, in 1970 Ernst Stewner and Heiko Pesch, both sexagenarians and partners in a glue, adhesives, and gelatin factory, sold their 105-year-old company to the Schering chemical concern. There was nothing wrong with their business, which had annual sales of more than DM 30 million, a payroll of 330 and had recorded a 1,100 percent increase in sales over the preceding eighteen years. But Stewner's and Pesch's children and heirs had no interest in taking it over and selling it seemed like the smartest thing to do.

In 1968, to cite a different example, Hermann Brunner-Schwer sold an 85 percent controlling interest in Saba Apparatus Company to the American-owned General Telephone and Electronics Corporation. At that time Saba, one of the leading manufacturers of quality radios, television receivers, and hi-fi equipment, had 2,800 employees and annual sales of DM 150 million. The company had been totally owned by several generations of the Schwer family since 1835. Schwer, who has continued as minority shareholder and general manager, explained that the sale was dictated largely by economic considerations. "As a family-owned business we had reached the point where our capital resources no longer sufficed to compete on a market where expensive research and efficient mass production are indispensable."

Tight credit, the growth of multinationals, rising labor costs, the labor shortage, and, as Ernst Wolf Mommsen, general manager of Krupp once put it, "technological advances which dictate consolidation of research and development capacities," force the absorption of smaller companies into bigger ones and induce the large ones to become even larger through mergers. The aim, of course, is ultimately to be more competitive, but as mergers and acquisitions have taken on a snowball effect, competition has actually given way to monopolistic positions in many of the key fields of West German industry.

In the mid-1960s, for instance, the four largest chemical companies—

three of them successors to the gargantuan I. G. Farben trust broken apart by the occupation authorities after the war—had a 40 percent share of the West German chemical, pharmaceutical, and plastic market. Today the same four—Hoechst Farben, Badische Anilin und Soda Fabrik, the Bayer Corporation, and the Henkel Group—control more than 70 percent.

The four largest steel conglomerates—Thyssen, Hoesch, Krupp, and Salzgitter—have a 90 percent corner of the domestic market compared to a "mere 58 percent" a little more than a decade ago. Almost 90 percent of the industrial research in West Germany is conducted by the hundred largest corporations and the eight biggest—Volkswagen, Siemens, BASF, Hoechst, Daimler-Benz, Bayer, Veba, and AEG-Telefunken—account for more than 25 percent of all West German exports.

Industry, trade, banking, and insurance in the Federal Republic today are run by a cobweblike network of interlocking directorates, supervisory boards, and holding companies which has led to a consolidation of wealth and power in the hands of a tiny group of industrial and mercantile oligarchs.

No more than six hundred persons—the owners and managers of the 130 largest manufacturing enterprises, banks, insurance companies, wholesale distributorships, and retail chains—actually control the West German economy.

Although the working masses have attained a standard of living, and the common man a degree of comfort, which would have been unthinkable thirty years ago, the rich have gotten superrich. More than 75 percent of West Germany's productive capital is owned by 1.7 percent of the total population. Some 5 percent of West Germans own 67 percent of the nation's entire wealth. There are nearly eighteen thousand men and women whose personal fortunes exceed DM 1 million. The thirty-four richest have annual personal incomes of more than DM 10 million. The biggest names are those of Flick, Siemens, Bosch, Quandt, Henkel, Henle, Oetker, Gerling, and Finck—nine families whose combined resources and wealth are five times greater than those of the more than thirteen million people in their employ.

Germany's community of multimillionaires and billionaires can be divided into a number of categories, distinguishable not by the size but the origins of their wealth. There is, first of all, the old aristocracy—the dukes, princes, counts, and barons left over from imperial days. They have no political authority, of course, and many are not rich at all. My circle of acquaintances includes nearly a dozen counts and barons, not one of whom is even moderately wealthy. I would describe their situation as comfortably middle class. Some of them are hardworking journalists with whom I have shared beats and stories in the Federal Republic, Eastern Europe, and the Soviet Union. Several are middle-ranking civil servants in the foreign ministry and the press and information office. One sells advertising space for an American news magazine. Another is public relations director for a large corporation. And a baroness once worked for me as a secretary—until she quit to marry a commoner and to become a housewife. But many of those who are wealthy are fabulously so. The richest clan of all are the princes of Thurn und Taxis, a family that began making millions in the seventeenth and eighteenth centuries with Germany's first postal service, which was probably also the first monopoly. Today they no longer deliver the mail but own banks, nonferrous-metal plants, vast expanses of land, and more castles than they can keep track of. "I'm never quite sure," Crown Prince Johannes von Thurn und Taxis once told a German journalist. "Is it eighteen or twenty castles?"

The second, and in a sense the most colorful and flamboyant group, are the self-made men. Most of them are newly rich, having made their piles since the war. A very few are masters of fortunes they personally began amassing in the early decades of this century. Among them the most famous and richest—indeed the richest German of all—was Friedrich Flick, who died at the age of eighty-nine in 1972. Flick was already a millionaire before the start of the *First* World War and a multimillionaire by the time it ended. He preserved his fortune throughout the Weimar Republic and the Third Reich, lost substantial portions of it under Allied edict, but having the touch of Midas, bounced back to build an even greater one in the 1950s and 1960s. A multibillionaire, he had either total, controlling, or partial ownership of some 350 enterprises, the biggest among them being Feldmuehle Paper Mills, Daimler-Benz Corporation, Buderus, Krauss-Maffei, and Nobel Dynamite.

It has been said that modern times and business conditions preclude the rise of another Flick. Perhaps. But there are a number of younger entrepreneurs in Germany today who are well on the way to emulating him. One of them is Willy Korf, forty-five, who started producing steel mats and grids for reinforced concrete in a small shop in Kehl on the

Rhine in 1954. Thanks to disciplined management and minimum profits, he was able to undercut the prices of his giant competitors. Two decades later, Korf has a half dozen steel plants spotted around the country, sales nosing the DM 1 billion figure, and a one-third share, along with Krupp and Salzgitter, of the contract for building what will be one of the world's largest steel plants in Kursk in southern Russia. Korf is an American-style businessman who drives himself and his employees to the physical limits. He regards an eight-hour day a light one, a six-day week an easy one, and is always on the go. When he barrels his Mercedes 350 SL down an *Autobahn* at 110 miles per hour, he usually has one hand on the wheel and the other on his car phone, which keeps him in touch with his plants around the country. At the rate he is going, and assuming he lives as long, he may end up some day being even richer than Flick was.

The third group comprises the heirs of the nineteenth-century industrial barons and mercantile princes—sons, grandsons, great-grandsons, sons-in-law, nephews—who, as heads of the empires their ancestors started, have succeeded in multiplying the family fortunes and power, thanks to the tail winds of the postwar Wirtschaftswunder. Among these fantastically wealthy tycoons are men such as Guenter Henle who, since 1940, following the death of his father-in-law Peter Kloeckner, has been head and majority owner of the Kloeckner-Humboldt-Deutz Group, a sprawling conglomerate in the iron, steel, mechanical engineering, and machinery fields, with nearly eighty thousand employees and annual sales in excess of DM 8 billion. Or there's Rudolf August Oetker, grandson of an inventive Bielefeld pharmacist who in 1891 started the family on the road to riches by concocting a popular and effective baking powder which he sold at 10 pfennigs a package, first to local housewives, then to the nation. By 1918, when old Dr. Oetker died, the baking-powder business had expanded to include cooking starches and pudding mixes. Today the Oetker group is still in the food business— ready mixes and frozen products—but it also controls a number of breweries and Germany's largest high seas tanker and freighter fleet. With a payroll of seventeen thousand and annual sales of close to DM 3 billion, Oetker ranks thirty-fifth among the giants of German industry. In 1974 he concluded what may be his company's shrewdest deal of all. In exchange for two cargo liners worth $24 million, he will build an ultramodern brewery with an annual capacity of seventy-nine million gallons of beer for the Soviet Union, where officialdom has launched a drive to persuade Russians to switch from vodka to less potent beverages.

Finally, there are the salaried rich—the field marshals and generals of German industry—who serve as hired general managers, general directors, and company executives. Though obviously not as wealthy as their employers, they often wield more power and influence. Their salaries frequently range in the seven-digit bracket and their personal fortunes—thanks to bonuses, gifts of shares, and shrewd investments—more often than not can be counted in eight.

Berthold Beitz, for many years general manager and now chairman of the supervisory board of Krupp, is a striking example of the salaried rich. Beitz has been a "hireling" since graduating from Gymnasium in 1934—first as a bank clerk in his native Pomerania, then as an executive of Shell Oil Company, for whom he managed a subsidiary in Poland. After a wartime stint as a Wehrmacht sergeant, he became an insurance executive. In October 1953 Alfried Krupp von Bohlen und Halbach, head of the legendary Krupp steel concern and just released from a war crimes prison, hired Beitz to be the firm's general manager. A handsome, flamboyant man, whom diplomats have described as West Germany's "most imaginative businessman" and whom other businessmen have called "a frustrated diplomat," Beitz not only put Krupp back on its feet but pioneered the Federal Republic's political, diplomatic, and commercial overtures to Eastern Europe and the Soviet Union. Thanks to his impeccable credentials—he had saved the lives of six thousand Poles and Polish Jews by hiding them from the clutches of the SS and the Gestapo—he had entree to Warsaw and, via Warsaw, to the Kremlin. It was Beitz who prodded and cajoled his countrymen and his government into looking eastward. It was Beitz who thought up the system of permanent trade missions in Poland, Hungary, Romania, and Bulgaria that for many years served as Bonn's quasi-diplomatic representations in the Communist world. It was Beitz, in fact, who laid the foundation for East-West detente. And as he carried the German flag eastward in one hand, he held up the three-ring banner of Krupp steel in the other. Now sixty-one, he is at the apex of the managerial caste and since the death of Alfried Krupp in 1967, virtually the embodiment of that legendary giant of German big business.

For all the class conflict that their dominance of the German economy may provoke, one thing can be said of West Germany's superrich: The majority do not flaunt their wealth. On the contrary, they seem embarrassed by it and often seek to hide it. There are notable exceptions, of course, such as Helmut Horten, billionaire king of one of the country's largest department store chains which he started after the war. Horten, who used a loophole in the German tax law to emigrate to Switzerland in 1969 with a tidy little tax-free fortune of DM 825 million which has multiplied manifold since then, displays his riches. He owns five Rolls Royce automobiles; mansions in Switzerland, Austria, and Southern France; a Caribbean island; an ocean-travelling yacht; a BAC 1-11 jet airliner for his personal use, and a beautiful blond wife, thirty years his junior, who has a jewel collection that would put Cartier's to shame. Somewhat of a hypochondriac Croesus, Horten is not only surrounded by lackeys and servants, but has a salaried personal physician who travels with him wherever he goes.

But bigger and richer men than Horten seem to make a deliberate effort to appear modest. When, in the 1960s, the Daimler-Benz Corporation first introduced its opulent Mercedes 600 limousine—Germany's answer to the Rolls-Royce and Cadillac—it had no trouble selling the cars to Arab sheiks and foreign heads of state. One car even went to the Republic of China for use by Mao Tse-tung, and another is assigned to the Kremlin motor pool. But West Germany's own billionaires and multimillionaires thought it too ostentatious. Berthold Beitz is said to have finally persuaded Alfried Krupp to buy one because Daimler-Benz is "one of our important customers." But Krupp himself was never seen in the automobile, preferring instead to drive himself about in his little Porsche sports car. Friedrich Flick, who used to brown-bag his lunch to his office, had little choice about taking and riding in a 600. He was majority owner of Daimler-Benz.

Flick's successor as the richest man in Germany today is Baron August von Finck, scion of a banking and insurance dynasty, whose personal fortune—based on his ownership of the Merck, Finck and Company banking house—is estimated at between DM 2 and DM 3 billion, give or take a few hundred million. Finck is so hypersensitive about the question of wealth that the only car he owns is a black Volkswagen beetle in which his chauffeur drives him to and from work in downtown Munich every day. Once asked whether a chauffeur-driven VW wasn't carrying understatement a bit too far, Finck replied: "It's not a question of modesty, false or real. The Volkswagen is the most reliable car I know of."

Philip Rosenthal, owner and head of West Germany's largest and best-known porcelain factory, prefers to bicycle from his mansion to the plant in Selb and has been known to drive to the annual Bayreuth Wagner festival, high point of the summer social season, in a Volkswagen bus. And instead of partaking of the opulent buffet in the lobby during intermissions, he invites his friends to the parking lot for a nip and tidbits out of the cooler he keeps in the VW.

Honors and titles seem to mean more to the German superrich than diamonds or gold. It is a rare multimillionaire who wouldn't grab at the first honorary doctorate offered him or who doesn't yearn to be appointed honorary consul—with the right to put diplomatic plates on his cars—for some foreign country. The buying and selling of honorary consular titles, in fact, is a big business unto itself, and the smaller and more obscure the nation, the more honorary representatives it is likely to have in the Federal Republic. One German businessman who ridicules the practice, once likened it to "the medals craze we all had during the Third Reich. Now that there are hardly any medals to be worn, everybody wants to be either an honorary doctor or honorary consul." And when Max Grundig, founder and head of one of the country's largest electronics firms, was named honorary consul of Haiti, Berthold Beitz is reputed to have turned to him at a party and said: "What's the matter Max, isn't the name Grundig big enough for you yet?" But then Beitz, who insists that he be called nothing except "Mister," is somewhat of an eccentric outsider anyway.

Next to titles and honors, the tycoons seem to want nothing more than to be loved and respected by their employees, to be regarded as philanthropists and humanitarians. This has led to a curious syndrome in German industry and trade—a paternalism and welfare system, based in turn on total loyalty to the company.

A Kruppianer in Essen is a man who has worked all his life for Krupp, just as his father and grandfather did. The house or apartment he lives in belongs to Krupp and he pays a minimal rent for it. When his children are ill they are treated in a Krupp hospital. He can vacation in company-owned hostels. The firm spends close to DM 150 million a year in social services to its workers who, in turn, are expected to feel like members of one big happy "Krupp family."

Gustav Schikedanz, septuagenarian head of the Quelle Group, Germany's largest mail-order house and department store chain, with annual sales of nearly DM 6 billion, has set up a nursery school at his company headquarters in Fuerth, where working mothers can deposit their children during the day at a monthly rate equal to about one hour's pay. He maintains a company hotel in the Bavarian Alps where employees are entitled to spend vacations at cut-rate prices.

Philip Rosenthal, much concerned about cultural uplift in the Bavarian backwoods area where his and most other porcelain plants are located, has brought to his plant auditorium in Selb Igor Oistrakh, Yehudi Menuhin, Marcel Marceau, Louis Armstrong, the Bamberg Symphony, a La Scala Opera ensemble, Guenter Grass, and dozens of other great names in music, art, literature, and the theater for guest performances, readings, and showings. Rosenthal also maintains a company rest home and sanatorium for his workers, and as a physical fitness fan, is not above leading them on endurance hikes through the countryside.

Kurt R. Koerber, an engineer who developed a machine for making cigarette filters which he now manufactures in his plant near Hamburg and exports around the world, is one of the most socially and politically conscious of all German entrepreneurs. The Koerber Foundation, for example, organized and put up the money for the Gustav Heinemann essay contest in which high school pupils around the country are encouraged to research and write about the significant democratic and revolutionary movements in German history. Among other things, Koerber also takes each of his two thousand employees and members of their families to private, closed performances of the Hamburg State Opera at least once a year.

Company clinics, kindergartens, vacation enclaves, rest houses, old-age homes, soccer teams, gymnasiums, athletic fields, orchestras, bands, craft shops, and adult education programs are to be found as part of the "social and welfare plan" of almost every large enterprise.

And one entrepreneur, Hanns-Heinz Porst, even gave his entire company away to his fourteen hundred employees. Porst, now fifty-one, is probably the most eccentric of all Germany's new superrich. With a matter-of-factness that defies description, he calls himself a "millionaire *and* a Marxist." And indeed, he is both, for not only is he worth millions, but he is a compulsive social reformer and Communist sympathizer who has spent sixteen months in prison following conviction on a charge of espionage for East Germany's intelligence agency. After World War II

Porst transformed his father's modest Nuremberg photo and camera business into Europe's largest mail-order and retail-chain photographic equipment business. Importing cameras, lenses, film, paper, and darkroom rigs from Japan, China, and the GDR and selling them under his own house brand at cut-rate prices, he built an empire with annual sales of around DM 200 million. In 1972 he turned the whole business over to his workers, setting up a complicated works-council structure similar to the self-management system in Yugoslavia. He stayed on as the firm's managing director whom, theoretically, the employees could fire any time. He pegged his own salary at DM 250,000, to which he adds approximately DM 1 million as interest on the capital investment which he donated to his employees.

Outlandish? Maybe. But not very much so in a country where labor representatives are already entitled by law to one-third of the seats on corporate supervisory boards and may soon occupy half of them and where the unions not only regard themselves as "social partners" of management but operate some of the country's largest enterprises and banks themselves.

West Germany's unions invariably baffle foreigners because they are so unlike unions anywhere else—both in structure and in behavior. During the past two decades they have called so few strikes that their strike funds now have billions of marks in them, and on the rare occasion when work stoppages do take place it seems like a national calamity.

Instead of small crafts unions, often competing with each other, or locals covering many enterprises, there are sixteen principal unions, organized in the *Deutscher Gewerkschaftsbund*, the German Trade Union Federation, each of which covers entire industries such as construction, mining, metalworking, and transportation. And instead of working out wage contracts with individual companies, collective bargaining is carried out for whole industries and branches of the economy. There being neither "union" nor "closed" shops, the contract agreements apply to everyone working in that industry, whether a dues-paying union member or not. Membership, however, is high, exceeding 80 percent among miners and nearly 70 percent in the metal trades, which includes the automotive industry. In fact, the *Industriegewerkschaft Metall*, that is the metal workers' union, is the largest autonomous union in the world, having more than two million members. Besides the Trade Union

Federation, there are several other umbrella organizations, the largest and most influential of which is the *Deutsche Angestellten Gewerkschaft*, an employees' and white-collar workers' union.

By law, any company having five or more employees or workers must also have a *Betriebsrat*, a shop council of elected worker delegates who represent the interests of labor vis-à-vis management. The larger the enterprise, the more involved the council becomes in the actual codetermination of company policies.

Virtually since war's end the approach of the unions has been to minimize class conflict, to prevent confrontations between labor and management, and to create a spirit of "partnership." It is a spirit reflected in the language itself. Collectively, labor and management are called *Sozialpartner*. The word for management is *Arbeitgeber*, literally "work-giver," and for labor, *Arbeitnehmer*, meaning "work-taker." The social conflicts that have thus far arisen tended to involve the work-takers intramurally, for there are still great distinctions in social standing between *Arbeiter*, meaning "blue-collar workers," and *Angestellte*, "white-collar workers," with an entirely new caste—*Leitende Angestellte*, "managing white-collar workers"—emerging. The latter are usually junior executives whose position between management and labor is not clearly defined and whose roles in the hierarchical structure have, in recent years, become the source of considerable controversy.

In many respects, the unions themselves are Arbeitgeber. The Federation of Trade Unions has some twenty-five thousand people in its direct employ, owns one of the country's largest real estate development and home-building enterprises, newspapers, insurance companies, and scores of manufacturing enterprises making everything from laundry detergents to furniture. Most important of all, the federation owns the Bank fuer Gemeinwirtschaft, West Germany's fourth largest bank, with nominal capital of DM 360 million and some two hundred branches around the country. It owns shares in some of the country's largest enterprises.

The degree of social and economic peace achieved by this unique spirit of partnership is indeed phenomenal and matched by no other country in the non-Communist world. How much longer it will last is a different question, however, for in the past few years the German economy has witnessed the rise of a new spirit of class consciousness. Prof. Helge Pross, a Giessen University sociologist, has described it as a "class-consciousness" and an "inimical attitude toward capitalism" which appears to have been "nurtured in affluence." She sees this new mood as being most prevalent "among the middle class, not the workers themselves," and "among a generation that has personally never experienced either poverty or unemployment."

"In fact," she says, "it is affluence and the stability of our democratic system that have provided the energies for the mounting criticism of capitalism. And it is a form of criticism which is primarily, though not exclusively, based on moral considerations. It is directed against the very fact that capitalism produces for profit rather than to fulfill social needs."

The most vociferous, articulate, and potentially influential critics are the militants within the Social Democratic party's own youth organization—the Jusos, or *Jungsozialisten,* as they are called. All three of the major political parties have youth organizations whose leaders and members stand well to the left of the mainstream of the parties themselves. But none is quite as far left as the Juso group and none has been as successful in gaining control of local and regional party echelons, giving them platforms as well as effective political power with which to exert pressure on the party leadership in Bonn.

The most radical of the Jusos, a faction calling themselves the *Stamokap* (state monopoly capitalism) group, has more or less been isolated since mid-1973. These were young intellectuals who contended that parliamentary democratic systems such as West Germany's actually encourage monopoly capitalism through subsidies, defense contracts, tax benefits, currency manipulations, and unemployment compensation. The essence of their argument was that, since there is no room for reform under this system of "state-supported monopoly capitalism," the only alternative is to get rid of the system—in other words, revolution followed by the establishment of a dictatorship of the proletariat. The Stamokap faction was never much more than a tiny but loud minority within the Juso group itself, and a number of its key members have in the meantime quit the SPD and joined the Communist party, where, ideologically, they belong. But there are plenty of "moderate" Jusos who argue that the system must be changed drastically to give labor a substantially bigger voice and the common man a larger piece of the national wealth. Their basic argument is that capitalism per se is both unjust and immoral because profit accrues only to those who have invested, not to those who produced it, and that managerial authority does not derive by consent of the managed.

Two highly controversial bills, drafted by the SPD/FDP coalition government in 1974 and awaiting approval by the Bundestag, are designed to remedy some of this "injustice" and "immorality." The most controversial of all is the *Mitbestimmungs,* or codetermination proposal, which would give labor an equal voice with management on the supervisory boards of all stock corporations having more than two thousand employees—roughly, six hundred West German business enterprises. The supervisory board, a unique institution under German corporate law, is a group elected for varying periods of service by the shareholders at their annual general meetings. The members of the board need not necessarily be shareholders or in any way connected with the company. Under present regulations, one-third of them must be representatives of labor, elected by the shop council. The supervisory board in turn appoints the board of directors which comprises the actual executive organ of the company; the general director, comparable to the president of an American corporation, is the chief executive officer. Under the proposed new legislation, all supervisory boards would consist of twenty members, ten elected by the shareholders, ten elected by labor. Of the ten labor representatives, one should be a *Leitender Angestellte,* that is, a "managing white-collar worker," who would be elected by a council of his peers.

Although there has been equal representation of shareholders and workers on the supervisory boards of companies in the coal and steel industries for more than twenty years, the bill extending codetermination to all industry has met with objections from nearly every conceivable quarter. Big business is opposed on the grounds that the shareholders take the principal risk and therefore their representatives should have the principal voice. The unions are opposed because they do not want any junior executives to have representation on the boards and because the bill, in its original form, precludes union officials from being elected: All labor representatives must be full-time employees of the company concerned. And the U. S. Chamber of Commerce in Germany, which represents all American-owned corporations in the Federal Republic, is against the measure because it would be "tantamount to partial expropriation of American-owned property."

The other major bill envisages a form of mandatory profit-sharing on the part of all large corporations, with money earmarked to go into special, tax-exempt workers' accounts, the object being to reduce the imbalance in the distribution of the national wealth.

Meanwhile, as the government battles to obtain passage of these measures, it is undertaking some tax reforms designed to ease the burden on the lower- and middle-income groups while extracting a larger share from the upper-middle classes and the rich.

None of this means, of course, that capitalism in West Germany is on its deathbed or that the country is on the brink of socialization. But it does mean, as Frank Vogl, for many years the London *Times* financial correspondent in Frankfurt, put it, that "the structure of West German industry is undergoing a major transformation. . . . New legislation such as tougher cartel laws, worker codetermination laws, tax reforms producing a fairer distribution of incomes . . . are producing major upheavals. The changes taking place are profound. . . . The German economy today is very much in the posteconomic miracle era and the present decade is going to be one of major transition. . . ."

8

Whatever Happened to Goethe?

GERMANY'S Zero Day—*Der Tag Null*—was when the awesome military machine that had steamrollered over most of Europe lay broken and defeated. It was the day—thirty years ago—when the arrogant Reich that was to last a millennium crumbled into chaos. Once-great cities were monuments of rubble. Throughout the ravaged country, millions wandered aimlessly and stunned—the driftwood of a tidal wave of war and a criminal ideology.

The physical ruin was total. But the moral bankruptcy, spiritual devastation, and intellectual vacuum left by only a dozen years of Nazi dictatorship, wanton aggression, and meticulously organized genocide seemed even greater. The German conscience, as represented by its *Dichter und Denker*—the poets and thinkers—had been muted. The works of the exciting, provocative authors and artists who had served as the intellectual backbone of the Weimar Republic and had made Germany of the 1920s a cultural mecca of Europe, had been burned and banned. Most of the significant writers, dramatists, cinéastes, painters, and sculptors had gone into exile and those who remained were either imprisoned, terrorized into silence, or in "internal emigration." Those writers who had dared to write at all during the Nazi era had written in parables which, fortunately, neither the Gestapo nor, unfortunately, most of their readers could understand. The young generation—those intellectuals who had grown to manhood during the Hitler years—had either been decimated on the battlefields or stunned dumb by the cacophony of propaganda and lies to which they had been subjected.

188

But just as Germany rose from the ashes to material prosperity, there is today, three decades later, a new German culture of note and a new generation of writers, artists, and intellectuals with talent.

There are some curious parallels and analogies between the intellectual renaissance and the economic and political recovery. In both spheres the first task was to clear away the debris. What the *Truemmerfrauen*— the rubble women—who cleaned the streets were to the economy, the *Kahlschlaeger*—the glade hackers—who cleansed the language were to literature.

"We had to start anew," the novelist Hans-Werner Richter once explained. "We had to hack glades in the jungle to revive the German language. After twelve years during which German had been reduced to a mumbo-jumbo of propaganda or the symbolisms of the 'internal emigrees,' even the simplest words had lost their true meanings. It was impossible for us to use such words as 'heart,' 'spirit,' 'blood,' 'soil,' 'folk,' 'fatherland,' because during the Third Reich they had acquired a sense and implication which those of us who returned from the war rejected. Our vocabulary was reduced initially to a few hundred words, free of any intimation or innuendo. . . .

"Then, slowly, we began to use traditional words and expressions again, though only cautiously, in order to give them once more their lost content and meaning."

Richter, now a sexagenarian, was not only one of the original glade-hackers himself but the driving force behind Germany's postwar literary renaissance. As impressario and ex-officio chairman of Group 47, an unorganized organization which dominated and influenced German letters for nearly a quarter of a century, Richter mentored to the top of the best-seller lists such postwar writers and dramatists as Heinrich Boell, Guenter Grass, Uwe Johnson, Sigfried Lenz, Martin Walser, Peter Weiss, and Peter Handke.

The group had its indirect beginnings in an American prisoner-of-war camp, where Richter and another writer, Alfred Andersch, founded a lively political-literary POW magazine, *Der Ruf* (The Call). Its editorial leitmotifs were militant antinazism, pacifism, literal interpretation of democracy, and application of the four freedoms—especially freedom of speech and the press. When they were repatriated to Germany in 1946, Andersch and Richter obtained a license to continue the magazine as a nationally distributed cultural-political biweekly. Slanted left and appeal-

ing to the embryonic idealism of the "new" Germany's young generation, *Der Ruf* soon set circulation records. But the editors apparently took
too literally the democratic lessons to which their American captors had
subjected them. After sixteen issues, U. S. military authorities in Munich
banned *Der Ruf* for being "overly nihilistic."

"The real trouble," Richter once told me, "was that we refused to
make a distinction between an elected and a military government and
criticized the latter as roundly as we would have the former."

The end of *Der Ruf*, however, was the start of Group 47. Richter
applied for a new military government license to publish *Scorpion*, an
apolitical, literary-satirical monthly. He had just called a conference of the
magazine's potential contributors when the permit was denied. With no
magazine in which to publish, they decided to read the manuscripts to
each other and to criticize them.

That first meeting, on a Bavarian farm in September 1947, attended by
Andersch, Richter, and four other writers, launched what was to become
the most influential force in postwar German literature. The name Group
47—for the year in which it started—was not attached until 1948 and was
actually a misnomer, for there was never really any group at all. It had no
by-laws, no officers, no dues, no criterion of membership except that
those who belonged were those invited by Richter to its annual sessions.
Richter kept most of the names in his head or, at best, on a grubby scrap
of paper in his pocket. From the original half dozen who started it, it grew
to an amorphous collection of more than 120 writers, professional critics,
publishers, and editors who met yearly to hear and criticize the
unpublished work in progress of twenty to thirty novelists, essayists,
poets, and playwrights.

Marcel Reich-Ranicki, one of West Germany's leading literary critics,
once described Group 47 to me as "a substitute for a literary cafe or salon
in a divided country which no longer has an intellectual capital or center
as Berlin used to be."

The meetings of this traveling literary cafe followed a set of unwritten
traditions and rules. The writers invited to read would sit in what became
known as "the electric chair," and be subjected, without the right of
rebuttal, to the frank and often brutal criticism of their fellow authors and
the professional critics in attendance. Frequently a session in "the chair"
became a major stepping-stone to fame for young and unknown writers.

There was a Group 47 prize, worth variously from $250 to $1,250 and invaluable in publicity terms. It was not awarded often—no more than a dozen times in twice that many years—but for its recipients it invariably meant that long-hoped-for professional breakthrough, publishers' contracts, and nationwide attention. Among the winners who owe their literary fame to the prize are Heinrich Boell, Guenter Grass, Martin Walser, and Peter Handke. The list of those writers who became successful without having won the approval of Group 47's critics is small.

In effect, Group 47 gave birth to and nurtured postwar literature in West Germany. There is hardly a poet, novelist, or playwright of note who does not have his literary roots and ties to the group. For all its contribution, however, Group 47 was the center of much controversy and far from being either generally admired or respected. It was often under attack for playing the role of imperious judge of literary tastes and criteria. And during the two decades in which the Christian Democrats were in power in Bonn, the group was regarded as the embodiment of dangerous left-wing intellectual radicalism.

Unquestionably, through its meetings and reading sessions the group did dictate literary standards. Rare, indeed, are the writers who failed to meet the standards but nonetheless achieved both critical and public acclaim. Its reading sessions, undeniably, were grueling trials for whoever took the chair to introduce new work—whether a novice or an established author. As one disenchanted member of the group once told me: "Nothing quite compares to a clique of highly neurotic, mutually jealous German intellectuals, all locked into a room together and just waiting to tear each other apart." And as Richter himself once admitted: "In the early days the proceedings *were* a little rough, I suppose. It used to be that the auditors just turned their thumbs down, Roman arena fashion, whenever they did not want to hear any more of a reading. I would then interrupt the author and send him—obviously dismayed and no doubt furious—back to the benches."

But at least those who sat in the chair were all treated equally. In applying the dreaded "treatment" that could make or break an author or a new work, no distinction was made between the famous and the unknown. And those who gave were also expected to take. Guenter Grass, for example, gained a reputation for being one of the most scathing and acid-tongued critics at Group 47 meetings. But in 1964, when he sat in the chair to read from a new play, *The Plebians Rehearse the Insurrection*, he was subjected to the longest and most acerbic criticism in the group's history. Two hours of tempestuous discussion followed his reading and ended with the consensus that the play was bad. Grass subsequently rewrote much of the script, but not enough to prevent the play from flopping abysmally when it premiered in West Berlin the following year.

As one publisher once put it: "I like to think of the group as protecting everyone from bad literature. Just imagine the benefit to the reading public had Ernest Hemingway submitted *Across the River and into the Trees* to Group 47-like criticism. He might have ended up fighting everyone in the room, but it would either have resulted in a better book or none at all."

The other charge—leftist radicalism—vastly overstated the case, of course. But there is no denying that virtually all writers rooted in or associated with Group 47—meaning, in effect, the literary elite of West Germany—were more or less left of center. Indeed, Hans Werner Richter wanted it that way. The group, he once explained, was founded by writers who regarded themselves as dedicated publicists first, literati second. "They wanted the new literature to help prevent a repetition of the past and to lay the foundations for a new, democratic Germany. I never knowingly invited a right-winger or a former Nazi to the meetings." This was a precedent-setting approach to literature and the arts in a country where intellectuals traditionally had tried to hide from the reality of their society in ivory towers. Thomas Mann may have warned that "it is impossible to devote oneself to culture and declare that one is not interested in politics." And even Schiller—a century before Mann—described Germany as a country in which "culture begins where the political realm ends." But the warnings and the laments about apolitical literati notwithstanding, the overriding current in German literature and art had been a neutral loftiness removed from sociopolitical realities. The impact of Group 47 in the postwar years was to drive the poets and writers out of their ivory towers.

Once on the ground, at least in the 1950s and 1960s, they were confronted by West German governments that were conservative and right-wing, and in the case of Chancellor Kurt Georg Kiesinger's administration, by a government headed by a former Nazi. Inevitably, virtually all leading writers and Group 47 members found themselves in opposition to such administrations. And they became an articulate opposition, demanding more democracy, more integrity in government, and social change. The government reacted with the predictable nervousness and irritation of all governments that find themselves under attack from the nation's intellectuals. As long, of course, as the attacks were limited to the outpourings of the writers' pens and typewriters, the official response was limited to insinuations and innuendos. However, once the writers became actively engaged in politics (for example, Guenter Grass stumped the country giving speeches on behalf of the Social Democrats and Willy Brandt during the 1965 election campaign), the arguments became more direct. Chancellor Ludwig Erhard was so rattled by Grass' persistent needling that he accused him of writing *entartete Literatur*—degenerate literature—an expression lifted right out of the ideological phrase book of the Third Reich.

Although most of the West German writers today do lean to the left, the majority do not lean much further left than the Social Democratic party. Moreover, most of them limit their political engagement to the social criticism in their works. Those who are actively involved as dues-paying, card-carrying members of any political party—invariably the SPD—are few in number and those who go beyond that to direct political participation are even fewer.

Guenter Wallraff, thirty-two, whose best-selling sociopolitical exposés of big business have made him the bête noire of the German industrial establishment, is one of those exceptions. In the spring of 1974 he went to Greece, chained himself to a lamppost on an Athens street, and distributed handbills protesting against the regime of the Greek colonels. Promptly arrested and beaten up by security police, he was sentenced to fourteen-months' imprisonment for "antigovernment agitation" and not released until the military regime collapsed nearly three months after his incarceration.

Dieter Lattmann, forty-eight, a Munich writer and graduate of the Group 47 electric chair, is not only the president of the German Writers' Association but a first-term Social Democratic Bundestag deputy.

Guenter Grass, forty-eight, not only stumped the country on behalf of Brandt and the SPD in 1965, but in 1969 and 1972 as well. In fact, his most recently published book, *Diary of a Snail*, is a belletristic personal report on his involvement in the 1969 campaign. The "snail" is symbolic of the SPD's long, slow climb to power in Bonn, as well as symbolic of "progress and social reform." Snails move slowly, Grass stresses, but they do move forward. He has described the current conflict between the SPD's moderates and the party's left-wingers, such as the Jusos, as a debate between "reformers and revolutionaries," between "snails that move at snail's pace and those that want to gallop or jump."

Siegfried Lenz, forty-nine, best-selling author of *The German Lesson* and one of the early members of Group 47, went on the hustings for the SPD in 1972. Martin Walser, forty-eight, whom critics have called the only writer of his generation with the potential for writing another *Magic Mountain*, was one of the first to become active on behalf of the SPD. He was also one of the first to have a falling-out with Brandt, whom he accused during a political rally in 1965 of being too soft on American involvement in Vietnam. Subsequently he turned toward the Communist party for ideological inspiration, only to abandon that end of the political spectrum cured of all illusions.

Even Heinrich Boell, the Nobel Prize winner and for a number of years the president of the International PEN club, has crossed the Rubicon from critical writing to direct political involvement on a number of occasions. At one point he was even erroneously suspected of sympathizing with and aiding the Baader-Meinhoff anarchist group.

Whatever Group 47 may have done for or to literature in the postwar era, it could do little, however, to control the centrifugal forces that have led to the quartering of German writing into four fairly distinct parts: West German, East German, Austrian, and Swiss.

The demarcation lines are not always clearly drawn, of course.

For example, although the novelist Max Frisch and the dramatist Friedrich Duerrenmatt are native Swiss and live in Switzerland, their greatest literary impact is in West Germany.

Rolf Hochhuth, the playwright, is a native of West Germany and first gained fame there with his drama *The Deputy*, his critical assessment of Pope Pius XII's position on the Jewish question during the Third Reich. But Hochhuth now lives in Basel, just across the German-Swiss border.

Peter Weiss, whose plays, *Marat/Sade* and *The Investigation*, won him international acclaim, is a native Berliner who fled with his parents in 1934 and has been living in Sweden since 1939. But he writes in German, and it is in the two Germanys where he is read and staged most frequently.

Ingeborg Bachmann, a sensitive and towering poet, dramatist, novelist, and short-story writer, who died in October 1973 of burns suffered when she fell asleep in bed with a lighted cigarette, was a native of Klagenfurt in Austria and made her home in Rome. But she gained fame through Group 47, and it was in West Germany where she was read the most and best known.

Peter Handke, perhaps the most provocative and exciting of the young writers today, is also a native Austrian, but he became known largely through Group 47 and his plays that were staged in West Germany. In 1973 he won the Georg Buechner Prize, the Federal Republic's most important literary award, and until early 1974, when he moved to Paris, he lived in Kronberg near Frankfurt.

Peter Hacks is East Germany's most important dramatist. He was born in Breslau (now called Wroclaw and a part of Poland), educated in Munich, and in 1955, motivated by political considerations, became a "reverse refugee" and settled in the GDR. But troubles with the Ulbricht regime for many years prevented his plays from being staged there. In West Germany, however, there is hardly a theater which doesn't have at least one of them in its repertory.

Wolf Biermann, the GDR's most scathing satirical poet, is a native of Hamburg who in 1953, at age seventeen, left his native West Germany to live in East Berlin and become an East German citizen. After a brief initial success there, he was silenced, and not a line of his work has been printed or a record of his songs made in the GDR since the mid-1960s. Instead, he is published and recorded in West Germany to which he refuses to return because emotionally and politically he regards himself more loyal to East Germany.

Notwithstanding these notable examples of intellectual border-hopping and literary cross-breeding within the larger framework of the German-speaking region of Europe, the trend in the postwar era has been toward the emergence of "four German literatures." To remain within the intended scope of this book, I shall narrow the focus to two of them: West and East Germany's.

The most significant development in both Germanys since the mid-1960s, it seems to me, has been the gradual shift of literary and theatrical attention from preoccupation with the Nazi past to the social phenomena of the postwar present. This is only natural, of course, as younger writers and dramatists emerge. But it is a phenomenon detectable in the works of older authors as well—those who have personal knowledge and experience of the Third Reich. Some are still in the transitional stage—a transition that in the works of Heinrich Boell, Guenter Grass, and Siegfried Lenz has often manifested itself in attempts to link the two eras or to demonstrate the impact of the past on the present.

Siegfried Lenz's *The German Lesson* is a striking example of this. Siggi Jepsen, the central character, is a delinquent youth doing time in a reformatory for a series of art thefts. He is ordered to write a composition about "duty and responsibility" in which, subconsciously, he links his contemporary antisocial, criminal behavior to his childhood experiences during the Third Reich. In the essay he relates the persecution of an avant-garde, anti-Nazi artist in his native village during the war. Siggi's own father was the village policeman who had to enforce the Gestapo ban on the elderly painter, whom Siggi loved like a grandfather. He helped the artist to keep one step ahead of the authorities, embodied by his own father, and to hide his nonconformist paintings which were subsequently destroyed in a fire. Siggi's postwar heists of art from museums and galleries are but a subconscious attempt to protect and secrete the works of his childhood idol, and his rebellion against authority is an expression of his contempt for his father, who was the local incarnation of Nazi injustice and dictatorship. The novel, which became an immediate best seller upon publication in 1971, draws an unbroken line between the Third Reich era and its impact on contemporary West German society. Coincidentally, it also marks Lenz as one of the most important writers in the Federal Republic today.

Guenter Grass' *Diary of a Snail* is another example of how some of the contemporary writers seek to link the two eras. Though ostensibly a belletristic reportage of his experiences as a campaigner for the SPD in 1969, it is laced with reflections about the Third Reich past in his native Danzig—the scene of so much of the action and narrative in *The Tin Drum, Cat and Mouse*, and *The Dog Years*. Explaining this in an interview when *Diary of a Snail* was published in October 1972, Grass said: "Whenever you want to tell a story about the German present, you have to return to the German past. I did so by bringing in Danzig's Jews—a subject with which I was familiar and to which I am inextricably linked by geographical origins. Moreover, it was a theme of special pertinence to my story of the 1969 campaign because the chancellor then in office was Kurt Georg Kiesinger, whose political roots are imbedded in the Third Reich."

Similar links to and reflections about the Hitler years run through most of Heinrich Boell's work. Indeed, it was not until publication of his latest novel in 1974, *The Lost Honor of Katharina Blum*, a fictionalized critique of the yellow press, that Boell devoted himself almost exclusively to a current West German theme.

Martin Walser, on the other hand, more or less broke with the past when his play *The Black Swan*, in which ruminations about the Third Reich and nazism play a central theme, proved too difficult and unwieldy for successful staging in the early 1960s. Since then he has dealt almost exclusively with the provinciality and materialism of postwar West Germany's economic miracle. A trilogy—*Half Time*, *The Unicorn*, and *The Fall*, the last published in 1973—is a social criticism of the Federal Republic as experienced by the central character, Anselm Kristlein, a travelling salesman turned advertising magnate and author who, in the latest of the three novels becomes a social waste product because at age fifty he is too old to compete.

Walser, who was born in Wasserburg on the shore of Lake Constance, now lives in a turn-of-the-century three-story house overlooking the lake, on the outskirts of Friedrichshafen, just a few miles from his birthplace. Much of his writing is influenced by and reflects his experience in that provincial southwestern corner of the Federal Republic. He is intellectually committed to the principle of writing only about what he knows best.

"One can write only about what one knows and has experienced," he once told me. "It would be difficult for me to write about the Third Reich—I was barely eighteen when it ended—or attempt to pass judgment on how people should have acted then. But I can write about how the people who were old enough to experience and remember the Nazi era should act today. Some of my friends wonder why I continue to live in Friedrichshafen or nearby. But in a sense I have the reality of Germany here. This town became rich through war production. It started with old Count Zeppelin who built and tested his dirigibles here in World War One. In World War Two it was the Dornier aircraft company and the Maybach factory which made panzer engines. And now weapons are again being made here. This is the reality I try to reflect in my writing."

For Uwe Johnson—massive, broad-shouldered, strong-handed, and now totally bald—reality for nearly two decades was Germany's partition. His first novels—*Speculations about Jacob, The Third Book about Achim,* and *Two Viewpoints*—all focussed on the division of Germany and Berlin. Johnson came from East to West Germany in 1957 and once implored me not to say that he "fled." "One cannot flee from one part of one's country to the other," he insisted. For years he devoted himself to that single theme "because that is my experience. I had no other experience." Then, in 1966 he went to the United States to edit, teach, and write, returning to West Germany in 1968. His most recent novel, the second volume of *Jahrestage* (Anniversaries), reflects both the new and the old experiences. The central character, Gesine Cresspahl, is a familiar one to fans of Johnson's often-convoluted prose, for she made her debut in *Speculations about Jacob.* She has emigrated to New York with Jacob's and her ten-year-old daughter because she cannot endure life in post-Hitler Germany—East or West—and attempts to come to terms with the United States of the late 1960s from which Johnson draws parallels to the Germany of the 1930s.

The West German present plays a dominant role in the works of less towering writers than Boell, Grass, Lenz, Walser, or Johnson—regardless of whether they are older than these men or members of the postwar generation.

Gerhard Zwerenz, now fifty, who fled East Germany in 1957, still considers himself a Marxist, and views both his old and his new homelands with a most critical Marxist approach that seems to leave officialdom on both sides of the border aghast with indignation. Zwerenz, as he puts it, left the GDR when "I began to recognize the difference between Communist theory and practice." Believing in the theory but appalled by the practice, he has sought in the eighteen years since his defection to make West Germany adhere to his own utopian and noble criteria. A novel about urbanization, real estate speculation, and pollution in Frankfurt, published in 1973, threw that city's Social Democratic mayor, Rudi Arndt, into a rage. The measure of Zwerenz's integrity, though it says nothing about his literary talent, can be deduced from the fact that East Germany has accused him of being a West German agent and in West Germany he has been suspected of working for the East Germans.

In 1974, Uwe Timm, a thirty-five-year-old literary novice, published the first novel about the student and youth rebellion of the late 1960s. Entitled *Hot Summer*, it attempts to explain the motivations, moods, and aspirations of the postwar generation, whose revolt against the social patterns and precepts of their parents proved to be a major turning point in recent West German history.

A number of authors also belong to a circle which calls itself Group 61. The year of their first meeting has less significance than the fact that all regard themselves as "proletarian" writers, whose themes inevitably are the factory, the working-class milieu, the blue-collar worker's alienation, and exploitation of the masses. Many of them being workers themselves who began writing in their spare time, they tend to be looked down upon by the literary critics and arbiters of taste, most of whom are Gymnasium and university graduates, making them members not only of an intellectual elite but of a caste. As a consequence, much of "proletarian literature" is relegated to the fringes of what we are told West German literature is all about.

There is, in fact, an awkward estrangement between the literary "mainstream" and the public at large, due in no small measure to a lingering German inclination to make a fetish of intellectualism, which is categorized and perpetuated by the schools, universities, publishers, booksellers (once described to me as "a cult all to themselves"), and the fringe hangers-on of the intellectual community. The traditional association of education and intellect with social-class standing has obviously left scars on the German psyche which will not disappear with one generation, perhaps not even with two. The inclination to "celebrate culture" in the way "mass is celebrated" will linger on for many years.

As one young renegade critic once put it: "Most Germans view a trip to the theater like going to church, and most of the books they buy are not bought to be read but to be given as gifts and to ultimately end up on shelves behind glass. When you talk about literature in the Federal Republic today you are talking about a subject that affects and interests less than five hundred thousand people. They are the ones who buy and read what we call literature."

This does not mean, of course, that only 500,000 Germans read and buy books, but that to the German intellectual only a small portion of the fiction and drama written and staged today counts as "literature." Authors whose works are likely to be serialized in daily newspapers or illustrated magazines are personae non gratae among the literati. Thus, Willi

Heinrich—phenomenally successful in the United States—barely gets mentioned except, perhaps, as an example of "America's curious literary tastes." Hans Habe, Hans Hellmuth Kirst, and Mario Simmel, three novelists whose political persuasions and story themes are greatly disparate, all write good, entertaining, if not exactly great, fiction. But they simply do not rate.

The problem then is partly one of attitudes and semantics. Germany's intellectuals do not expect literature to entertain but to enlighten, uplift, and influence. The cultural arbiters—the critics, literary historians, professors of *Germanistik*—look with suspicion even upon those established literati—Boell, Grass, Lenz, Walser, Johnson—whose books do land on the best-seller lists. Boell's novels consistently sell more than 100,000 copies in hardback and Grass' *Tin Drum* reached the phenomenal figure of 700,000. But on the whole, a best seller is any work selling between 30,000 and 50,000 copies and even recognized authors are happy with a sale of 5,000, while new writers consider themselves lucky if a first book sells more than 600 copies.

Of course, things are changing. Book clubs—with more than five million members—are gaining in popularity. The advent of the pocketbook and the paperback has at least helped to break down the financial obstacles to making literature available to a larger audience. And, most important of all perhaps, there is the impact of drama.

Mark Twain once commented that "whenever the German literati dives into a sentence, that is the last you will see of him till he emerges on the other side of his Atlantic with his verb in his mouth." I would not want to make a survey of the number of German literati who go for long dives each day. But when they write for the stage they have little choice except to swim on the surface with their verbs quite visible. That physical requirement of theater, bolstered by the fact that most of the leading German Dichter und Denker also write plays and most playwrights also write for television and film, has contributed to the remarkable liveliness of Germany's dramatic arts. On the stage, and TV and motion picture screens there is little of the aloofness so often associated with German literature. And while it may be true that the average German does enter the theater with the same awe he senses upon entering church (in contrast to the opera house, which he approaches as nonchalantly as an American does the baseball stadium), he does enter it. Should he prefer not to, however, he can readily turn to his "boob tube" which delivers, by far, the most literate—not to mention the newsiest and most informative—television programming in the world today.

Obviously, not everything produced for the West German stage is accessible to the "nonintellectual" with equal ease. But the barriers between the play-writing literato and his audience in such cases are less a problem of verbiness than verblessness. Peter Handke, for example, first penetrated the unsuspecting German consciousness in the late 1960s with a drama called *Publikumsbeschimpfung* which can best be translated as "Offending the Audience." And that, precisely, is what it was, for from the moment when the curtain rose until, fortunately, it dropped again, the actors on stage did little more than scream, bellow, and shout insults, curses, and obscenities at the poor innocents squirming in their seats. Handke, regarded by some as the brightest genius on Germany's literary and dramatic horizon today, has obviously gone on to write more articulate and coherent works. He would have had to, in order to win the coveted Buechner prize. His latest play, premiered in Zurich in 1974, is about entrepreneurs and their feelings, or lack of them.

Nor are all the novelists, poets, and essayists necessarily good dramatists. Guenter Grass' *The Plebians Rehearse the Insurrection*, a controversial dramatization of Bertolt Brecht's behavior during the June 17, 1953 workers' uprising in East Germany, was not his only stage flop. Martin Walser's dramas—he has been working on a musical about one of the medieval German peasant revolutionaries—are about as stageable as a verse reading of a *New York Times* editorial.

But on the whole, drama in West Germany today, in content, staging, and acting—whether live or on film for television and motion pictures—is both vibrant and socially relevant. Moreover—the critics will surely protest, but Goethe, Schiller, and Brecht will understand—it is also entertaining.

To catalogue or even just skim over the entire drama scene in the Federal Republic today would entail a chapter by itself. But a number of currents in postwar theater and several of the playwrights and filmmakers deserve closer attention.

For all the debate aroused by those who consider him brilliant and those who consider him mediocre, Rolf Hochhuth has won a permanent niche in the theatrical hall of fame. And he carved it in 1963 with *The Deputy*, a play which stirred passions on five continents by contending that Pope Pius XII shares in the guilt for the Nazi murder of six million Jews. As the first play of more than purely parochial interest and impact, it did much to extricate German theater from the ideological restrictions and the esthetic and intellectual doldrums in which it had been mired since the end of the Weimar era.

For years after the war, the German stage had been a wasteland. With the exception of the few actors and directors who had returned—Therese Giehse, Ernst Deutsch, and Fritz Kortner—the Jews who had once helped to make German theater the best in the world were gone. Except for a few, such as Erwin Piscator, who had come back, the non-Jews who had stood for engaged political contemporary theater were also either dead or in exile. A few, such as Bertolt Brecht and his wife Helene Weigel, had tried to find a new intellectual home with their erstwhile Communist friends in East Germany—only to be sorely disillusioned by the autocratic nature of that regime. And those who were not dead or who had not gone into exile were suspect because of their ambivalent relationship with the Nazi *Kulturmacher* during the Third Reich. The younger generation had either been decimated on the battlefields or were too numbed and stunned to translate their bewilderment into literature for the stage.

The war, moreover, had also devastated the theater physically. The great playhouses of Berlin and Hamburg, Dresden and Munich, Frankfurt and Leipzig, were heaps of rubble. Some 86 percent of all theaters were destroyed and more than a hundred new ones have been built since 1945—mostly with federal, state, and municipal funds.

Once the debris had been cleared away and the facilities restored, a renaissance began. But it was a renaissance only of performance and staging. The willingness to stage contemporary pieces and the readiness to experiment soon attracted foreign playwrights the same way George Bernard Shaw had been attracted to Germany in the 1920s. But there was little about the German theater that was really German. A survey of all German-language theaters in 1963, including those in Austria, Switzerland, and the GDR, revealed that the German-language plays performed most often were Duerrenmatt's *The Physicists*, Max Frisch's *Andorra*, Lessing's *Minna von Barnheim*, and Gerhard Hauptmann's *The Beaver Coat*; two contemporary Swiss works; two classics. The rest of the repertories consisted mostly of translated French, British, and American plays. Hochhuth's *The Deputy* marked the turning point.

Hochhuth himself once sought to explain the development to me. "For years," he said, "everybody was busy attending to the basic essentials of living. No one had time to be artistic for the first decade or so. There was also a natural gap in cultural life caused by the depredations of the Nazi era and the loss of countless young men and women who would otherwise have been at their most productive in the 1940s and 1950s. War and defeat and expulsion were such traumatic events that for years nobody wrote about anything but their own wartime or Nazi experiences, and few people outside Germany were interested. There was also considerable prejudice and resistance abroad to what little German dramatic writing there may have been—at least until the Brecht boom started in the 1950s. And by the time that boom really got underway, Brecht was dead. But now that a younger generation of playwrights has matured and the era of concern about material recovery is over, I think we can expect a whole new wave of productive and creative activity."

Hochhuth not only triggered that wave, he inspired a different one as well: a deluge of documentary plays which held so closely to historic reality that some critics refused to call them dramas but "reportages for the stage." Dramas or nondramas, it was a new style that imbued German theater with a hint of the electrifying air of controversy and messianic spirit that had typified it in the 1920s.

The Deputy was followed by Heinar Kipphardt's *In the Case of J. Robert Oppenheimer*, a stage version, based on the documentary record, of the 1954 security hearing. The play not only advanced Kipphardt's contention that a scientist's duty to humanity takes precedence over his duty to country, but it was almost as huge a commercial success as *The Deputy*. Following its premier at Piscator's Freie Volksbuehne in West Berlin, *Oppenheimer* was performed more than a thousand times at some thirty West German theaters that included it in their repertories. Kipphardt followed up *Oppenheimer* with *Joel Brand—The Story of a Transaction*. The play was a stage documentation of Adolf Eichmann's attempt to trade the lives of one million Jews for ten thousand military trucks. Joel Brand was the Hungarian Jew who tried to convince the Allies to engage in the deal.

But whereas Hochhuth had been a total newcomer to drama and

Kipphardt the author of a number of previous flops, Peter Weiss, who tried his hand at the documentary genre in 1965, was already an established master of total theater. His *Marat/Sade* had been a worldwide sensation and his *The Investigation* became one too. Subtitled *An Oratorio in Eleven Cantos*, with electronic music by Italian composer Luigi Nono, it was a thinly dramatized distillation of the day-to-day record kept at Frankfurt's marathon trial of former Auschwitz concentration camp guards. It had no plot, no action, and only a modicum of gesture. Premiered simultaneously in four West German and ten East German theaters, it was the epitome of the documentary style, relying exclusively on facts and documents and raw brute actuality with not even a hint of artistic imagination. If *Marat/Sade* had been total theater, then *The Investigation* was total nontheater. But, to cite merely the example of one playhouse, Berlin's Freie Volksbuehne—during the first season in which *The Investigation* was in repertory, nearly eighty thousand people saw the play; this was sixty thousand more than had attended the real Auschwitz trial in Frankfurt during the nearly two years it was in session.

There was a spate of other documentaries as well. Felix Luetzkendorf wrote a melodramatization of Lee Harvey Oswald's life as seen through the eyes of the Warren Commission, which was called *Dallas, November 22nd*. Hans Hellmuth Kirst, a very popular novelist, wrote one about the July 20, 1944 assassination attempt on Hitler. The same theme was used for a play and subsequently a documentary TV film by Guenther Weisenborn, a highly respected and eminently talented director, playwright, novelist, and essayist.

Certainly the style was controversial and at the time the controversy raged I had the opportunity to interview a number of the protagonists. Munich critic Joachim Kaiser told me: "Being a playwright also means having something to say. All these plays are terribly true to life but they develop no theses, present no real argument, and leave no room for interpretation or original thought. None presents a viewpoint through the fate of one individual as Sartre did so successfully in his *The Condemned of Altona*. Both *Oppenheimer* and *Brand* were great ideas but—and this is true for most of the documentaries—I have yet to meet someone who has wanted to see them twice. And whatever Peter Weiss' talent may promise, in *The Investigation* he did nothing more than to set the Auschwitz trial record to blank verse. The playwright who does that is no longer a dramatist but an arranger."

Fritz Kortner said shortly before his death: "No compilation of facts and documents can replace a writer's own power of conviction. A plain statement of facts convinces no one. To demonstrate that Nazis were Nazis and acted as such does not make a play. If theaters feel compelled to stage them, we must be awfully short of dramatists."

And yet, when Piscator's Freie Volksbuehne staged an evening of *discussion* about *The Investigation*, some eight thousand West Berliners asked for tickets. No more than eighty had been expected to attend. Theater which can unleash that sort of a reaction obviously has something to it.

Perhaps the sagest comment at the time was made by Group 47's Hans-Werner Richter. "The documentary form," he said, "is a natural outgrowth of the effort to comprehend what happened in Germany. It reflects an artistic and political need. But the documentaries are only a beginning of a whole movement which will not confine itself to theater alone but to all forms of art."

How right he was. Rolf Hochhuth, the man who started it all, also ended it with his 1967 play *The Soldiers*. No less a worldwide sensation and success than *The Deputy*, it was a documentary, with Winston Churchill in the center, which challenged the morality of wartime bombings of civilians and raised the allegation that Churchill had been implicated in a plot to kill Poland's General Sikorski, who died in an aircraft crash off Gibraltar in 1943.

Like the other dramatists, Hochhuth has since turned to different theater. He has written comedies and his latest, *Lysistrata and NATO* is a modern version of Aristophanes' classic. The story: Lysistrata and the other women on a Greek island deny sex to their men because the men want to sell some of their farmland to NATO for construction of a military base.

One of Peter Weiss' latest plays, placed in repertory by sixteen West German theaters in the 1971–72 season, was *Hoelderlin*. It is a uniquely powerful drama about one of Germany's greatest poets who, in his early years, was inflamed by the promise of the French Revolution and the figure of Napoleon but became increasingly disillusioned and bitter. Retiring from the world of politics into an inner world, Hoelderlin spent the last forty years of his life in an encroaching darkness that culminated in total insanity. One critic described it as Weiss' "most poetic and least histrionic drama to date. His mood is pensive, and while he is still crying out against the same wrongs, his voice is subdued, and so we listen more closely." A Marxist, despite his increasing estrangement from and disillusionment with the Communist countries, Weiss has the young Karl Marx visiting the dying and far-gone Hoelderlin in his tower room in Tuebingen during the last scene in the play. His most recent piece is a dramatization of Franz Kafka's novel, *The Trial*, which was premiered in Bremen in June 1975.

Kipphardt, the other leading playwright of the documentary period, after a brief, successful, but tempestuous and controversial stint as dramaturgist at Munich's prestigious Kammerspiele, which ended with his summary dismissal because his repertory selection was too leftist for the Munich city administration's taste, has returned to writing. His next play is to be about Tupamaros and city guerillas in Latin America.

With the documentary wave over, but the theater revitalized, a whole new crop of younger playwrights has emerged. Most of them are graduates of, and were influenced by, the youth rebellion of the 1960s, so they are—like the majority of other writers—leftist-oriented and inclined to concentrate, sometimes stridently and sometimes quite subtly, on social criticism. More often than not, despite the complaints of older, conservative critics and the drama establishment, their work is also very good theater. Along with the new dramatists there has been a rise of young drama companies and collectives which rebel against the artistic, and sometimes political, strictures imposed by the managements of West Germany's nearly two hundred state or municipally subsidized playhouses.

Typical of such groups is Munich's Red Beet collective, founded in 1971 by the graduating class of the city's Falckenberg School of Acting. Disillusioned by what they called the "tediousness, stuffiness, and unimaginativeness" of Munich's official drama establishment, and dedicated to the idea of a "political theater that can also be fun," the nine young men and women—all in their early twenties—formed a "working and living commune." They moved into a villa in the suburb of Gruenwald and began to build a cohesive team. They write, direct, and stage their own pieces; make their own sets and props; give each other continuing training in voice projection, breathing techniques, gesturing, and gymnastics. Legally constituted as a limited corporation, each member draws the same pay—DM 670 monthly—from which equal shares for taxes, health, unemployment and old age insurance, and rent and food costs are deducted, leaving each with DM 200 monthly as pocket and private spending money. Any member who takes on outside film, television, or stage work must contribute three-fourths of the fee he or she receives to the common kitty. They jointly own a car, a Volkswagen bus, five dogs, a cat, and one goldfish. They share cooking and housekeeping duties, and their only condescendence to "bourgeoise morality" is the stipulation that steady couples are allowed a little privacy, either in a room or a corner to themselves. Their repertory is a lively collection of socially critical agitprop pieces and political cabaret. And they perform all over West Germany wherever they can find audiences: in discotheques, experimental playhouses, corner taverns, youth centers, and, in an attempt to revive the street theater of medieval times, on the streets. They estimate their combined monthly expenses, including each member's pay and rent for a practice stage, at DM 12,000, and they admit frankly that receipts for their performances just barely keep pace with the outlay. But they are obviously enjoying themselves while at the same time demonstrating how lively *and* relevant theater can be.

Among the younger dramatists, a number of whom write and direct and feel equally at home working for the stage, films, or television, three in particular merit closer attention: Rainer Werner Fassbinder and Franz Xaver Kroetz, both native Bavarians; and Peter Turrini, an Austrian. Although all three are under thirty years of age, they have more in common than youth. They are sons of the peasant-oriented Alpine region, speak the same south German dialect, and have a penchant for "antitheater."

Fassbinder, the most versatile, restless, and internationally acclaimed of the three, is somewhat of a *Wunderkind* of the West German stage, films, and television. He writes, directs, acts, produces, and, according to those who work with him, exudes a magnetism that is almost irresistible.

The son of upper-middle class, intellectual parents and a Gymnasium dropout, he has been on the drama scene since 1967 when, as a twenty-one-year-old, he joined Munich's Action Theater. Avant-garde as that group may have been, it wasn't farout and aggressive enough for Fassbinder. Together with some of its actors, notably Hanna Schygulla whom he has launched to international stardom, Fassbinder founded a commune and drama collective known as the *anti-teater*. He was chief playwright and director.

When the plays and productions, such as *The Bitter Tears of Petra Kant*, failed to win the acclaim Fassbinder demanded, the group began filming gutty, violent, socially critical films that shocked German motion picture and television audiences with their stark revelations about the cruelty, brutality, and meanness of human nature. Starting in 1969 with *Love Is Colder than Death*, Fassbinder and his team ground out scripts and films at a rate of more than two a year.

There seems to be no form or theme he will not try or touch: thrillers, science fiction, homosexuality, lesbianism. For television he wrote and directed a five-part serial—each part a full-length, ninety-minute feature film—about a blue-collar family in the Ruhr. In *Katzelmacher* which he wrote and directed, he himself plays the lead—an Italian guest worker who is hounded and persecuted by a clique of youths in a Bavarian village. It won him a packet of prizes. On the other hand, his film version of Kroetz' brutal peasant saga, *Game Crossing*, won him a packet of complaints from Kroetz, who called the movie "crass pornography."

His most recent effort is a film, with Hanna Schygulla in the lead role, based on Theodor Fontane's nineteenth-century novel, *Effi Briest*. In Munich, where it was premiered in the summer of 1974, it had an unprecedented seventeen-weeks' run in the first house where it was shown—a record no film has ever matched in Germany.

Franz Xaver Kroetz has, thus far, restricted himself to writing plays, but plays that show his fellow Bavarians in a peasant rawness which not even their severest North German critics would have ascribed to them. The central figure in the most recent one, *Stallerhof*, which premiered in Hamburg in 1974, is a myopic teenage Bavarian farm girl whose bad eyesight leads her roughhewn father to regard her as retarded and to treat her cruelly. In the course of the play she is raped by a sixty-year-old farmer, an act, so Kroetz implies, which is hardly unusual in the Bavarian mountains.

Peter Turrini writes in the Kroetz peasant genre, only with even greater brutality. A Gymnasium education in his native Carynthia notwithstanding, he has been a steelworker, warehouseman, advertising copywriter, hotel manager, bum, and has served a hitch in the Austrian army. By the time he was twenty-seven he had written a novel published in West Germany, three radio dramas, and four one-act plays of which *Sauschlachten*—literally "Pig Slaughter"—touched off a storm when it was premiered in Munich's experimental, state-subsidized Werkraumtheater in 1972.

The narrative of *Sauschlachten* is simple and direct enough: Valentin, the younger of two grown sons in a mountain peasant family, suddenly stops talking and begins to grunt like a pig. The more his parents, brother, and neighbors try to cajole him into speaking again, the more he grunts; and the more he grunts, the more they treat him like a pig, ultimately taking him out to slaughter behind the barn. For Turrini the grunting is symbolic: "Deliberate silence designed to provoke." When Turrini was asked by an interviewer whom Valentin is rebelling against, he replied: "Against the family, and he has stopped talking because speech leads only to lies and misunderstanding." He sees his play as a parable, for "ultimately Valentin is treated like any outsider anywhere—like a pig." Turrini, who rejects "leftist theater that is written by intellectuals, for intellectuals in the language of intellectuals," chooses dialect "because that is the way people really speak." And he has no interest in "formulating ideologies. I want to provoke them."

Revitalized as West German theater may be, the greatest impact on it in the early 1970s has been by East German dramatists, two of whom in particular—Ulrich Plenzdorf, forty, and Peter Hacks, forty-seven—find their work performed more frequently in the Federal Republic than in the GDR.

Plenzdorf, as versatile as Fassbinder, writes novels, plays, and film scripts, of which *Paul and Paula*, mentioned in a previous chapter, has been by far the most successful. The novel and play that have moved him center stage as an enfante terrible of East German literature, glibly thumbing his nose at official Communist orthodoxy, is called *The New Sorrows of Young W.* It is based on the suicidal young eighteenth-century Werther, hero of the novel which made Goethe famous in 1774. The "Werther" of Plenzdorf's play is Edgar Wiebau, a dropout from East German society for whom American-style blue jeans are "not so much a pair of trousers as a way of life." Young Wiebau, like young Werther, tells his story from the beyond, with the significant difference that, unlike Werther who committed suicide, Wiebau accidentally electrocutes himself with a machine he has invented and is trying to perfect in the garden shack where he has taken refuge from the collectivized mainstream of East German life. The character of Wiebau, which some critics have likened to Holden Caulfield in J. D. Salinger's *Catcher in the Rye*, presents a whole catalogue of ideological imponderabilities for the official guardians of East German moral values. His protest and rebellion are totally apolitical. He neither rejects communism nor the East German regime as such—merely everything the Establishment stands for and officially propagates. His rebellion is that of the young generation against the old, a highly sensitive theme in a society that denies the existence of a generation gap because neither Marx nor Lenin ever considered it. In a sense, young Wiebau speaks for millions of young East Germans and—thanks to Plenzdorf's obviously acute ear—also speaks their pseudo-hip slang. The reason he is building his machine by himself, rather than as a member of some factory research or engineering team, is because "I wanted to do something I could call my own. People should have their pride." At another point in the play Wiebau says, "My great idol is Wiebau. I want to be the way he'll be some day. Nothing more." And in a final passage he declares: "Idiot that I am, I always wanted to be the winner."

In an acid comment on the play in the summer of 1973, Erich Honecker, the East German party chief, expressed "doubts whether . . . it contributes to a socialist way of thinking and acting." But it is a sign of the changing times and attitudes that, despite officialdom's obvious discontent with the drama and its message, it has not been banned and has played to enthusiastic audiences in the GDR. But the response has been even more enthusiastic in West Germany where—to the amazement of the GDR's Kulturmacher, I am sure—young theatergoers readily acknowledge that Plenzdorf's young Wiebau speaks for them as much as he does for their East German cousins.

Peter Hacks has been called "the Aristophanes of our age." His oscillating fortunes with East German censorship are a reliable weather vane for the directions in which the winds of cultural policy are blowing. In the mid-1960s, when his plays *Moritz Tassow* and *The Sorrows and Power* were banned and Hacks was under persistent attack from officialdom, the winds were cold and unfriendly, for a long, harsh artistic winter had settled over the GDR. Since early 1974 they have been blowing more warmly and favorably. Nearly a half dozen of Hacks' plays were being performed in East Berlin theaters, including his latest, *Adam and Eve*, which is a hit in both Germanys.

An allegorical play, *Adam and Eve* could be understood as little more than a light-veined dramatization of the classical Bible story. But it is far more than that. God, Hacks admitted to a recent interviewer, is the "absolute monarch at the apex of society." Gabriel is representative of "the party secretaries who serve as the administrative links between the "monarch and the people." Adam and Eve represent the mass. The serpent symbolizes "the technocrats who, with their productive stupidity, produce obstacles." Hacks implies that Adam and Eve, through their sin, are "released into freedom to realize themselves." He says God, by his very nature, could not have created a "perfect man" because, though perfect Himself, He had not been created. Man's imperfections and contradictions are the prerequisites of his freedom and essential for his continuing efforts at self-perfection. Such allegorical writing is not unusual in a country where it has frequently proven to be the only way to publish if the writer has something socially critical or provocative to say.

The plight of writers and intellectuals in the GDR—or in any authoritarian society for that matter—was allegorized eloquently some years ago by Reiner Kunze, an East German poet who only recently has been freed of most of the restrictions placed on his work. In a short poem entitled "The End of Art," he once wrote:

> Thou shalt not, said the owl to the grouse,
> Thou shalt not sing of the sun.
> The sun is not important.
>
> The grouse promptly deleted
> The sun from its song.
>
> You are an artist,
> The owl praised the grouse.
>
> And it was already dark.*

Kunze, forty-two, was for many years a literary unperson in the GDR. But since late 1973 and early 1974, he has become its most fashionable poet. He not only gives public readings and is permitted to travel to the West but, after a five-year hiatus during which not a line of his work saw print, a collection of his poems—*Letter with a Blue Seal*—was officially published: not in just one, but in two editions, with a total press run of thirty thousand. In one of his poems, in which he compares the art of poetry and fishing, Kunze says: "Poets and anglers must be able to wait."

Kunze had to wait for many years.

Except for a brief period of relaxation, from 1962 to 1965, the GDR

* Reprinted by permission of Rowohlt Verlag. From *Das Ende der Kunst* by Reiner Kunze © Rowohlt Verlag GmbH, Reinbek bei Hamburg, 1969.

long ranked as the culturally most restrictive of all the Communist countries. Its party officials and ideological watchdogs demanded from writers and artists either total conformity to the Stalinist precepts of "socialist realism" and partisan engagement on behalf of communism, or silence.

The limits were strictly spelled out by Walter Ulbricht, who once said: "Our artists and writers are completely free to shape and create anything as long as it is useful to our state and our society. But I would consider it incompatible with their ethical standards if they took liberties which harmed our state and our party. It behooves them to close ranks around the party, to fight ideological diversions and the poison of skepticism, and to oppose negativism."

Art was to be optimistic and representational, with no abstractions or experiments in form permitted. Literary heroes had to be positive, and the themes of novels, drama, and poetry worker-related. As Hermann Axen, then editor-in-chief of the official Socialist Unity party daily *Neues Deutschland*, now a politburo member and SED party secretary, once told an assemblage of writers: "You have no idea how much material you will find for gripping, dramatic human situations in the struggle of our steelworkers at the smelter in Fuerstenberg or at some of the other furnaces and rolling mills in our republic."

The ideal painting depicted upward-looking, happy tillers of the soil and builders of factories. The most praised poems were those which were eulogies to Ulbricht. And the heroes of novels and plays were expected to be in love with their tractors and their construction cranes. Fulfillment of the economic plan was considered their chief goal in life. Although criticism per se was not proscribed, it had to be "constructive" criticism that would help to resolve "the conflicts which still exist in the building of socialism." And above all, it dared not be criticism of the system itself.

Although the Ulbricht regime welcomed the Communist and leftist returnees from exile abroad, it imposed upon them cultural dictates that either drove them to flee to the West or to produce for their desk drawer. Even Bertolt Brecht, the most gilded figure in the regime's entourage of postwar returnees, was not spared. Though he developed his Berliner Ensemble into one of Europe's most successful theaters, he never wrote another significant play after returning to Germany and settling in the GDR in 1948. Had he been a man of lesser fame, he probably would have foundered somewhere between the shoals of official ideology and the reefs of the state security service. Only his reputation as Europe's leading living playwright protected him. He was honored with prizes, to be sure, but his relationship with the Ulbricht regime remained a tenuous one at best. His plays were criticized for being "formalistic," a Stalinist expression for works of art in which form predominated over content. A number of them were barred from performance in East Berlin. While making a cult of Brecht and then his widow, Helene Weigel, and the Berlin Ensemble Theater, the authorities continued to view his work with skepticism. It was no accident that he never became an East German citizen but retained an Austrian passport instead. Brecht was the name with which the regime could boast—as long as the Ensemble Theater was filled with admiring tourists from the West. But when the East Berliners themselves queued at the box office, officialdom smelled heresy in the air. When he died in 1956, Brecht was a disillusioned man.

Those intellectuals, less famous than Brecht, who failed to hew to the official party line and dared to publish abroad or managed to slip into print during the brief three-year period of cultural liberalization in the early 1960s, eventually found themselves the targets of official censure and repression.

One of the darkest moments in postwar East German cultural history was the December 1965 plenary session of the SED's central committee at which Erich Honecker, then Ulbricht's crown prince and heir apparent, delivered an hour-long attack on cultural and intellectual heresies, describing them as subversive influences inspired by the West. In his monologue he singled out a number of writers and editors and cultural officials who had not been "sufficiently vigilant," subjecting them to vitriolic personal diatribes. Among them were Peter Hacks; the poet Wolf Biermann; the novelists Stefan Heym and Christa Wolf; and Robert Havemann, a Humboldt University professor and veteran Communist who had outraged the party hierarchs with popular lectures in which he suggested there was room for parliamentary opposition under socialism.

The outcome of the plenum was that Biermann was forbidden from performing publicly—a ban that has not been lifted to the present day. Heym was ostracized. The editor of *Neue Deutsche Literatur* was fired from his post. Countless artists and writers and minor cultural function-aries were reprimanded or sidetracked in their careers. Havemann was fired from his university post, expelled from the party and purged from the GDR's Academy of Sciences. Hans Bentzien, the minister of culture, was dismissed and replaced by Klaus Gysi, a far more tractable and manageable functionary. The Writers' Association engaged in self-criticism. Party and ministerial advisory councils were established to supervise literature, films, and the theater. Political cabarets such as Leipzig's Pfeffermuehle (The Pepper Mill) and East Berlin's Distel (The Thistle) were ordered to revise and mellow their satirical programs. And a new law was enacted to prohibit writers from publishing their work abroad before first offering it to East German publishing houses. It was appropriately called "Lex Biermann," after the upstart young singing poet whose verses had been widely printed in collections and anthologies in West Germany.

The GDR even attempted to impose its cultural policies on its Communist neighbors. Fearful of the "heretical" thawing winds blowing from the other countries, SED functionaries, with Kurt Hager—then as now the politburo member and party secretary for culture—usually in the lead, made numerous pilgrimages to Warsaw, Prague, and Budapest to persuade authorities there to muzzle their intellectuals. "The works of modern Polish, Czech, and Hungarian writers," Hager said in conjunction with one such journey, "pave the way for counterrevolution."

A new winter settled over East Germany, lasting until Honecker replaced Ulbricht as party chief in May 1971. Ironic as it may seem, it was Honecker himself who introduced the second thaw with his dictum that there be "no cultural taboos" for those writers and artists who proceed from "firm socialist positions." As a result, the GDR became somewhat of an ideological and cultural wonderland within the Soviet bloc. Within a year or so of Honecker's taking over, novels and films, some of them held back for as long as fifteen years, began appearing in print and on the screens.

A third novel by Hermann Kant, *The Masthead* was cleared for printing in an edition of forty-five thousand copies, after having been withheld for several years, and became an immediate best seller.

Christa Wolf, whose first novel, *Divided Heaven*, had established her in both East and West and on both sides of the Atlantic as a major writer, was also permitted to come out of limbo. Although not reelected to the party's central committee, of which she had been a candidate member from 1963 to 1967, her third and thus far most sensitively written novel,

The Quest for Christa T., was published in a first edition of thirty thousand copies. For East Germany it is a most remarkable work, because it scarcely has a plot, is "negative" in its tragedy, and is highly introspective, concerned with humanity itself. Christa T. is a woman of forty-six-year-old Frau Wolf's own generation, and like her, a writer; she has died of leukemia, leaving her husband with three motherless young daughters. In her role as narrator, Frau Wolf "reflects" posthumously on her friend through memories, some of her letters, and her writings. Autobiographical to an extent, it is a search for identity but also a clash between the writer's commitment to moral integrity and the often discouraging realities of East German life which Frau Wolf, despite her consistent support of the regime, does not attempt to hide in this work any more than she did in *Divided Heaven*. But if it was her frankness in *Divided Heaven* which got her into trouble in 1965, today she is justly revered.

Poets, playwrights, and novelists at odds with the regime for a decade and longer—not only Peter Hacks, but Paul Wiens, Heiner Mueller, Volker Braun, and Guenther Kunert—have suddenly found the restrictions on publishing and staging their works remarkably relaxed. New writers, too, have blossomed into print with work that would have been unprintable just a few years ago because what they write is either highly critical of social conditions in the GDR or highly personal, devoid of any involvement with the "building of socialism." Thus Rolf Schneider, forty-four, has made the East German best-seller list with *The Trip to Jaroslaw*, a youth-rebellion novel about a teenage East Berlin girl who drops out of East German society and heads for Poland in search of sex and excitement. Her story—a denial of all the upbeat official propaganda about the socialist enthusiasm of GDR youth—is set against a grim background, painted gray on gray. The GDR Schneider's heroine leaves, only to return to reluctantly in the end, is a place where sausages "taste of sawdust," new appliances break down after three months, store shelves are always empty, the "police watch your every step," and the new class of functionaries is committed to bourgeois consumerism.

One of the most promising younger writers is Helga Schuetz, thirty-eight, who has published two novellas thus far. In one she is concerned with her pre-GDR, wartime environment in Silesia, and in the other, in a very quiet, personal, and wryly humorous way, with the GDR of the present. Though often critical, hers is a criticism based on full acceptance of East Germany as her homeland, as a different Germany—

not necessarily better or worse, just different—from that of the Federal Republic.

What has transpired in East Germany since Ulbricht's departure from office cannot, of course, be compared with the sensational developments in some of the other Communist countries in the 1960s. And the seesaw still goes up and down.

First some of the cultural and ideological arbiters in the party hierarchy had to be gotten rid of, and some of them dragged their heels for quite a while. It was not until February 1973, for example, that Klaus Gysi was eased out of the ministry of culture, sent to pasture as ambassador to Italy, and replaced by Hans Joachim Hoffmann, a forty-three-year-old who had demonstrated his liberalism in the provinces. But both Kurt Hager and Hermann Axen are still very much around and no less vocal than they ever were in their demands that literature and art must be "thoroughly partisan and committed to socialism and the class struggle." Honecker himself expressed his second doubts when he criticized both Ulrich Plenzdorf's film *Paul and Paula* and the play *The New Sorrows of Young W.*

Some of the nonconformists ostracized in 1965 have remained in official limbo, balking at what appears to be Honecker's outstretched hand of reconciliation. Wolf Biermann is still not being published and Robert Havemann remains an outcast. The poet Peter Huchel, sacked from the editorship of *Sinn und Form*, the East German literary monthly in 1960, then ostracized for eleven years until he was permitted to "emigrate" in 1971, remains in exile in Rome and has no desire to return to the country whose greatest living poet he was. "Friends have told me that matters have gotten better under Honecker," he told a recent interviewer. "I have my doubts. But if that is the case, then I can only say how glad I am for all the friends I left behind."

In the visual arts—a field in which West Germany is again making an international name for itself with the works of Horst Janssen, Guenther Uecker, Horst Antes, Gerhard Richter and Gotthard Graubner, not to even mention the Duesseldorf Academy's eccentric Professor Joseph Beuys—the GDR remains a wasteland, just one step ahead of "socialist realism." Thus, although the winter is over, no one is yet prepared to predict how warm the spring will be and whether there will be a summer. "As yet," Stefan Heym said recently, "I would not even call it a thaw—more a gesture, an approach to reason."

There is no better litmus test of cultural policy in East Germany than the attitude toward Stefan Heym, the unchallenged dean and master of East German literature but for nearly two decades also its most prominent pariah. The trouble, as a West German reviewer said in 1965 when Honecker accused Heym of "negativism" and of painting a "false picture of life in the GDR and the Soviet Union," is that "Stefan Heym is a very headstrong, obstinate man. The Americans became aware of that when he lived in the United States. Now the high priests of East German culture and literature have made the same discovery."

One might also add that Stefan Heym is a Marxist who drinks his socialism pure—a potent beverage in a country where all manner of mixtures and adulterations are prescribed. Born in 1913 as Helmut Flieg, the son of a Jewish shopowner in Chemnitz, Saxony, now called Karl-Marx-Stadt, Heym first broke into print as a teenager in 1931 with a poem, "Export Business," which bitterly attacked the Weimar Republic for its cynical arms trade with Chiang Kai-shek's Kuomintang. After a brief stint in leftwing journalism in Berlin, he fled Germany for Prague when Hitler came to power. In 1934 he went to the United States and on a Jewish scholarship enrolled at the University of Chicago, changing his name in a futile attempt to protect his parents in Chemnitz from Nazi retribution.

After a series of odd jobs—he was a dishwasher, clerk, travelling salesman, and translator—and publication of an influential pamphlet entitled *Nazis in the U.S.A.*, he became editor of the antifascist, exile weekly *Deutsches Volksecho* in New York in 1938. In 1942 he published his first, highly praised novel, *Hostages*, which was filmed by Paramount, with William Bendix and Luise Rainer in the lead roles. The following year he took out U. S. citizenship, joined the army, received a commission, and was sent overseas as a psychological warfare officer, winning a Bronze Star for bravery in the Battle of the Bulge. When the military government was established, Heym was assigned to the staff of the American daily *Neue Zeitung* in Munich, then being edited by Hans Habe.

Dismissed from the paper because he refused to write the anti-Soviet and anti-Communist editorials Habe wanted him to do, Heym returned to the United States and wrote his novel *The Crusaders*, which became a long-running best seller in 1948—sixth on the list behind Norman Mailer's *The Naked and the Dead*. There was to be one more book, *The*

Eyes of Reason, before Heym, disillusioned by American cold war policy and the Korean involvement, resigned his army commission, renounced his U. S. citizenship, sent his medals and decorations to President Eisenhower, and left America to settle in East Berlin.

In the GDR Heym was panegyrized and showered with prizes, but his literary intractability soon collided with the regime's cultural dogmatism. There was one more novel, *Goldsborough*, then nearly a decade of silence, interrupted only by occasional essays, reportages, and short stories until 1964, when Heym gave vent to his frustration and disillusionment with the system in *The Papers of Andreas Lenz*.

A historical novel centering on the revolution of 1848–49, it told the story of the popular German folk poet Lenz who had fled to America and died, a Union soldier, in the Battle of Gettysburg. Its publication in the GDR was possible only because of the 1962–65 thaw, for it was a novel whose pages bristled with heresies such as these:

"What should I tell the people now? That we fought against one tyranny merely to replace it with another?"

"The only consolation I can draw from the absurdities of the revolution is the knowledge that the absurdities of the counterrevolution are just as great."

"That would be a great idea, a marvellous future: a world without any police, without police informers. But do you really believe you can get along without them? You say that you won't need me after the revolution. But you will, like every government, because I know a lot. You will need my information about your enemies and about each other."

"He is an intellectual! A writer! A man who can turn the mute, inchoate feelings of people into words, into a threat, into dynamite under the seats of the powerful."

Following the attacks on him by Honecker at the December 1965 plenum, Heym found that the only way to get into print was to publish in the West. His next two books, a biography of the nineteenth-century Socialist leader Ferdinand Lassalle and a novel about Daniel Defoe, *The Queen Against Defoe*, full of overtones for writers and rulers in the

Communist world, were published in the Federal Republic and Switzerland. Once asked how he got away with such actions, Heym just shrugged and said: "Simple. I ignore the rules." One rule is that he must submit contracts with foreign publishers to the GDR's State Bureau for Authors' Rights. His failure to do so with the Lassalle book netted him a 300-mark fine. The bureau didn't bother him about the Defoe novel or his next and probably greatest work, *The King David Report*, published in West Germany in 1972, and in the United States and Great Britain a year later.

More than any of his other work, *The King David Report* establishes Heym as East Germany's most preeminent living writer—indeed, as one of the leading German writers of our time—even if he did write it first in English, as he does all of his work, and then translate it into German himself.

When Peter Hacks read the finished manuscript he presented Heym with a copper engraving of Saul, David, and Solomon, inscribing the following couplet on the back:

> David slew Goliath,
> The Philistines were confounded.
>
> Stefan slew David,
> Again they were astounded.

Indeed, its publication confounded the Philistines in both East and West, for *The King David Report* is a political parable of scathing timeliness. In it Heym proves himself a pertinacious historian who approaches the Old Testament with the skepticism of a sleuth. Weaving quotations from I and II Samuel and I Kings with the product of his own fertile imagination into the narrative, Heym not only slew the personality cult of David but the universal establishment that propagates such cults.

The story line is simple enough: At the court of King Solomon a commission has been formed to write "The One and Only True and Authoritative, Historically Accurate and Officially Approved Report about the Remarkable Ascent, the Pious Life, as well as the Heroic Deeds and Wonderful Accomplishments of David Ben Jesse, King of Juda for Seven and of Both Juda and Israel for Thirty-three Years, the Chosen of the Lord and Father of King Solomon," which henceforth is to be referred to by its working title: *The King David Report*.

The commission chooses Ethan the Ezrahite to edit the report. Of Ethan it has been said that he is one of the wisest in Israel. Only King Solomon himself is wiser. Unfortunately, Ethan, the protagonist of the novel, is too wise, and the disparity between what Solomon wants written into the report and what Ethan's own research about David turns up as the truth becomes an unbridgeable gap between Temple politics and reality. Ethan is an intellectual who recognizes the ritualistic glorification of David as a blatant attempt to legitimize his son Solomon's questionable succession and progressively tyrannical rule.

Setting out on a politically dangerous path, Ethan eschews the official records, which have been carefully adulterated to meet post-Davidian political exigencies and set before him by the royal commission. He ignores the accounts of the "licensed tellers of tales, myths and legends." Instead, he sifts and sorts hidden and forgotten clay tablets and papyrus rolls. He seeks out David's surviving wives and concubines for first-hand information. He consults the Witch at Endor. He meets clandestinely with Joab, who has become an "unperson." He confers with the son of Ahitophel, David's counselor who joined with Absalom in revolt and then committed suicide. In short, he searches for the truth about David.

It is an ugly truth, for it reveals the appalling trail of blood and the mountain of corpses through which the guileless young shepherd David hacked his way to supreme power and to become the Chosen of the Lord. But it is a dangerous truth, and the more of it that Ethan finds, the tighter becomes the net of Solomon's secret police that closes around him, and the more devious the machinations of David's political heirs.

Ultimately Ethan is put on trial, charged with high treason for attempting to infuse "The King David Report" with "doubts, undesirable thoughts and nefarious opinions" and "for cloaking said doubts, etc., in language which appears harmless and seems agreeable in the Eye of the Lord." Ethan is found guilty, of course, but Solomon proclaims a "Solomonic judgment." Ethan is not to be put to death. Instead he is to be "silenced to death." The report is to be suppressed forever and the commission writes its own version, the one to be read in the Old Testament today.

"It seemed to me there was more to the Books of Samuel and Kings than a parable or Oriental fairytale," Heym told me shortly after the novel's publication. "Behind the accounts of battles with giants, sayings of prophets, beautiful women and bloodbaths, I saw the report of a revolution which apparently culminated in David's ascendency to the throne and the creation of a state. But the intent of the biblical report also seemed clear: to legitimize the rule of David's successor, Solomon. Theological research suggests that the story of David was written not too long after his death and sewn together with information from various, often contradictory sources. The seams are rather obvious."

So are the analogies which Heym draws to life in contemporary dictatorships. Ethan's Israel could easily be Heym's GDR or Alexander Solzhenitsyn's Soviet Union. The book is pregnant with references to literary censorship, the rewriting of history, secret police surveillance, midnight knocks on the door, forced confessions, summary trials, slave labor, prison camps, political unpersons, power struggles, corruption, lagging production, and economic malfeasance of the sort that seems endemic to East Berlin and Moscow.

In one passage, for example, Ethan arrives in Jerusalem to start work on the report and is assigned to a new government apartment. Like those one finds in Eastern Europe, it is an instant slum, ripe for condemnation before the first tenant moves in.

When Ethan seeks an official signature on a document, he loses his way in a maze of government bureaus and is told by one cynical clerk: "A signature means nothing. He who signs it today may not be at his desk tomorrow and his signature is worthless. Only the Lord Yahweh knows how many names remain on the secret list the dying King David gave to his son Solomon."

And during one debate in the commission, Ethan is told: "We must be consistent. If we agree that David is the Chosen of the Lord, then everything he did was to Israel's benefit. Since knowledge of the bare facts, however, can lead people to dangerous thoughts and opinions, we must report the facts in such a manner as to guide the thoughts of the people in the proper channel."

The prospects for publication of *The King David Report* in East Germany seemed slim indeed. But to everyone's surprise, including Heym's, it came out in an edition of twenty-five thousand copies in December 1973, as a sort of belated sixtieth-birthday present to the author. And when, in the spring of 1974, both the Lassalle and Defoe books were also published, there no longer seemed any doubt that Heym was back in the regime's good graces and that a cultural thaw had indeed set in.

But how much ice will melt still remains to be seen, for Heym's latest work, *Five Days in June*, published in West Germany in October 1974, is still awaiting clearance in the GDR. It is a novel about the June 17, 1953 workers' uprising in East Germany on which he has been working intermittently for more than twenty years, periodically revising it and periodically trying to get it published. Why it was banned in its orginal form remains inexplicable, for when Heym set out to write the book after painstaking research, it upheld the original fiction that the rising had been inspired and organized from outside by the West Germans and the American CIA.

The revolt, crushed by Soviet tanks, has been cultivated into a legend on both sides of the border. In West Germany, where June 17 is still celebrated as National Unity Day, it is viewed as a rising by the downtrodden East German masses clamoring for German reunification and free elections. In the GDR the official view is still that the revolt was organized and led by the West, and that most of the rebels were *agents provocateurs* from West Berlin. The truth is far different. The revolt began as a protest against higher work norms for the construction laborers on East Berlin's Stalin Allee and got out of hand because of the inefficacy of Ulbricht and his men in dealing with it. Only then did Western intelligence and propaganda agencies, in particular RIAS, the U.S.-controlled radio station in West Berlin, attempt to capitalize on the rebellion.

In ferreting out these truths, Heym has toppled sacred political cows in both Germanys. "The West," he said, "provided the fuse. But we supplied our own dynamite."

Heym, still a Marxist, is saddened by the East German ministry of culture's ban on the book: "I really believe that after twenty-five years of the GDR's formal existence, the workers in our state are astute enough to reflect upon themselves and their own past. We demand that they be mature enough to assume responsibility for industry and government. If they are mature enough for that, they are also sufficiently mature to read."

Erich Honecker obviously disagrees, and his disagreement reveals where the limits of his cultural thaw lie.

In one passage of *The King David Report* King Solomon says of Ethan: "I have seen men swallowing knives and others eating fire, but never have I seen a more agile dance on the edge of a sword."

The dancer is Stefan Heym—and every other honest writer and artist in the German Democratic Republic.

9

Please Don't
Walk on
the Grass

WHILE taking a walk in my Munich neighbor-
hood one balmy summer day in 1974, I spotted a sign of the changing
times:

Bitte den Rasen Nicht Betreten, it said. Please Don't Walk on the Grass.

Two thoughts entered my mind. One was that old line of Lenin's (or
was it really Stalin?) that the Germans could never stage a revolution if it
meant stepping on a lawn, the stepping on which was *Verboten.* And the
other was about all the signs one used to see which read: Walking on the
Grass Is Strictly Prohibited.

There are innumerable other such signs of changing times, or of what I
prefer to consider the gradual "de-Germanization" of the Germans, a
phenomenon of the past three decades that understandably, of course, is
far more prevalent and apparent in West Germany than in the relatively
isolated and economically less prosperous GDR.

To call it an "Americanization" of language, taste, living styles, and
behavioral patterns would be an oversimplification. "Internationalization"
is probably the better term. Although the huge neon sign outside
Munich's Riem Airport, proclaiming there are now *eight* McDonald's
hamburger joints in the capital of beer and pretzels where Hitler got his
start, makes me wonder whether I am sufficiently circumspect in the
choice of terms.

Undeniably, the traditions of centuries obviously run deep and the
Germans, who place great value on the old and historic, certainly try to
preserve them. In the East I occasionally have the impression that they are

bottled in formaldehyde. Titles, both professional and aristocratic such as *Herr Rechtsanwalt* (Attorney) *Schmidt* and *Hermann Baron von und zu Somewhere-or-other* are still in vogue, though inclined to be less popular and less used with each passing year. Newspaper obituaries, especially in the southern parts of the country, do from time to time still proclaim that the deceased was a "senior streetcar conductor" or a "railway switch-man's widow."

By its very nature, the German language with its formality tends to preserve traditions too.

There are still castles and vineyards on the Rhine and splendid baroque churches and monasteries in Bavaria. The famous Cologne cathedral still stands; Nuremberg's medieval wall has been completely rebuilt; Charle-magne's tomb can be seen in Aachen; Beethoven's house stands unchanged in Bonn, and the really nostalgic can still lose their heart to Old Heidelberg. The villages—especially in Bavaria, Lower Saxony, Schleswig-Holstein, and parts of Hesse and Wuerttemberg—with half-timbered houses, steep tiled roofs, painted facades, narrow twisting streets, and market squares, do look almost as quaint and picturesque as the travel folders make them out to be.

Afternoon coffee and creamy cake is still a custom—especially on Sundays. The village inn, where men spend interminable hours playing a card game called Skat and drink more beer than their wives approve of, remains a part of the scene. Carnival continues to immobilize the Rhineland from 11:11 A.M. each November 11 until Shrove Tuesday. In Bavaria one will find more than four thousand amateur brass bands, their members colorfully costumed in green hunting jackets and leather breeches, which play at weddings, funerals, beer festivals, and Saturday night dances. The Germans still shake hands upon meeting.

Germany is still Germany, that is true. But far more striking than the residual patterns are the departures from them—the new mores, lifestyles, and attitudes—especially in the West.

Americanisms and English words and phrases are creeping into the language and are already commonplace in advertising copy. The *Kaffeeklatsch* is giving way to the *Kocktailstunde,* just as scotch and bourbon whisky are replacing *Schnaps.* German cities are being truncated by superhighways, pockmarked by shopping centers, and surrounded by suburbias. Youngsters listen and dance to American pop music, read comic books, eat breakfast cereals, prefer hamburgers to dumplings and sauerkraut, and wouldn't "be caught dead" in anything but denims. Traditional German thrift is losing out to the credit card and the installment plan, the corner Gasthaus to the discotheque.

It is not yet a "pink plastic" society, but the impetus is there, the trend unmistakable. More quickly than West Germans realize, or care to know, theirs is becoming a country of split-level houses, laundromats, dishwashers, two-car garages, keeping-up-with-the-Joneses, TV dinners, crowded schools, unbreathable air, polluted rivers and lakes, nervous tension, ulcers and heart attacks, urban ghettos, and spiralling crime rates.

One of the most striking developments is what is happening to the language.

For some time, actually since 1958 when a "study committee for spelling rules" met at Wiesbaden, pressure has been building to lowercase the almighty German noun. For two centuries the noun in German, no matter where it stood in a sentence has had its first letter capitalized. The rule is complicated, however, by the fact that words other than nouns frequently play noun roles in sentences, while nouns themselves often function as other parts of speech. The debate among educators, linguists, and grammarians is a hot one. The proponents of change point out that the complicated rules not only make German one of the most difficult languages to learn to spell properly, but places it out of step with the times. Only one other language observed the noun capitalization rule into the twentieth century—Danish, which underwent revision in 1948. The opponents contend that change "would go to the very heart of our language, to something that is vital to us," and that it would alter or confuse the meaning of sentences.

The dispassionate observer cannot help wondering what the argument is all about in view of the fact that so many Anglicisms are creeping into the language anyway that in a few more years German, as it used to be "gespoken" or "gewritten," may be dead anyway. For Germans today it seems almost natural to express their thoughts in a curious mixture of "Engman" or "Gerlish." In advertising, in business, the military, government, on radio and television, and certainly among the young generation, English words and phrases are used so liberally and frequently that I sometimes do not know which of the two languages predominates.

Thus clothing is now manufactured for German men who prefer "good taste *und den* Country Look." The smart rum drinker imbibes it "*mit* Coke, *mit* Tonic, *mit* Bitter Lemon *oder* on the rocks." The best of music is naturally reproduced on "compact *casetten,*" which one plays on a "hi-fi stereo *casetten-recorder*" whose manufacturer offers "full service" in the event it should go *kaputt.*

For decades, even before Adolf Hitler appeared on the scene, the pure Germanists were trying to purge the language of borrowed foreign words—most of which had a French origin. But they were relatively unsuccessful. The Nazis, however, countenanced no lengthy discussions and simply decreed that un-German, non-Aryan *Fremdwoerter*—foreign words—had no place in the language. That this, as is the nature of the German language, required a lot of additional tongue-twisting, made no difference.

Thus, the *Trottoir*—sidewalk—had to be a good old German *Buerger-steig.* A *Portemonnaie*—money purse—became a *Geldboerse.* Newspaper-men were no longer *Reporter* but *Berichterstatter,* and their editors, once known as *Redakteure,* became *Schriftleiter.* Instead of the *Radio* Germans began listening to their *Rundfunkempfaenger.* Rather than use the old *Telefon* to make a call, they picked up the *Fernsprecher,* and when looking for a number, no longer searched in the *Telefonbuch* but in the *Fernsprechnummernverzeichniss.*

Since the end of the war, however, efforts to keep the language *urdeutsch*—pure German—have virtually ceased. Though some of the expressions are still in use, many of the French words have come back and, more importantly, English—the language of the U. S. and British occupation forces, subsequently West Germany's principal allies and commercial partners—has infiltrated and spread with amazing speed.

It is not just the young generation that laces its speech with Americanisms and Anglicisms: for the older Germans, too, English words and phrases have become standard and are considered chic. When Frau Schultz wants to set her hair, she uses a *Haarspray.* Her new dress is probably made of *Syntheticstoffe* and will undoubtedly be *fully fashioned.* In the mornings her husband will lather his face, not with good old German *Rasierseife* but good old German *shaving soap,* then rub it with *aftershave lotion* instead of what used to be called *Rasierwasser.*

There still being a major difference between Deutsch as it is "gespoken" and English as it is "gewritten," the hair spray is likely to be pronounced *shpray* and the shaving soap *chafing sop.* But what's der difference if der meaning comes across?

Herr Mueller works not in the good old, picturesque *Innenstadt*—as downtown used to be called—but *in der City.* At lunch he is likely to eat a *sendvitch* at a *kvickimbiss*, which means a sandwich at a quick-lunch counter. West Germans inevitably smoke cigarettes that are *king size mit filter und extra light,* fly *nonstop* and read in their newspapers about *filmstars, playboys,* and bank robberies committed by *gangsterbanden.*

The reasons for the de-Germanization of German are many. Some expressions have become necessary simply because there are no German equivalents. An advertising man, for example, has no German substitute for the word "layout." The government official who wants to tell newsmen about something must do it in a "briefing" because there is no German word to describe such sessions. There is also the pure snob effect of lacing one's speech with foreign words. The thirty-year-long impact of AFN and BFN, the American and British forces' radio networks, both of which estimate that they have five times as many German as U. S. and English soldier listeners, must be considered too. English-language newspapers and magazines, or their German editions, and books by American and British authors, translated but still sprinkled with original expressions, have all contributed.

Thus, in industry one speaks of *big business, marketing, der self-made man,* and what appears to be Germany's most popular ailment: *die manager krankheit,* which can be anything from ulcers to heart disease.

Products for which there are no German names—at least not saleable ones—have been introduced. I suppose one could say *Maisflocken* or *geroestete Reiskoerner* but any halfway savvy *marketer* knows that calling them *corn flakes* and *reis krispies* is likely to improve their sale, especially now that the *supermarkt* is replacing the corner grocery store. Every merchandiser, of course, offers *top service* or *all-around service,* and to sell what they make, West German manufacturers need *gute junior produkt manager, produktingenieure,* and *servicelabortechniker. Ein public relations fachman* doesn't hurt either, to keep up das *produktimage,* of course.

In sports, terms such as *knockout* and *sprinter* have long been in use. But even I couldn't believe my ears not long ago when I heard a television sportscaster describe a track meet thusly: *"Schmidt hat einen guten* lead. *Als das* gun off shot *hatte er den* best start. *In dem* pinch *in der* curve *zeigt er grossen* speed."

In view of this massive Americanization of the language, what seems inexplicable is the extent to which Germans Germanize the titles of

American movies. There seems to be a compulsion to give American titles—which already jar the nerves of the authors on whose novels they're based—an even juicier box-office ring on *Hauptstrasse*—Main Street—in Germany. To the frequently voiced charge in the Federal Republic that Americans seem to be obsessed with crime and sex, one German movie critic said caustically: "We are the masters of that. The Americans could learn a lot from what we do to the titles of their movies. Ours are mired in eroticism, violence, murder, and manslaughter."

When the Gondolas Are in Mourning was the German title for *Don't Look Now*. Terence Young's *The Klansman* has been billed in the Federal Republic as *They Are All Cursed*. The German for *Omicron* was *Doctor, the Corpse Is Alive*. Remember *September Affair*? In German it was called *Love Rage on Capri*. The German title for *Escape* was *With 1,000 Volts into Death*," while *Look in Any Window* was called *In the Frenzy of Sensuality*.

The Fist in the Nape of the Neck was German for *On the Waterfront*, while *The Fist in the Face* was the translated title of *Requiem for a Heavyweight*. Duccio Tessari's *Tough Guys* came out as *Two Fists of Heaven*, and an Italian film, innocently entitled *The Magnificent Adventure*, was Germanized as *With Fists and Daggers*.

"We seem to be addicted to fists," said the critic. "I can only assume the translations match our mentality."

Be that as it may, one thing seems certain: The German mentality itself is changing. Once upon a time, the Germans lived to work. Nowadays they work to live. The result is that the once-admired—and feared—*furor teutonicus* has been replaced by a national preoccupation with *Feierabend*—quitting time—plus the length of vacation periods, holidays, lunch hours, and shortening the work week.

While this may be healthy in many respects, it can be frustrating for anyone trying to get things done, and according to many economists may eventually price German goods right off the international market. "I just can't get used to it," one German businessman, back from an extended stay in Italy and France, said several years ago. "In Italy they work on construction sites on Saturdays and the TV repairman will come as late as midnight on the first call. Here they even paint the white lane markers on the streets during rush hour because no painter will touch a brush after six P.M."

"We're reaching the point," complained one Bonn housewife, "where we'll have to start making appointments even with the garbage collector. You already need one with your garage mechanic, your plumber, and the repair service for the washing machine."

The West German worker today earns more per hour and actually spends fewer hours on the job each year than any worker in Europe. Holidays and vacation account for much of this leisure time. Not only do West Germans celebrate every conceivable major and minor religious holiday, but they usually celebrate them twice as long as any other people. Christmas is not a one-day affair, but three days long, beginning around noon on December 24, when all stores close, and including the 25th and 26th, both of which are legal holidays. Easter is celebrated not just on Sunday, but on Monday, and because Good Friday is a legal holiday as well, it becomes at least a four-day weekend, with some people taking off on the preceding Thursday and the following Tuesday too. There is not only Whitsunday, but Whitmonday; Ascension Day; Corpus Christi Day; Assumption Day; All Souls Day; Labor Day; German Unity Day; New Year's Day; and in Bavaria, Three Kings' Day on January 6. Rhinelanders take off at least a week to bring the carnival season to a liquid and happy conclusion. Nearly every German village has at least one day set aside to celebrate the anniversary of its founding or the dedication of its church back in A.D.-something-or-other. Minimum legal vacation time for most workers is now twenty-one working days, plus the Sundays, Saturdays, and holidays that fall within the period, which means that, in practice, they have more than a month off with full pay. Some firms are even paying an additional per diem so their workers can enjoy themselves.

The West German today seems preoccupied with *Freizeit*—leisure time—and the German workhorse of yesteryear has been replaced by the *Freizeitmensch*, today's man of leisure. An entire new leisure industry has arisen. When stores are open for business, which is not long because many close for two hours for lunch and federal law requires everyone to shut down at 6:30 P.M. on weekdays and 2:00 P.M. on Saturdays, they sell *Freizeit* suits, *Freizeit* dresses, *Freizeit* shirts, *Freizeit* shoes, *Freizeit* furniture, *Freizeit* appliances, *Freizeit* foods, and *Freizeit* just-about-everything. Psychologists and sociologists are now concerned with the problems of *Freizeitgestaltung*—or how the Germans should best use their leisure time—while enterprising businessmen and real estate dealers promote *Freizeit* parks and recreation areas replete with heated swimming pools, artificially lighted solariums, zoos, skating rinks, *trim-dich-fit* installations, golf courses, and tennis courts.

As a result of changing attitudes toward work, completely new terms have entered the language. One of them is *Arbeitsdenkmal,* literally meaning "work statue," which is applied, for example, to those road- and building-construction workers who can frequently be seen leaning motionless on their tools and equipment, gazing off into space. Or there's also the *Krankheitswelle*—the sickness wave—a consequence of the fact that since 1957 the health insurance plan entitles everyone to six weeks' paid sick leave a year. Indeed, with an annual loss of some 250 million workdays through sick leave, every West German worker must be taking an average of 10 days a year off for illness. When he does, he no longer says, *"Ich bin krank"* ("I am ill"), but *"Ich feiere krank,"* which means, in essence, "I am celebrating an illness." Another frequently heard remark: "I think it's a good time to have my grippe." And even more common is the comment: "I'll take my six weeks now."

Germany's health insurance system, the oldest and most comprehensive in the world, has certainly freed the average man from the fear of being ill. But more than that, because no one need fear or worry about high medical bills or loss of income (the insurance pays all), Germans tend to be hypochondriacs, utterly obsessed by the malfunctions of their own bodies.

Although the Federal Republic has more doctors per capita than any other Western country, including the United States, the "shortage of physicians" has been a major issue for years, and the average doctor is so busy that he can devote only a few minutes to each patient because his waiting room is usually crowded. With more than 700,000 beds in nearly 3,600 hospitals and clinics, West Germany also has the highest hospital capacity per population of all non-Communist countries. But to accommodate all the patients, hospitals are forced to place emergency beds in hallways and corridors. The reason for these seeming contradictions is that people make undue use of the medical facilities available. The average stay for a patient in a hospital is nineteen days, compared to only eight or ten in U. S. hospitals. Since the insurance pays all, no patient is under financial pressure to leave, and physicians have become so attuned to the system that they prescribe much longer care than is needed.

Absenteeism due to illness, claimed and real, increased by nearly 50 percent during the five-year period from 1968 to 1973; to cite but one example, more than 8 percent of the workers at the Volkswagen plant report in sick each day.

Wherever one turns there are indications of the German preoccupation with illness and health. Advertisements for products ranging from margarine to hair tonics, from deep freezers to office chairs, all use the same pitch: "It's good for your health."

"We have become the greatest nation of hypochondriacs in the world," an insurance specialist lamented to me once. "Many of us would not like to hear it, but Monsieur Argan in Molière's play *The Imaginary Invalid* could well have been a German."

One explanation for the syndrome is unquestionably the health-insurance system instituted nearly a century ago under Bismarck. The way it functions today, if a worker is ill he is entitled to six weeks on full salary, with graduated reductions for longer periods. During that time he enjoys full medical benefits. But that is only the beginning. He is also entitled to convalescent leave called *Erhohlungsurlaub* and an additional period of postconvalescent treatment, called *Schonzeit,* in which he must not be overworked. The system is most flexible. I once heard of a bookkeeper who suffered a minor heart attack, and upon returning to work after his sick leave, announced: "I think I'll postpone my convalescent leave until September. The Riviera resorts are more pleasant then."

The most determined of the chronic hypochondriacs appear to be those who must have their annual *Kur*—a cure—at one of the Federal Republic's more than six hundred spas. The branch of medicine, almost unknown in the United States, concerned with their treatment is called balneology. A major specialty, it deals with baths and mineral waters as medicinal treatment.

The Kur is by no means restricted to the wealthy, although the more exclusive resorts such as Baden-Baden and Wiesbaden still try to preserve that air of nineteenth-century gentility which existed when only aristocrats, merchant princes, and industrial barons took the waters. Nowadays physicians regularly prescribe visits to spas for millions of patients covered by compulsory insurance which, of course, pays not only for the cost of treatment but for living expenses in resort hotels.

The preoccupation with rest, health, and leisure has also made the West Germans probably the most peripatetic people in Europe. Nearly half the total population goes on a vacation trip of at least one week's duration every year; and of those travellers, more than 45 percent go outside Germany, with Austria, Italy, Spain, Switzerland, and Yugoslavia being the most popular countries, though visits to North Africa and the United States are catching up fast in the statistics. In fact, thanks to the decline in the value of the dollar and the rise in the value of the deutsche mark, vacation travel to the United States increased by 15 percent in 1974 compared to the previous year and nearly 400,000 Germans invaded America.

The invasion has not gone unnoticed. During the tourist season, camera-laden Germans are now as prevalent around the Statue of Liberty, Rockefeller Center, the Capitol, and the White House as camera-bedecked Americans used to be—when the dollar still got them somewhere—on the streets of Heidelberg, Munich's Marienplatz, or around the Cologne Cathedral. As the usually staid *New York Times* pointed out early in 1974: "Eins, Zwei, Drei, Vier: Hans und Fritz Are Coming Here." And for the average Hans und Fritz the trip, by charter flight, including a week of sightseeing that usually includes New York, Washington, and Niagara Falls, costs less than three weeks' take-home pay.

German preoccupation with things American, especially Wild West American, predates the travel wave by a number of years. In fact, in the late 1960s, Americans visiting the Federal Republic might well have believed they had gotten on the wrong plane and had landed instead in Wyoming, Colorado, Texas, or Arizona. The reason was the *Wildwest Welle*—the Wild West craze—when it seemed every second German was trying to imitate *den Cowboy look*. Though the wave has ebbed a little, all large cities still have at least one Western store which serves as "headquarters *fuer echte* Cowboy-*Ausruestung*." There one can buy Winchester rifles that *"knallen und rauchen"* (bang and smoke) and *"texanische Stiefel*—Texan boots.

The craze was actually originated by Karl May, a turn-of-the-century German author who wrote a whole library of books about the American West without ever leaving his native Radebeul near Dresden. May was the creator of such figures as old Shatterhand, Old Surehand, and Winnetou, who kept the grandparents of today's Germans in the grip of suspense and who, thanks to the motion picture industry, have been imbued with a new breath of life. Thanks to the continuing impact of May's novels, there are some forty-five cowboy and Western clubs in the Federal Republic whose members meet to study American history, pioneer lore, and to practice fast-drawing, sharpshooting, lassoing, and trick riding. They publish a magazine and hold an annual council attended by more than a thousand members. Should the yearly clambake ever prove dull, the cowboys can always tangle with the Indians, for there are nearly as many Indian clubs, comprising several thousand members who will go on the warpath at the drop of a ten-gallon hat.

Westerns easily account for an average of 10 percent of West German movie billings. The Cartwright family from Bonanza Valley has one of the highest viewer ratings on television. And until it burned down in 1973 (arson was suspected), there was a "Hot Gun Town" amusement park in the Bavarian Alps not far from Munich.

Germans are prevalent not only in the United States these days. They virtually dominate the beaches of Italy and Spain, the white sands of Tunisia and Morocco, and in recent years have been pushing ever farther south into Africa, where they are offered package-tour photo safaris and exotic jungle experiences. One species of West German tourist that continues to bemuse psychologists, sociologists, and other students of human behavior is the single—married and unmarried—female who embarks on a perennial exodus to southern climes, obviously in search of far more than just a place in the sun. What they look for is *amore*—Latin style. And more than just a flirt. Some 20 percent of German married women go on vacations alone and of these nearly one-fourth have admitted to vacation romances that went far beyond the initial sparring stage—invariably with dark-haired, dark-eyed Lotharios in the beach towns of Italy, Spain, and Yugoslavia. For the native males—ranging in age from fuzzy-cheeked teenagers to experienced casanovas in their best years—the annual influx of sex-seeking German maidens is a boon. Many have honed their tactics to a fine precision; some have developed them into an art. According to one survey, some 27 percent of divorces can be traced to vacation-time adultery.

Travel and broadened horizons have changed West German lifestyles at home, especially the eating habits and tastes in food. Finding a "typical" German Gasthaus which serves traditional German food, generally considered to be "plain, heavy on fat and grease, but wholesome and hearty," can be quite a challenge these days. Even the least pretentious place now has a menu which it describes as "international." True, a *Wiener Schnitzel*, boiled beef with sauerkraut, pot roasts with lots of potatoes and thick gravy, and all manner of clear soups with dumplings, can still be found in most of them. But some traditional German dishes are becoming increasingly difficult to obtain. Instead of *Sauerbraten und Kloese* the West German taste now runs to spaghetti and pizza, beefsteaks and filet, raznicci, roast beef "English style," Spanish paella, shrimps and oysters, and—especially among the young—to hamburgers, which despite their German name are as American as apple pie.

Munich, for example, has more than a dozen Chinese restaurants, some thirty Italian ones, several specializing in Indian and Indonesian cuisine, at least fifteen that serve passable Yugoslav and Balkan dishes, several excellent Swiss places, and scores that feature Greek, Hungarian, Spanish, Russian, Mexican, and pseudo-French cooking. And because the Germans have become almost compulsive weight watchers, steaks are in. The steak craze was launched by forty-year-old Baron Hans-Albrecht von Maltzahn, who in 1969, following a trip to Argentina, started a chain of "Churrasco" steak houses in West Berlin, Hamburg, Frankfurt, Bonn, Munich, Cologne, and a half dozen other cities around the country, where Argentinian beef is grilled to perfection by genuine Argentinian *parrilleros* and served by waiters in *gaucho* costumes. Maltzahn's Churrasco chain proved so successful that it has found innumerable imitators such as the La Pampa, Asado, Rodeo Steak, and Block House restaurants with outlets all over the country.

Styles and tastes in home cooking have changed beyond recognition too. Virtually every German household now uses frozen food of which some 250,000 tons were sold in 1974 compared to only 14,000 tons five years previously. The figure, by the way, does not include frozen chicken, sales of which have increased by nearly 600 percent during the past two decades. Packaged and semiprepared dishes of every kind, many of them American imitations, others manufactured by the West German subsidiaries of the large U. S. food manufacturers, fill the shelves of supermarkets from Hamburg in the north to Munich in the south.

In the early 1960s cheese in Germany was still something people put on sandwiches. Only the most wealthy, travelled, and sophisticated of gourmets viewed it as a dessert or had the money to eat it as such. But the Common Market has changed all that, and French, Italian, Dutch, and Danish cheeses now take up most of the space in supermarket cheese sections, account for most of the cheese sales, and cheese itself has been transformed from something you put on your *Butterbrod* to an after-dinner and snack science.

The same thing has happened to other products most Germans had never heard of as recently as fifteen years ago. Tomato juice, once regarded something for health addicts, is becoming a standard appetizer. Oranges and grapefruits, imported from Israel, Spain, Italy, and South Africa, are now as common as apples and potatoes. In the mid-1960s the average German wouldn't have been able to tell a corn flake from a rice crispy, let alone know what to do with either. Today cereals are common breakfast foods.

Just as typical German food and the typical German restaurant seem to be losing out to "internationalization," so, too, are German drinking habits changing. Although beer is still the most popular alcoholic beverage, with wine running second, West Germans are turning increasingly from their own clear grain spirits and potato-based schnaps to Scottish, Irish, and American whiskies and to vodka.

Although the village tavern with its *Stammtisch*—a bare round table in a corner, reserved for regular patrons who come to play cards or argue sports and politics—is holding its own, in the cities the traditional *Eckkneipe,* the tavern on the corner, is fast losing out to expresso cafes, discotheques, and nightclubs. According to one 1974 survey, only one in four urban residents claims to have a *Stammlokal,* a regular pub in the neighborhood, and even among that minority, visits to the pub are becoming fewer. Curiously, those people living in new residential areas, invariably short of traditional German *Gemuetlichkeit,* complain that what they miss most is a good corner tavern. But in the older parts of cities, where these still exist, they are being patronized more and more infrequently. The days of German Gemuetlichkeit and the rustic old tavern where burghers came to discuss the world's problems over a leisurely stein of beer or glass of wine appear numbered. "If in fact," as the weekly magazine *Stern* lamented a few years ago, "they are not already over."

One consequence of the change in drinking habits and styles appears to be a dramatic rise in alcoholics and problem drinkers. In the past ten years, according to government statistics, the number of alcoholics and chronic drinkers has nearly doubled from 350,000 to an estimated 600,000, of whom at least one-fourth are under thirty years of age.

Consumption is certainly prodigious: 144 liters of beer per capita annually; 18.7 liters of wine; 8.2 liters of spirits. The total national expenditure for alcohol is almost twice that which is spent on education, books, newspapers, magazines, theaters, concerts, and other cultural pursuits and almost as high as the national defense budget. Consumption of alcoholic beverages has been increasing steadily over the past two decades and most sociologists attribute this to economic prosperity, as well as to the pressures of urbanization and the competitive achievement society.

Statistics indicate that alcoholism and problem drinking are, proportionately, most prevalent among the upper-income groups. But nobody is quite certain whether this is an expression of social and professional pressures or of the affluence and greater purchasing power at these social levels. The well-stocked living room bar being a status symbol, more and more drinking seems to be done at home, where the tendency toward habitual and excessive alcohol consumption is greater.

"I fear that this is a symptom of our age," the proprietor of a famous winehouse in Bonn once told me. "There was a time when Germans drank alcohol to quench thirst and drinking a glass of beer or wine was as natural to us as drinking water is to Americans. For wine, especially, one needs leisure and time to enjoy a good glass and contemplate. But nowadays there seems to be a real compulsion to drink, almost a desire to down something fast, reach a state of inebriation and feel the effect quickly."

Whether the same pressures are the cause for the spiralling suicide rate, no one is willing to say with certainty. But the increase—nearly 8 percent a year during the early 1970s—is considered alarming. In 1973 more than thirteen thousand people committed suicide in the Federal Republic and West Berlin; the 1974 figure was expected to exceed fourteen thousand. The number of known attempts was five times as high.

Industrialization, urbanization, rising living standards, and consumer aspirations have not only changed West German lifestyles but are continuing to alter the face of Germany itself—and not necessarily to its advantage. For, that which the war did not destroy has been falling victim to superhighways, shopping centers, office construction, vast housing projects, and whatever else enterprising planners and profit-hungry entrepreneurs seem to regard as "urban renewal" and "modernization." When World War Two ended, West Germany's reservoir of "historic architecture" had been reduced by 73 percent. Due to neglect and deliberate demolition in the three decades since 1945, another 12 percent has been whittled away so that a scant 15 percent remains. The process, moreover, has not been halted, despite a nationwide outcry, the activities of citizens' initiative groups, and the advent of a generation of younger municipal planners who express horror at the diminishing quality of urban life, the dwindling individuality of Germany's cities, the rise of bedroom suburbias, the spread of ghettos, and the creeping cancer of pollution and ecological imbalance.

Old Heidelberg, one of the few larger German cities to escape wartime destruction, is currently being raped in the name of urban renewal. Plans call for construction of a four- to six-lane superhighway along the banks of the Neckar River, thus separating the town from the stream that gives it its special romantic atmosphere. In the old quarter, several blocks of historic houses are already being razed to make way for a shopping center and high-rise parking facilities. In the Westphalian town of Lemgo, city officials want to condemn nearly half the houses in the center to make room for office buildings and department stores. The Gothic center of Osnabrueck has been sacrificed to a four-lane freeway. The old town of Stade, west of Hamburg, once a gem of Renaissance and Gothic architecture, is to be surrounded by a freeway ring, and current plans call for demolition of more than 50 percent of the old houses in its center. Frankfurt, badly damaged during the war, has long been called the "Chicago of Germany" because of its devotion to commercialism, its high crime rate, and architectural facelessness. But the label, frankly, is an insult—to Chicago. Frankfurt is the embodiment of everything that is wrong with urban living in the world today.

A number of complex factors contribute to the steady erosion of the quality of German urban life; pervasive motorization and real estate speculation are only two of them. One problem, for example, is the taxation system, which leaves city and town government so poor that they are induced to attract industry and shopping centers which can be legally squeezed for trade tax, a municipal administration's main source of revenue. The federal "urban renewal" law also serves as an incentive to raze old sections of cities, regardless of their condition or architectural and historic value, and to replace them with new buildings. Federal grants for such work help to subsidize the construction industry, which has more or less reached a saturation point with home and apartment building.

There are, of course, countermovements to halt and prevent further sacrifice of West German cities on the altars of motorization, real estate profiteering, and a clearly misconceived and misguided urban renewal policy. Under pressure from citizens' groups, three of the oldest and most picturesque cities in West Germany—Regensburg, Bamberg, and Luebeck—have banded together in a "monuments preservation association," whose aim is to protect, renovate, and modernize the towns' "historic and architectural substance." Their program calls for refacing the facades of hundreds of old buildings, treating them with newly developed chemicals so as to make them resistant to erosion by pollutants, and modernizing their interiors, many of which now lack the sanitary facilities and amenities tenants expect. The costs of such projects are phenomenal, however, and are expected to run close to DM 2 billion in Luebeck and DM 1 billion each in Bamberg and Regensburg. Where that kind of money is supposed to come from, city officials do not know. But at least they are agreed on the urgency of doing something.

Some of the city officials are banking on volunteer help, and in Bamberg they have been getting it. In the summer of 1974, for example, five hundred youths—students in their late teens and early twenties belonging to an action group that calls itself the "Protective Association for Old Bamberg"—converged on the city for a "painting and plastering festival." While popular folk and protest singers such as Colin Wilkie and Shirley Hart spurred them on with music in the streets, the youngsters erected scaffolds and refaced dozens of venerable downtown buildings.

"What we want," said one of the organizers of the festival, "is more than just exterior renovation of course. To keep people living in or attract new tenants to houses that are two and three centuries old, the interiors have to be modernized and professionally equipped with bathrooms, kitchens, and central heating. Otherwise people will just naturally drift away, leaving uninhabited shells and lifeless old quarters that will become prey to speculators and profiteers. Repainting exteriors is not enough—in fact it could lead to making some of these sections and some of our old cities into nothing more than architectural museums."

The city that has been most successful in breathing new life into its center is Munich. It closed off almost its entire downtown area to vehicular traffic, invested billions in an underground rapid transit system and turned its main shopping streets into permanent pedestrian malls replete with trees, benches, and old fountains. The historic center is now vibrant with life and the Munich experiment draws admiring city planners from around the world. Attractive and exemplary as Munich may be, however, the work could never have been done had the city not received massive transfusions of Bavarian state and federal money to prepare it for the 1972 Olympic games and had its former mayor, Hans-Jochen Vogel, now the federal minister of justice, not decided to fight the further incursion of the automobile.

Vogel, elected to his first term as Munich's mayor in 1960 when he was only thirty-four years old, made a name for himself soon after inauguration by riding the streetcar from his home to city hall.

"With every million a city invests in road and street projects," he once told me, "it hastens its own destruction. A city simply cannot afford to capitulate to the explosion in private automobile transport by building more and wider streets and roads to accommodate the cars. The consequence of such a policy is inevitably irreparable harm to the existing, and often historical, substance of the city's architecture, which is to say, to the very essence of its urban character."

His streetcar-riding beginnings as mayor notwithstanding, Vogel started in office as ready to capitulate to the car as anyone else. He set out by destroying a lot of architectural substance himself with the construction of two "defensive" four-lane automobile rings around the city. The inner ring follows the old medieval fortification line around Munich. As originally conceived, it was to have high-rise parking facilities placed strategically along it in an attempt to induce motorists to leave their cars there and then walk the rest of the way into the center, the diameter across downtown being only a mile or so. "But we discovered," Vogel said, "that with each parking facility we built, the number of cars converging on the city just increased."

The only alternative was a total ban, in effect since 1971, coupled with a subway and rapid-transit system whose underground hub is the very center of Munich itself—Marienplatz and the neo-Gothic city hall.

Exemplary as Munich may be, it is an example no other city can afford to emulate. Construction of the first stage of the subway system cost nearly DM 1 billion and had it not been for the 1972 Olympics it is doubtful whether it would ever have been built.

One unhappy consequence of urbanization and the dehumanization of urban life is the rising crime rate, a phenomenon in both West and East Germany. By American standards, of course, West Germany's is a crime "wavelet" and, in turn, by West German criteria what is happening in the GDR is a ripple.

More murders, for example, are committed in the three largest U. S.

cities—New York, Chicago, and Los Angeles—each year than in all of
the Federal Republic, and more in Newark, New Jersey, than in the
entire GDR. There were fewer robberies in West Germany than in
Washington, D. C. and fewer in East Germany than in Greensboro,
North Carolina.

But such comparison statistics provide Germans no more comfort than
the news that the Federal Republic's inflation and unemployment rate is
the lowest among the industrialized Western nations. And the sharp
increase in the incidence of crime in both Germanys—about 10 percent
annually during the five-year period from 1968 through 1973—has
predictably spurred calls for law and order and caused alarm.

The alarm has been sounded loudest by Hans-Werner Hammacher,
chief of detectives in Cologne, who predicts that by 1980 the crime
incidence in West Germany will be almost as high as it was in the United
States in 1970. He sees a doubling in the West German murder rate and
three times the number of armed robberies and burglaries by the end of
the decade and has warned that uniformed police will be riding guard on
subway trains within the next five years. Hammacher, who gained
nationwide attention and fame in December 1971 when he offered
himself as hostage to two bank robbers in Cologne, also believes that most
of the increase in crime will be attributable, as it is in the United States, to
socially underprivileged minority groups—the children of foreign workers.

The increase in the GDR is so alarming—and apparently so embarrassing to the regime which has traditionally regarded crime as strictly a
phenomenon of capitalism—that the authorities have stopped publishing
the figures. Starting in 1973, and for the first time in twenty-four years,
the GDR's *Statistical Yearbook* no longer discloses data dealing with crime
and punishment.

Although Hammacher stresses that much criminal activity in West
Germany is prompted by American crimes that are not only widely
publicized but, on occasion, glorified in the Federal Republic, there are
significant differences in the crime pattern. On the whole, the streets of
German cities are still peaceful and safe at night, and neither muggings
nor rapes are really a serious problem. On the other hand, to be a bank
employee in West Germany these days is to be in a high-risk profession.
No country has as many small neighborhood branch banks as Germany.
In the metropolitan area of Munich, for example, there are more than five

hundred, some with only three or four clerks and tellers. And nowhere are as many banks robbed. In Munich it is not uncommon to have two bank robberies in one day. As banks have taken protective measures, such as the use of bullet-proof glass in tellers' cages and the installation of alarm signals, the taking of hostages as a means to obtain money has increased.

Another phenomenon is the spread during the past decade of "rocker gangs"—leather-jacketed, heavily tattooed, Nazi-emblem-wearing, motorcycle-riding bands of young toughs who emulate America's Hell's Angels. Armed with blackjacks, brass knuckles, bicycle chains, knives, and, lately, guns, they have terrorized a number of large cities, especially Hamburg and Munich, demolishing cafes, bars, inns, youth clubs, and occasionally attacking people on the streets. Robbery is rarely involved in their rampagings, but there is always violence, wanton destruction, and crass brutality and, once in a while, gang rapes. Police in Hamburg and Munich have set up special squads to deal with the problem. Hans Juergen Wolter, the head of the Hamburg squad, has a register of three thousand rocker youths belonging to "packs" with anywhere from six to twenty-five members. Although there are striking similarities to ghetto gangs in the United States and the youths have adopted Americanized names such as The Bloody Devils, Tiger Rocks, Black Spiders, and The Chikagos, there are also striking differences. They rarely fight each other to protect their "turf." Instead, indiscriminate marauding is their thing—an expression, as Wolter puts it, of "their inferiority complexes, antisocial feelings, belligerence toward society, low-grade intelligence, limited education, and laziness." The majority come from lower-class families and broken homes and are school dropouts.

The rise in crime has understandably triggered hysterical demands for more law and order and stiffer penalties. The increase in the murder rate has spurred calls for reinstituting capital punishment, which was abolished in 1949. Such reactions inevitably touch raw nerves in a country where one can still hear members of the older generation proclaim that "under Adolf this kind of lawlessness would have been unthinkable." It was after all, as recently as the fall of 1971 that irate courtroom spectators shouted, "We need Hitler back!" and "Chop off his head!" during the trial of a young sex deviate sentenced to life for the murder of three young girls.

Yes, there are still those who shout for a return to old-style law and order and who equate the Nazi era with public peace and safety, conveniently forgetting or denying that Hitler's law and order was in itself the epitome of lawlessness and criminality. But fortunately, they are a dwindling minority, subject with each passing year to the natural attrition of age.

The overwhelming majority of Germans know that the solution to the growing crime problem is to seek out its origins and social causes and remove them, and to reform and modernize their nineteenth-century penal and correctional system whose only tangible achievement seems to be that of making even more hardened criminals of those who get caught in its ruthless machinery.

"Of course we shall need better police protection," says Cologne's Hammacher. "But that is only an inadequate and temporary solution to a problem we will not really solve until we systematically research its social and political causes."

"Harsher penalties," another law enforcement official said to me, "are really no answer. The public is going to have to realize that the increase in violent crime parallels the experience of all other industrially advanced countries. The solution is to reduce the economic and social strains brought on by industrialization."

In a country where the traditional solution to social ills was always to pass more laws "forbidding" and "prohibiting" them, those comments by two cops, it seems to me, are another way of saying: "*Please* don't walk on the grass."

10

Divided They Stand

NOT another seat was to be had in the tavern on East Berlin's Boetzow Strasse the evening of June 22, 1974. The patrons were leaning against the walls, sitting on the tables, and perching on the edges of the windowsills. The barkeep was perspiring profusely as he drew beer after beer, and the waitresses looked as close to exhaustion as they claimed to be.

Through the haze of acrid cigarette and cigar smoke you could see, if your eyes didn't smart too much, the screen of the television set with its broadcast, live and direct, from Hamburg's Volkspark Stadium. And over the babble of noise in the tavern one could hear the din from the stadium where West Germany's and East Germany's national teams were locked in mortal combat in the semifinal round of the World Cup soccer championship.

From the TV set came a chant familiar to soccer fans everywhere: "Deutschland, Deutschland! Deutschland, Deutschland!" The last "Deutschland!" shouted by thirty thousand enthusiastic West German fans was still echoing across the bleachers when a small delegation of fifteen hundred flag-waving East Germans, huddled defensively against the overwhelming majority, yelled back defiantly: "D—D—R, D–D–R, DDR!"

"We can cheer all we want to, but there's no way we're ever going to win this game," said one of the East Berliners in the tavern, sounding about as enthusiastic as a man being led to his own hanging.

"Look at him, he's already licking his chops," said another, as the screen showed a closeup of one of the West German players.

"You know what that stupid woman did?" exclaimed one man, jerking a disgusted thumb at his wife sitting forlornly in a corner. "She bet on us instead of them. Boy, that shows you what women know about football!"

Obviously not much, to judge from the East German odds against an East German victory: three cases of beer against one bottle. But obviously, too, what women may lack in knowledge they more than compensate for in intuition, for a strange thing happened that evening to the East German team. Ninety minutes after kickoff, when the final whistle blew, the stunned but elated underdogs walked off the field victorious—1 to 0.

There was pandemonium in the little bar. "I knew it, I knew it," shouted the "stupid woman's" husband, thumping her on the back. "I could kiss 'em all!"

There was even greater pandemonium in Hamburg's stadium where the fifteen hundred East German fans frenetically waved their black-red-gold flags, with the hammer-and-compass emblem of communism, while the thirty thousand moaning, groaning, head-shaking West Germans, their black-red-gold flags without the emblem, hanging limp, trooped slowly toward the exits, looking very much as though they had just lost the war all over again. And if one can believe the psychiatrists who call soccer "a form of ersatz war," perhaps they had.

There have been many important dates in the history of the German-German confrontation ever since January 1, 1947, when the United States and Great Britain merged their zones of occupation, thus laying the foundation for Germany's ultimate division into capitalist West and communist East. But the day that may prove to be the most significant, though the historians, being historians, will probably not even record it, was that of June 22, 1974, when East defeated West in an upset soccer victory in Hamburg's stadium.

The game embodied all the elements that have made the division of Germany one of the strangest phenomena of our age, not to mention their roles as symbols in the cold war between two sociopolitical ideologies.

Take the two coaches, for example. West Germany's Helmut Schoen and East Germany's Georg Buschner are both Saxonians and were born a scant hundred miles apart in what is now the GDR—Schoen in Dresden, Buschner in Gera. They speak the same singsong dialect, both have sons in college, both are model family men, both own poodles, both have devoted most of their adult lives to professional soccer. Yet both are symbols of Germany's division and the rise of two so different and yet so remarkably similar Germanys. Buschner is typical of the successful athlete who has placed his skills in the service of East Germany's glorification of sports and has been recompensed lavishly with all the privileges and amenities his society has to offer. The same is true of Schoen, who has led West Germany's national team to more titles than any coach before him. But there is one important difference: Schoen is a "refugee" from East Germany—one of those three million who, before the Berlin Wall was built to prevent their exodus, turned their backs on the East for economic, family, or political reasons and fled to the West.

Then there was the upset itself. In the "ersatz warfare" of sports, athletic victories have become the triumphs of governments, political systems, and ideologies. The loss shook West German self-confidence in a system which West Germans looked upon as the better one, while bolstering that of the East Germans who, despite the propaganda which daily inundated them, had long felt and regarded themselves as the "poorer relations," the ne'er-do-wells. But there is an interesting soccer-related anomaly here. The reason for the East German soccer teams being so weak for so many years that no East German would have wagered on a victory over powerful West Germany was that the regime had applied its sociopolitical principles to the game. In 1957 it had abolished all the traditional "bourgeois" local athletic clubs which had fielded teams, reorganizing them under trade and industrial union sponsorship similar to the arrangement in the USSR. Venerable old athletic associations with dues-paying members and wealthy patrons were replaced by spiritless "industry clubs," with such names as the Magdeburg Turbines or Leipzig Locomotives. In 1973, however, the system was scrapped and the local clubs reestablished, and East German soccer began experiencing a renaissance.

Or consider the shouting matches in the stadium. Here were the teams of two Germanys, with the fans of one team repeatedly screaming, "Deutschland, Deutschland!" (or "Germany, Germany!" to put it in English), thus implying that there is only *one* Germany. Yet the *other* German team refused to utter the word "Deutschland," using instead only the initials GDR, which stand for the name of its state. The implication on the Western side, of course, is that there is but *one* Germany, whose official representative is the Federal Republic. Yet that claim—maintained for nearly three decades—is automatically nullified by the game itself and the presence of the other Germany's team on the field, as well as its fans in the bleachers and its official quasi-ambassadorial representative, Dr. Michael Kohl, who shared a grandstand box with Chancellor Helmut Schmidt.

Alice would wonder at a land where so much history, so many unresolved issues, so many unanswered, and perhaps unanswerable questions come all wrapped together in a soccer ball. Fifteen years ago when I wrote of Germany's "schizophrenia" I was attempting to describe the ailment of a people trying to come to terms with their recent past; of a government that was paying out millions to victims of nazism while also paying millions to erstwhile Nazis; of a state trying its own war criminals in courts presided over by judges who had committed crimes themselves. The schizophrenia of today, if one dare call it that, is the split personality of each Germany in its relationship toward the other and in their often absurd efforts to rectify their division with their common history.

Germany's postwar division is, of course, a product of the cold war between the United States and the Soviet Union. For nearly one generation, as that war became colder, the gap between them widened inexorably. The two halves of what had been a unified nation—albeit unified for only seventy years under Prussian hegemony—became antagonists in a vitriolic and acrimonious confrontation. Each refused to recognize the other. West Germany, maintaining the fiction that there was but one Germany for which it alone had the right to speak, refused even to recognize the existence of the GDR. East Germany, maintaining the fiction that nazism had been the logical consequence of capitalism, insisted it was the only true "new" Germany because it had abolished capitalism. Their governments became victims of their own propaganda, their leaders prisoners of their own prejudices and preconceived notions. Each claimed to embody the better and more viable economic and political system and became committed to imposing it on the other as the only avenue toward reunification. Each competed ruthlessly for the loyalty, allegiance, and physical control of the German people. Economic hardship in the East, attributable to a variety of factors, among which the inefficacy of socialism is merely one and not the most important, motivated millions of East Germans to seek their luck and fortune in the miracle economy of the West. But despite the economic considerations that had motivated their flight, they were hailed in the West as "voters with their feet who chose freedom," while the East equated their migration with treason. And while each half blamed the other for causing the split and for widening it, an objective analysis of the record will reveal that each is equally to blame insofar as both were not pawns of their superpower mentors: Washington and Moscow.

To recapitulate the story of Germany's division—its tragedies, absurdities, legal intricacies, diplomatic complications, and human suffering—would go beyond the scope and intent of this book; besides, the story has been chronicled, analyzed, and interpreted often enough by others. Suffice it to say that since the start of this decade, the two Germanys have moved toward a different kind of relationship from that of the 1950s and 1960s, toward a tenuous form of peaceful coexistence.

The turning point was the October 1969 formation of the left-liberal SPD/FDP coalition government under Willy Brandt as chancellor and Walter Scheel as vice-chancellor and foreign minister in West Germany. Until then West German policy had been predicated on eventual reunification through the incorporation of the GDR into the Federal Republic and the restoration of Berlin as the capital of that reunited state. How this was to be accomplished by a West Germany which had solemnly forsworn to use military action was never clearly spelled out. The general notion, however, was that the majority of East Germans favored such a move and would support it in "free elections" and the East German Democratic Republic could somehow be "purchased" or negotiated out of the Soviet orbit where it had become, next to the USSR itself, the second most important power.

It was this policy which gave rise to many of the political burlesques of the past quarter of a century. Because Bonn was considered a temporary capital, virtually no endeavors were made to develop it into a functioning one. For decades government ministries and political parties, including the SPD, headquartered in barrackslike structures or the requisitioned mansions and scientific institutes of what had once been a comatose little university town, famous largely for the fact that Beethoven had been born there (leaving as soon as he was old enough), that Robert Schumann had gone mad and died there, and that Queen Victoria had first met Albert, a student at Bonn's University, in its romantic environs. Parliament continued to sit in the same former teachers' college where the West

German constitutional convention had first met in 1948. As recently as 1967 the British embassy was still called "Her Majesty's only mission in a cornfield" and my office, a block from the Bundestag, faced a meadow on which a shepherd grazed his flock every Friday afternoon. On the other hand, vast amounts of money were invested in the reconstruction of governmental buildings in West Berlin, such as the old Reichstag destroyed by the infamous fire in 1933 and further devastated by bombing raids during World War Two. And there was the Hallstein Doctrine, named after its author Professor Walter Hallstein, the first president of the Common Market Commission, which held that West Germany would not recognize and would break its ties to any nation that established diplomatic relations with East Germany.

Whatever the aspirations East Germany's Walter Ulbricht may have harbored for eventual reunification—and he expressed them periodically and forcefully—they were motivated by an equally unrealistic dream. For what Ulbricht, a veteran of the German Communist party's infant days and a Communist Reichstag deputy during the Weimar Republic, envisioned was a unified Communist Germany.

Both these approaches merely served to drive the two halves of Germany farther apart—politically, ideologically, diplomatically, and economically—and to harden their positions vis-à-vis each other.

Willy Brandt, upon taking office, devised a completely new formula for dealing with the "German problem." Although there is but one German people, one German "nation," this did not, he maintained, preclude the existence of two German states. At some future date they might reunify by peaceful means. Until then there was no alternative but to recognize their independence from each other. Brandt argued that by reducing cold-war tension; by eschewing postwar West German territorial claims to East Germany, to the Polish-controlled former German provinces of Silesia and Pomerania east of the Oder and Neisse rivers, and to East Prussia which had been jointly partitioned by Poland and Russia; by abjuring the 1938 Hitler-Chamberlain Munich pact under which Czechoslovakia had ceded the Sudetenland to the Reich; and by recognizing the existence of the GDR and treating it as an equal and mature state, West Germany would not only come to terms with reality but there might be a chance to reweave some of the ties that had been broken by two decades of propaganda and confrontation.

It was a risky and courageous approach, for it meant destroying innumerable political sacred cows. It meant risking the ire of millions of refugees and expellees from East Prussia, the Oder-Neisse territories, and East Germany who for decades had had dangled before them the prospect of return to their homelands by the paid functionaries and propagandists of their respective lobbies and "homeland leagues" and by politicians in Bonn. It entailed obtaining concessions from the USSR and the Soviet bloc, especially regarding guarantees concerning the territorial inviolability of an area permitting access to West Berlin—a hundred miles from the West German border and deep in the heart of East Germany—and promises of greater freedom of movement between the two Germanys themselves.

Brandt and his chief advisor, Egon Bahr, always took pains to stress that, despite their policy, relations between the two German states might never be good. But, they insisted, "this is still an improvement over the present situation in which we have no relations at all."

Within a few weeks after Brandt took office, his administration embarked on a path of multifarious, parallel negotiations involving the Soviet Union, Poland, East Germany, and the three Western powers—the United States, Great Britain, and France, who are legally still the occupiers and the guarantors for isolated West Berlin. Bahr began with Soviet Foreign Minister Andrei Gromyko the talks that were to lead to the Soviet-West German nonaggression treaty. In March 1970 Brandt travelled to the East German city of Erfurt for a summit meeting with Willi Stoph, at that time the GDR's prime minister and now its titular president. That initial "Willy-Willi conference," as the papers called it, was the first time representatives of the two Germanys had talked to each other officially. Soon after, Stoph came to the West German city of Kassel for a return engagement. Negotiations were also begun with Poland and Czechoslovakia. And in the meantime the Four-Power Agreement on West Berlin was being hammered out by U. S., Soviet, British and French representatives. By early 1971 a whole series of East-West German meetings was under way to regulate communications, traffic, and trade; to ease personal contacts; to promote cultural exchanges and legal and judicial cooperation; and to establish border delimitations, diplomatic relations, and transit rights between West Germany and West Berlin. The aim was to find means for the two states to coexist peacefully.

Finally, in December 1972 the Basic Treaty between the two Germanys was signed. In it both countries renounced the use of force against each other; promised to respect their social, economic, and political systems; and agreed to exchange permanent diplomatic representatives who would be ambassadors in all but name. The treaty, moreover, provided for a relaxation of previous travel restrictions. It enabled West Germans and West Berliners to go to East Germany as ordinary tourists, without formal invitations from their relatives, for the first time in more than two decades. It provided for twenty-two additional road and rail crossings at the heavily fortified and tightly guarded border. It entitled some 6.5 million West Germans and 2 million East Germans living close to the border to travel back and forth for one-day trips as often as thirty times annually. (Unfortunately, this privilege was extended to the East Germans only on paper.) It set up certain guarantees for the independence and security of West Berlin and for its links to West Germany, the most important being that automobiles and trucks are no longer subject to East German search and inspection, and border formalities upon entering East German territory at both ends of the transit routes have been reduced to a perfunctory minimum.

In June 1973, after the treaty had been ratified by the West German Bundestag and East German Volkskammer, a symbolic ceremony took place in Bonn's Palais Schaumburg, the offices of the chancellor. Facing each other to exchange signed, sealed, and leather-bound copies of the treaty, stood the two men whose months of tough, nit-picking negotiations had made it possible: Bahr and East Germany's Michael Kohl. Both were Germans and both spoke the same Thuringian dialect, for both had been born in that same German province in villages less than fifty miles apart. Both had served in the wartime Wehrmacht and for almost half of their lives had been citizens of the same German Reich. Yet the documents in their hands signified the first formal recognition of the two Germanys by each other.

Another year—punctuated by Willy Brandt's resignation when his administrative assistant, Guenther Guillaume, turned out to be an East German spy—was to pass before Kohl took up residence in Bonn as East Germany's quasi-ambassadorial plenipotentiary and Guenther Gauss, former editor-in-chief of *Der Spiegel* presented his credentials as West Germany's representative in East Berlin. But in the meantime scores of other countries—the United States among the last of them—extended formal diplomatic recognition to East Germany. A number of additional Communist countries established diplomatic ties with West Germany.

And both German states were admitted to the United Nations as separate countries. Although division now seemed irreversible, relations between them had entered a new era of peaceful coexistence that would have seemed inconceivable only a few years ago.

The new relationship is producing profound changes of attitudes and behavior domestically, and it is altering their roles vis-à-vis their respective partners and allies. East Germany is no longer a pliable instrument of Soviet foreign policy and West Germany no longer considers itself a diplomatic and political dwarf. Both are unquestionably flexing their muscles and acting more independently, though with a spirit of realism. And while East Germany is turning into a genuine nation state with national consciousness and public pride in its achievements, West Germany has resigned itself to the status quo of which Bonn's transition from a provisional to a permanent capital with widespread new construction is but one example.

Only the older generation in West Germany really views what has happened since 1970 as political and diplomatic resignation. For the majority of West Germans—the younger generation—it represented the enactment of a logical policy, indeed the only policy to follow, and one which both Germanys could have enacted many years earlier had they not been prisoners of their own inflexibility and victims of their own propaganda and grandiose dreams of lost nationhood.

Of course, the new relationship between the two Germanys has not brought instantaneous harmony. Numerous old problems remain unsolved and seem to defy solution. Anachronisms and anomalies bordering on the illogical and the absurd persist. The Wall dividing West from East Berlin, which is the GDR's capital, is still there, as is the 835.8-miles-long border between West and East Germany. Wall and border still bristle with barbed wire, mesh fences, watchtowers, searchlights, plowed strips of no-man's-lands, ferocious dogs, two million mines, and a network of shrapnel-shooting booby traps. Each year the GDR still spends an estimated $350 million to maintain the frontier and to pay the sixty thousand soldiers of the National People's Army who stand guard there. And those soldiers still shoot to kill any of their countrymen who attempt to cross it in flight to the West.

The Wall and the border have become incredibly porous since the signing of the treaty, that is true. But only in one direction: from West to East. Between spring of 1972 and the end of 1974 there were more than

ten million visits by West Germans and West Berliners to the GDR and
East Berlin—an influx of human contact and potentially "subversive
ideologies" which has frightened East Germany's rulers. In late 1973, it
frightened them so much that they doubled the mandatory daily exchange
of currency required of all visitors in the hope—borne out by subsequent
events—that the minimum daily exchange of DM 20 to visit Aunt Minna
or Sister Clara would keep the West Germans away. It did. Travel to the
GDR decreased by 40 percent. But the West Germans, who regarded
this as a violation of the spirit of the treaties, were not without leverage.
Hinting darkly that they would curtail the interest-free credit which East
Germany has enjoyed under inter-German trade—a facet of relations
between the two Germanys I will examine in greater detail later in this
chapter—they were able to force a reduction in the currency requirement
in October 1974. The fee—for that is really what it is—was reduced from
DM 20 to DM 13 per day. While that did not bring it down to the
original DM 10, it is an amount West Germans are willing to live with in
a period which is rather inflationary anyway.

Spying upon each other, a practice that has made the two Germanys
the most spied-upon countries in the world, will apparently continue with
the same abandon as in the past. Indeed, detente and relaxed travel
restrictions between East and West have made spying easier, since they
provide greater access and opportunities to recruit and infiltrate agents.
The case of Guillaume, besides toppling Brandt, the architect of the new
relationship, unquestionably soured relations between the two Germanys
for a while. Guenther Gauss, for example, delayed presenting his
credentials as Bonn's permanent plenipotentiary by more than a month.
But that act of diplomatic pouting is not likely to reduce the espionage
war. Indeed, East Germany sees no reason why it should be reduced.
Commenting on the Guillaume case, *Neues Deutschland*, the official
Socialist Unity party daily, stated there is "no contradiction whatsoever"
between improved relations and espionage. "Nothing in the treaty
between the two German states," the paper said, "would require the
abolition of intelligence activity by either side." If that is a clear statement
of East German intentions, then it is also clear that the East Germans
suspect the West Germans of the same intentions. People who watched
the construction of the East German mission in the Bonn suburb of Bad
Godesberg couldn't help but notice and chuckle at how GDR security
men checked every brick, every stone slab, and every girder for bugging

devices before it was put in place, then kept a twenty-four-hour watch on the construction site.

The flight of East Germans, the original cause for construction of the Berlin Wall and fortification of the borders in 1961, remains a major issue between the two Germanys. Indeed it has become a bigger one since the signing of the treaties. Relaxation of surveillance and restrictions on the transit routes between Berlin and the Federal Republic have opened new avenues of escape. Compared to the exodus of more than three million that took place before the Wall went up, the westward flow has been barely a trickle: less than forty thousand in the fourteen years since the borders were sealed. Two reasons can be cited for the reduction: the mounting difficulties and risks to life and limb entailed in escaping, and the dramatic improvements in East German living standards which serve as an inducement to stay put. But even the trickle is a source of ire, embarrassment, and concern for East German authorities, who have been trying to stop it completely. Between June 1972 and August 1974 they caught 221 professional and semiprofessional "refugee smugglers" and in July 1974 began placing them on trial, at the rate of several a day, conspicuously publishing the sentences, which ranged up to fifteen years' imprisonment, in the daily press. It was an obvious signal to Bonn to do something about the "underground railway." But there is little the West Germans can or want to do, politically and legally, about the traffic in human lives which raises complicated moral and image questions on both sides of the border.

The underground railway began operating soon after the Berlin Wall was built. While the original operators of the system were largely idealists, many of them students, in recent years it has become more and more a business for profit, attracting professionals from the world of gun-running, espionage, mercenary soldiering, and smuggling as well as criminals known to both West and East German police. The techniques, starting with the tunnels dug under the Wall in the early 1960s, have become increasingly sophisticated and increasingly expensive. The average price per escapee is now about twelve thousand dollars and some of the "body runners" even advertise their services openly in the classified columns of West German newspapers under such headings as "Family Reunions" and "Problems with Relatives in the GDR?"

The tools of the trade include automobiles with false-bottomed trunks and gas tanks, counterfeit documents and passports, ingenious mechanisms for switching car-license plates with the flick of a switch on the dashboard, and a whole network of clandestine operatives spanning the European continent from Scandinavia to Turkey, from Poland to France. Since the transit agreement providing for uncontrolled vehicular traffic between West Berlin and West Germany went into effect, truck drivers and ordinary tourists, too, have gotten involved. All a trucker need do when picking up a refugee enroute is break the seal on his van, hide the escapee inside, and put on a new, forged seal. If he has not been spotted by a passing patrol, his chances of entering West Berlin or West Germany are high. Inspection has become so perfunctory and road traffic so heavy since the signing of the treaties, that the forged seal is likely to escape notice.

Technically speaking, such a pickup violates the four-power Berlin and East-West German transit agreements. But legally speaking, no individual—only governments—can be held liable for breaking them. East Germany has an impressive array of laws against "fleeing the republic" and "trafficking in human lives" which it applies against those who are caught; but except for minor infractions, such as falsifying documents, the trafficker violates no West German law.

Morally and politically there is nothing the West German government can do at all. One of the peculiarities of the inter-German relationship, dating back to the time when the Federal Republic claimed to represent Germany as a whole, is that West Germany does not really recognize East German citizenship. The escapee is an automatic West German citizen the moment he crosses the border and there is nothing illegal about helping someone "return to his homeland." On the contrary, the smuggler, even if he is a known scoundrel who assists escapees only for pay and profit, is still hailed as a hero for helping a hapless victim of tyranny flee the "inhumane wall-building East German regime."

All discreet attempts by the government of Helmut Schmidt in the summer of 1974 to reduce the human traffic brought the chancellor nothing but virulent attacks from his Christian Democratic opposition which implied that he was in collusion with the GDR. But his failure to do anything also opened him to accusations of treaty violation by East Germany and brought about their periodic harassment of traffic on the transit routes to Berlin, which in turn enabled the CDU to contend that East Germany was breaking the agreements.

Berlin itself remains a continuing bone of contention between the two

Germanys, due in part to the ambiguity of the language in the Four-Power Agreement, especially in the Russian text and its two German translations, one East the other West. The heart of the argument, of course, is that East Germany and the Soviet Union regard and attempt to treat West Berlin as a separate political entity, as a quasi *third* Germany, but consider East Berlin an integral part of the GDR as well as its permanent capital. West Germany considers West Berlin an integral part of the Federal Republic, the quasi *eleventh* West German federal state. Nominally, it is under U. S., British, and French occupation, and the Soviets have some rights there too, although the USSR steadfastly denies that East Berlin is also still occupied or that the Western Allies have any rights there.

Indeed, it is much easier to say what West Berlin isn't than what it is. Between the extreme positions concerning its status and in the equivocal linguistic void of the various treaties, there is plenty of room for interpretation, misinterpretation, and ways to treat the city and its official representatives.

Whenever the Soviets and East Germans stage a trade fair, for example, they insist on assigning West Berlin a separate pavilion and displaying its flag. West Germans and West Berliners, however, invariably insist on exhibiting together. Compromise is not always reached. West German athletic teams have boycotted international matches whenever Soviet and East German organizers have refused to accredit West Berlin sportsmen on the team. When the Berlin Philharmonic last played in Moscow and the West German ambassador feted the musicians at a diplomatic reception, Soviet officials refused to attend. In fact, they attempted to spirit the orchestra out of town beforehand by claiming they would not be able to land in Leningrad, their next destination, because of "expected fog." This was during a summer month. When that ploy failed, the Soviet foreign ministry arranged to cut off the catering service to the embassy so that from a gastronomic point of view, the reception was a failure.

Although the status of West Berlin remains so obscure that its deputies in the Bundestag (who are appointed by the city-state government instead of being elected by West Berliners), have limited voting rights, the Bonn government makes every effort to expand West Berlin's role as a "second capital." It has established the headquarters of all manner of federal agencies there, the most recent being the environmental protection bureau whose opening in the summer of 1974 touched off one of those seemingly perennial little "Berlin crises," replete with harassment on the transit routes, formal demarches by the three Allied governments, and a one-month's delay in the scheduled U. S. diplomatic recognition of the GDR. And, of course, whenever the Federal Republic negotiates with the USSR or any other Communist country about anything, its aim is always to include West Berlin in the agreement. Thus the multibillion-dollar deal through which West Germany will sell the Soviet Union two atomic power stations in exchange for twenty years of electric power calls for including West Berlin in the grid as the central relay point.

The existence of two German states and their quasi-diplomatic recognition of each other notwithstanding, West Germans continue to have a variety of protocolar, semantic, and political inhibitions when dealing with the GDR and matters East German. For example, Bonn's terminology for the trade between the two, now that the cold-war expression "interzonal" has been dropped, is *intra*-German, while the GDR insists on calling it *inter*-German.

West Germany's mission in East Berlin has no consular service because, as a mission spokesman pointed out, "it would be a self-contradiction for us to issue visas or entry permits to people whom we regard as our own citizens. To us the East Germans are not foreigners."

The establishment of the two missions and the accreditation of their chiefs, Kohl and Gauss, raised semantic and protocolar questions of a magnitude unprecedented in the world of diplomacy. First of all, according to the Basic Treaty, they are not embassies but "permanent representations," and their heads are not ambassadors but "leaders of the permanent representations" who are not entitled to full diplomatic status but to the "equivalent of full diplomatic status." Kohl, for example, does not have diplomatic CD plates on his car but a license number starting with O, like that of the highest West German officials.

"I have never seen anything more legalistically Teutonic than this," said a veteran American newsman who has been covering German affairs since the end of the war. "The negotiations over these points have been going on for months and if they prove anything, then it's that despite their division, they both remain Germans to the marrow of their bones."

In practice, they have proven to be far more flexible than the terminology of the treaties would indicate, with each side feeling free to interpret them as they choose. Kohl, for example, unlike other heads of "foreign missions," is not accredited to the West German foreign ministry but directly to the chancellor's office, and when he was to present his credentials to President Gustav Heinemann, there was endless discussion as to whether he and Kohl should wear the traditional cutaway for such occasions or business suits. Business suits were agreed upon, as Kohl is "not an ambassador." But since East Germany has given him the formal title of both ambassador and minister, he calls himself and is addressed as "Mr. Ambassador."

The East Germans, anxious to stress the two-Germanys concept, accredited Gauss to their foreign ministry in the same manner as they did all other ambassadors, put him through the regular presentation ceremony, complete with honor guard and the playing of both national anthems, and attached diplomatic plates to his car. But Gauss' residency in East Berlin is pro forma. On weekends he commutes to his villa and family in a suburb of Hamburg. And his staff, like those of all the more than one hundred other embassies now in East Berlin, do their shopping, entertaining, and relaxing on the other side of the Wall in West Berlin where, after all, the living is more than just a mite better.

Perhaps the knottiest problem of all arose on October 7, 1974, when Kohl staged a reception in Bonn on the occasion of the twenty-fifth anniversary of the GDR's formal establishment. The notion of celebrating in the West German capital an event which only so recently West Germany officially regarded as a nonevent, had every diplomat and journalist in town eagerly alert to the developments. For Kohl there was the ticklish problem of whom to invite; and for those invited, there was the even more precarious matter of whether to attend. To the bafflement of all concerned, Kohl sent an invitation to Egon Franke, the minister of intra-German affairs, then discreetly let it be known that he wouldn't be sorry if Franke "finds it impossible to attend." But Franke came, and when asked by a mob of journalists whether he was going to congratulate Kohl on the anniversary of the GDR's founding, said with a smile: "I intend to say 'good day.'" Predictably, the opposition CDU/CSU and the papers of the right-wing, ultranationalist Axel Springer chain waxed indignant against those who had displayed "patronizing servility" by turning up for the occasion. No prominent CDU or CSU politician did. "No other free government in the world would inflict such an indignity on itself or its subjects," said Dieter Kiehl, official spokesman for Franz-Josef Strauss's CSU in Munich. "People need time to get used to reality," Egon Bahr commented laconically as he downed East German sausages and beer at the party.

Reality is not necessarily what such diplomatic beerbusts may make it appear. Although the two Germanys now have peaceful relations with each other, ideologically both remain armed to the teeth against one another. Mutual distrust remains a permanent fixture in the relationship between them, and while West Germany spares no effort to stress what unites, the GDR is determined to emphasize what divides them.

The degree of their division was never more apparent to me than it was one day in Bonn some years ago when I was browsing through a bookshop and noticed a new paperback by a group of West German journalists reporting on their trip to the GDR. It had a thought-provoking title: *Journey to a Faraway Land.* Have the two Germanys really grown *that* far apart? There is no easy answer to the question. I know many West Germans who will say: "East Germans seem more foreign to me than the French." Of eleven teenagers who wrote letters to *Die Zeit's* weekly youth forum recently, each one said flatly: "Paris seems closer to me than Leipzig." Said one of the contributors: "I can hop the next train to Paris and be there in a matter of hours. The idea of going to Leipzig would never occur to me." All blamed the growing alienation between West and East Germans on the ideological and intellectual barriers raised by the GDR, barely stopping to think how many propagandistic restrictions their own government had imposed. They were of one mind, of course, that contacts should be improved and deepened, not because of any emotional commitment to Germanism or German nationhood, but rather because of a desire to improve human relations with "all peoples in Eastern Europe." One eighteen-year-old said: "For someone like me who was born after Germany was already divided, the GDR is a foreign country like any other."

Most West Germans know so little about that country that in one recent survey less than 10 percent were able to say with reasonable accuracy how many people lived there and only a scant 6 percent had ever heard of Willi Stoph. A television study about what schoolchildren knew about the GDR and what was to be found in their social science textbooks produced results that in their own way were even more shocking than Juergen Neven-duMont's study fifteen years ago about the teaching of Third Reich history. The pupils are confronted with propagandistic clichés in which West Germany is portrayed paradisiacally, East Germany as prisonlike. Blame for Germany's division is assigned unilaterally to the Soviet Union, and the fact that West Germany established a separate state more than a year before the GDR was even founded is conveniently, or perhaps deliberately, deleted from the instructional materials. Virtually all the pupils queried believed that the refugee exodus has been motivated by "a desire for freedom," when in fact the overriding reason was pure and simple economics. Of scores of textbooks examined for the study, some were nearly a decade old and the only one that presents an objective picture of conditions in the GDR has been banned in a number of West German states because local politicians consider that picture "too favorable." Conversely, of course, what East German schoolchildren are taught about West Germany is even more of a propaganda cliché. In most of their textbooks and lesson plans the FRG is pictured as a decadent playground where Nazis, war criminals, militarists, imperialists, and capitalist exploiters run rampant, subjugating the downtrodden working masses.

Official statistics show that nearly 20 percent of all West Germans still have family ties to inhabitants of the GDR. But those ties, despite the relaxation of travel restrictions, seem to grow looser from year to year. Even those who visit with relatives regularly can be heard to remark: "We seem to have less in common and less to say to each other each time."

Strong divisive forces are at work in the language as well. A number of years ago a professor at East Berlin's Humboldt University predicted in all seriousness that the day might not be far off when shop windows in other countries could logically display signs reading, "East and West German spoken here." *Freiheit*, the Socialist Unity party daily for the East German city of Halle, once stated flatly that "the social development of the GDR and West Germany has taken so different a course over the years that a unified German national language no longer exists." While matters have not quite yet reached that point, a sort of East-speak, West-speak German is definitely evolving. There are already striking differences between the Eastern and Western versions of the *Duden*, the German equivalent to *Webster's Dictionary* and the ultimate law on all matters linguistic and grammatical. *Duden* (West) is published in Mannheim; *Duden* (East) in Leipzig. In the most recent editions more than four hundred words do not appear in one or the other, and the two books disagree in their definitions of two hundred more. The problem is not so much one of Russianisms creeping into East-German, for there is little of that, nor of the anglicization of West-German, for many Americanisms have crept into East-German as well—to the dismay of language purists and the ideological watchdogs who regard such terms as "meeting," "cocktail," "darling," "hobby sets," "suntan lotion," and "Oxford shirt" in newspaper and advertising language as "incompatible with our socialist way of life." But it is the infusion into the language of Germanic and Germanized expressions which are endemic to the society. The Mannheim *Duden*, for example, does not list "class struggle" or "class society," while the Leipzig *Duden* deletes "leisure time," "expression of opinion," "world travel," and "codetermination"—expressions which are single words in German and therefore belong in a dictionary.

On the other hand, until the signing of the Basic Treaty and the opening of East Germany to millions of West German visitors, the problem of alienation was confined mainly to West Germany. The GDR was indeed a "faraway land." But thanks to West German television, the majority of East Germans not only had a daily window on the Federal Republic but were remarkably well informed about conditions, problems, and sociopolitical developments there. No East German would have, or would today, gape with vacant stupidity when asked to identify Konrad Adenauer, Ludwig Erhard, Willy Brandt, Gustav Heinemann, Helmut Schmidt, Walter Scheel, or lesser-known Federal Republic leaders.

"Much has been written about the difficulty of crossing the wall," Stefan Heym once said. "But any electron jumps it with ease. Western radio broadcasts reach everywhere and West German TV can be clearly received in all but two districts. The brand names and advertising slogans of West German products have become household words in the GDR, and films shown by West German television are matters of public discussion on our trains and streetcars every morning."

The same cannot be said of East German TV. Even where it is readily receivable, that is, along the border and in West Berlin, it is rarely watched. West Germans have closed their minds to it because they regard it as too propagandistic. What they do see of it is replay material purchased by the West German networks or film clips shown on programs such as "Kennzeichen D"("Nationality Sign D"), devoted to comparing life in the two Germanys.

Only more travel is likely to expose larger numbers of West Germans to East German life and attitudes, but for all the great strides taken in that direction since 1972, they are but a start. Should East Germany's leaders continue to impose restrictions for fear of "ideological infection," that start will remain a halting one.

A far stronger link, though even more, perhaps, a pronounced anomaly in the inter-German relationship, is the massive trade between the two. Inter-German trade (or *intra*-German, to use Bonn's terminology which is more accurate in this case) amounts to almost DM 6 billion annually. After the United States (for the FRG) and the Soviet Union (for the GDR), each Germany is the other's second largest trading partner. And being based on the fiction that there is but one Germany—a thesis the GDR challenges vehemently in all situations except, of course, this one—it is a most privileged form of trade. Being considered intra-German, it is free of duties, taxes, and all the normal restrictions. It also makes East Germany a backdoor member of the West European Common Market, with all the benefits but none of the disadvantages of membership, a fact which has caused considerable grumbling among the allies of both Germanys. Moreover, East Germany has been granted the privilege of interest-free credit on amounts up to DM 600 million annually by the West German *Bundesbank*. This arrangement, called the "swing overdraft," enables the GDR to import more than it exports without having to pay for the imports immediately. The advantages to the GDR are enormous, but considerable for West Germany, too, which can always use the trade agreement as a lever to extract political concessions from East Berlin. The increase in the tourist visiting fee would surely not have been rescinded by the GDR had not West Germany threatened to cancel the overdraft privilege. And whenever the GDR also wants to cash in on West German investment and development projects the way Poland and the Soviet Union have done, it tends to be most conciliatory in its relations with the Federal Republic.

Much about inter-German trade appears contradictory. To repeat, the GDR, usually so insistent that it be regarded and treated as a separate, independent state, is only too happy to underscore the single-Germany concept when it comes to trade. West Germany, which for decades attempted to portray the GDR as an economically backward and deprived country, is only too happy to import some of the GDR's sophisticated goods, especially a vast array of household appliances which are sold under the brand names of mail-order houses and department store chains without the buyer ever knowing that they were manufactured in the GDR. West Germany also imports a considerable amount of agricultural produce from East Germany and has done so for years, although for decades, of course, Bonn's propaganda mill has portrayed the GDR as a country going hungry because it collectivized the free and independent farmer. Actually, East German per-acre farm yields—despite, because of, or regardless of, collectivization—are now among the highest in Europe, West or East.

The propagation of fictions and the indulgence in opportunism, such as in trade, have been developed into a sophisticated form of propaganda in the decades of Germany's division. Nowhere is this more apparent than in the GDR's claim to be the "better Germany" and the emphasis on its "Germanness" throughout the 1960s and early 1970s. Identifying itself with all of German history that was "good," it attempted to transfer the evil eras and villains to the West German ledger. It claimed to be the "true German fatherland" in a social and historic sense, a fatherland in which "the rich have been expropriated and deprived of power, a fatherland which has nothing in common with that of Hindenburg, Krupp, or Eichmann," although the GDR is no more above doing big business with Krupp these days than the Soviet Union, Poland, or Romania.

Walter Ulbricht once said: "One should never forget that Germany has two cultures and two traditions. One is the nonculture and barbaric tradition of German imperialism which expressed itself in the slaughter of millions at Auschwitz and today raises its ugly head in support of American aggression. . . . The other culture is the progressive tradition of the German nation and its humanistic heritage, represented by the forces of the working masses in the GDR. . . ."

The GDR conveniently arrogated all those figures of the German past that it considered part of that humanistic heritage. Goethe and Schiller may have been born and raised in what is now West Germany, but since they did most of their writing in Thuringia, the GDR staked a claim on them. Weimar, where Goethe lived from 1775 until his death in 1832, has developed a Goethe cult. The houses he lived in have all been restored and are visited by some 800,000 tourists annually. The town's bookstores seem to sell nothing but the works of Goethe or literature about him, and there is a flourishing souvenir industry which turns out plaster Goethe statuettes and medallions by the tens of thousands. Whatever Goethe was—and he was a highly complex man whose vanity was always in competition with his genius—the GDR portrays him as an antecedent of the class struggle. "His thought," says one Weimar guidebook, "raised and answered questions which serve as the foundation of our socialist society. His vision of man has been fulfilled by socialist man." Although Schiller also spent the last twelve years of his life in Weimar, it is the nearby city of Jena, where for a brief period he held a professorship, which claims him. And the Schiller cult in Jena is propagated just as assiduously as that of Goethe's. As one East German writer who disapproves of this sort of historic piracy has said: "Schiller became a citizen of the GDR when he settled in Jena in 1789."

The composers Bach, Handel, Schumann, and Wagner, all born in what is now East Germany, are naturally regarded as precursors of socialist music. Even Martin Luther, Thuringia's most prodigal son, was taken into the fold of what is, officially at least, an atheistic Communist state. For the purpose of the 450th anniversary of the Reformation, Luther was portrayed as a German national hero, a progressive force, a forerunner of socialism, and a kind of spiritual godfather of the GDR.

The official attitude toward the heritage of Prussia has been equally opportunistic. As is the case with Protestantism, the GDR happens to have the meccas and symbols of Prussian power on its territory and in a curious bending of historical fact, they have been turned about to serve the purposes of Germany's "first workers' and peasants' state." The historic architectural heart of Berlin is in East Berlin, much of it on Unter-den-Linden Avenue, nearly all of whose buildings and monuments have been meticulously rebuilt and restored. At one point in the late 1960s there were even rumors that Ulbricht wanted to return the equestrian statue of Frederick the Great to its original place on the avenue from the courtyard of Sans Souci Palace in nearby Potsdam, to where it had been sent during the war for safekeeping. In Potsdam itself, Frederick's favorite city of residence, as it was of all the Prussian rulers who succeeded him, the palaces and symbols of Prussian power have all been carefully preserved and attract an estimated one million visitors annually. And whenever one of them asks why a Communist state would go to such pains to protect and display the relics of German absolutism, he is told: "But they were built by the toiling masses."

The epitome of East German devotion to the Germanic spirit is the preservation of the Kyffhaeuser monument. The Kyffhaeuser is a forest-covered mountain in Thuringia that plays a central role in German nationalistic mythology. According to a centuries-old legend, Barbarossa, the twelfth-century Hohenstauffen emperor of the Holy Roman Empire, and, after Charlemagne, perhaps the most powerful of the medieval Germanic rulers, sleeps bewitched in a limestone cave deep inside the mountain. There he is awaiting the time to come forth and restore Germany to its former greatness and glory. In the late nineteenth century a huge monument, with an equestrian statue of Kaiser Wilhelm, was erected atop the mountain close to two ruined castles. The monument has served ever since as a symbol of German unity under Prussian hegemony. The Barbarossa legend and Kyffhaeuser symbolism serve the East German regime as effectively as they have all previous German regimes, albeit with the addition of a few Communist condiments. Inside the monument a bronze bas relief was installed in 1968. It depicts fist-waving, rebellious workers and peasants paying tribute to the spirit of Barbarossa. Explanatory texts and guidebooks to the monument claim that all revolutionary movements in German history have looked to the Kyff-haeuser legend for inspiration and that some of the peasant rebellions of the sixteenth century even began at the foot of the mountain. While East German authorities seem less enthusiastic about the statue of Kaiser Wilhelm under whose aegis the three-hundred-foot stone monument was built, justifiably calling him the "embodiment of arrogant Prussian-German militarism," they show no eagerness to remove the statue. For the tens of thousands of visitors who clamber up to the monument each year, the statue is one of the chief attractions. The horse, they say, "is so lifelike. You can see all its muscles and veins."

Starting in 1972 with the signing of the Basic Treaty between the two German states, the East German pendulum began swinging away from glorification of things German toward a policy of strident de-Germaniza-tion. Erich Honecker, in a dramatic about-face from the policy of his predecessor, Ulbricht, launched a drive to erase as many reminders of the common German past as possible, eliminating nearly all references to "Germany." Radio Germany, the principal broadcasting network, was renamed Voice of the GDR. The Association of German Journalists became known as the Association of Journalists of the GDR. Coins were taken out of circulation because they had the word Germany on them. The old nationality stickers for automobiles—a capital D for Deutsch-land—used in both West and East Germany were declared void, and since January 1974 East German cars and trucks display a sign reading

DDR, for Deutsche Demokratische Republik. In virtually all references to their state, East German officials employ only the initials to avoid use of the word German as much as possible. Even the national anthem is no longer being sung, merely hummed or played by an orchestra, because there is a passage in the verses that refers to "Germany, our united fatherland."

The drive for "de-Germanization" is part of Honecker's policy of *Abgrenzung*—demarcation—from West Germany and all things German since the signing of the Basic Treaty which propagates the view that although there are two German states there is but one German nation. The more Bonn has stressed that formula and interpreted it as the long-range implication of the treaty, the more East Berlin has endeavored to divorce itself from the common German heritage and to carve out its own identity.

The culmination of this policy was a series of amendments to the East German constitution which went into effect October 7, 1974, the twenty-fifth anniversary of the GDR's founding. The amendments erased all references to the unity of the German people and substituted new phrases intended to underscore the GDR's position in the common-wealth of Soviet-led Communist states. Eliminated from the preamble, for example, was the phrase, "imbued with the responsibility for showing the entire German nation the road to a future of peace and socialism. . . ." To replace those words, the Volkskammer introduced the phrase: "continuation of the revolutionary tradition of the German working class." Also deleted was a phrase that had committed East Germany to strive "to overcome the division of Germany." Particular stress was laid on the introduction of phrases which emphasize the "permanent" ideological ties between the GDR and the USSR.

Honecker's "de-Germanization" policy raises the question of whether the allure of the West is still so great, loyalty to the GDR so fragile, and the East German regime itself so unstable that it must fence itself off physically and ideologically? I cannot answer with certainty, but my impression, and that of many objective East German intellectuals such as Stefan Heym, is that this is no longer a problem. Honecker and those in his political entourage who propagate "demarcation" and "de-Germanization" are, in all probability, victims of their own propaganda and fears—like many politicians in many countries, and not just those of the Communist world. There is, it seems to me, a striking similarity between

Honecker's demarcation policy and the policy in West Germany, now jettisoned, which compelled the government to pronounce claims to the Oder-Neisse territories long after it was apparent to all that those claims would never be honored and could never be upheld. To renounce them, however, seemed like political suicide, for it was axiomatic that all those millions of refugees and expellees would vote against the party which took such a stand. Actually, the expellees—loud and militant as their professional spokesmen and lobbyists might sound—had long ago lost interest in returning to "homelands" where life would be infinitely less pleasant and affluent than in the economically miraculous Federal Republic. Willy Brandt was the first politician to be either aware of this or willing to take the risk. When and if such a politician will ever come to power in *East* Germany remains to be seen.

One thing is certain in the GDR. The standard of living has improved so dramatically in recent years that the economic sparkle of the West, which has dimmed considerably under the pressures of recession, no longer induces people to flee. If they continue to escape, and the rate has certainly increased since it has become easier again, then it is largely because of the regime's continuing restrictions on the westward travels of their own citizens. People do not want to be fenced and walled in.

"I wouldn't dream of defecting," an East Berliner told me. "I have a comfortable life and security here. All I demand is to be treated like an adult by this regime and to be free to vacation in West Germany, France, or Italy."

The mood was expressed succinctly by an East German physician who told me, a few years after the wall was built: "Now that it is there and I can no longer travel back and forth as I used to, I'd consider walking across the border barefoot to get out of here. But were the Wall to come down, I'd want to remain here, for I would then be free to come and go, wouldn't I?"

But the regime is so unsure of itself, so incapable of forgetting the trauma of the pre-1961 exodus, that it is afraid to lift the restrictions, and points to the increase in escapes as proof for the wisdom of its policy, failing to understand that the restrictions themselves are what motivate the defectors.

Honecker has surprised all those who have watched his rise to power over the years by turning out to be far more flexible and less orthodox in his rule than anyone would have predicted. But he is hardly an East German Dubcek nor does there appear to be a Dubcek waiting in the wings of power in the GDR. This is the tragedy of "liberal" Communists, some veteran Social Democrats, and "new left" intellectuals in the GDR—together a tiny minority—who dream of a freer, more liberal, really democratic way of "building socialism." Some of them placed hope in the SPD's coming to power in West Germany and harbored illusions of a "third road" to socialism in tandem with the SPD. But Brandt's fall and the SPD's waning electoral fortunes in the face of economic recession have more or less destroyed those illusions. And like their soulmates in other Communist countries, they see the tide of history moving against them. They remember only too well what happened to the most recent attempt to combine communism with genuine democracy in Czechoslovakia in 1968. The Soviet Union crushed it with tanks and guns.

Brandt's policy certainly brought Germans closer together than at any time in the previous two decades. Did that policy also pave the way toward eventual reunification? The prospects seem more remote with each passing day. Most Germans seem to realize it too. A decade ago nearly 50 percent of West Germans believed there was a chance. Today a scant 9 percent consider it a possibility, and of that small minority, most are over fifty years of age.

Of course, nothing in politics is impossible. Although unity, romantic nationalism, and chauvinism are dead issues for the overwhelming majority of young West and East Germans today, there is no guarantee that given the right political and economic constellation, it will not grip their children or grandchildren like a fever some day. But for the foreseeable future, as long as the present postwar generation of East and West Germans dominates the scene, it seems there will be two Germanys.

"We think," says Erich Honecker, "that this is an advantage to the world."

And he is probably right. Though for the people in those two Germanys one can only hope that eventually their relations with each other will be like those between other independent and sovereign peoples, that no wall will divide them, and that their border becomes as easy to cross as West Germany's boundary with Austria, Switzerland, France, Belgium, or Denmark, or as East Germany's with Poland and Czechoslovakia. Once there is free movement of peoples and ideas in both directions between the two German states, they will really be sovereign and independent, and the question of unity or division will hardly matter.

11

Profiles of
the Future

TEN years ago, just before the September 1965 Bundestag election, I wrote an article about the generational revolution that would take place in the West German parliament, regardless of which party scored best at the polls. From the list of candidates it was apparent that no matter what the outcome in the election, approximately one-third of the faces in the new house would be new and, for the most part, young. The era of the wise (and sometimes not-so-wise) old men whose public careers had spanned two generations and three German governments—the Weimar Republic, the Third Reich, and the Federal Republic—was drawing to a close. The generation which had been in its teens or in short pants and pigtails when the war ended, was grabbing for the rudder of West Germany's ship of state.

In the article, a yellowing copy of which is still in my files, I described it as "a generation of young managers and professionals raised right along with the Americanization of Europe and Germany. It is, in a large sense, materialistic, and accepts as only natural the high standard of living of postwar West German society. For the most part it is a generation free of emotional or close family ties to East Germany or the Oder-Neisse and Sudeten territories, and therefore disinclined toward sentimentalism or chauvinism, yet innately aware that the Wall in Berlin and the barbed wire on the East German border, the shootings of refugees constitute a gross injustice and act of inhumanity. But it is also a generation realistic enough to appreciate that it may have to treat the rulers of the other Germany as equals if the Wall and the wire are ever to be removed. It is a generation free of illusions. It is a generation raised in an atmosphere more worldly, more tolerant, more directed toward the U. S., Britain and the European neighbors than any Germany has known in the past. It is a generation which condemns the crimes of its parents but refuses angrily to be held equally responsible for those crimes."

This is the generation which is now in power in the Federal Republic. In the article I profiled briefly a half dozen of the prospective young deputies—all then in their thirties. Looking back, it turns out to have been a surprisingly prognostic list, which was not the intent at the time. It consisted of two Social Democrats, Dr. Hans Apel and Karl Ravens; two Free Democrats, Hans-Dietrich Genscher and Dr. Hans Friderichs; and two members of the CDU/CSU, then the governing party, Dr. Bernhard Vogel and Dr. Heinrich Geissler. All six are now government ministers at the federal or state level, men who, disregarding the fortunes and misfortunes of partisan politics, are already guiding and will, for years to come, continue to guide the destiny of West Germany.

Apel, born in 1932, is the minister of finance and the youngest member of Helmut Schmidt's cabinet. Friderichs, a year older, is minister of economics and the second youngest cabinet member. Genscher, now vice-chancellor, minister of foreign affairs, and national chairman of the FDP, was born in 1927, the same year as Ravens, who is federal minister of urban affairs. Bernhard Vogel, forty-three, is minister of culture and education in the Rhineland Palatinate and chairman of the CDU in that state, a position he won in 1974 following a hotly contested party election in which the rival candidate was Geissler, forty-five, the state's minister of health and welfare.

Vogel, who replaced Helmut Kohl, the forty-five-year-old national CDU chairman and potential future chancellor, as the Rhineland-Palatinate's state Christian Democratic leader, is somewhat of a political anomaly in West Germany. He is the younger brother of Dr. Hans-Jochen Vogel, himself only 49, the former mayor of Munich, now federal minister of justice and state chairman of the *Social* Democratic Party in Bavaria. In a sense, the Vogel brothers represent everything that is new and different about politics in West Germany today. Both are pragmatic, unemotional, highly intelligent managers of government, committed to the principles of honesty and integrity in public affairs. As leaders of the two major opposing parties, albeit in different states, they are also dedicated, as Bernhard Vogel once put it, to "imbuing politics with a spirit of fairness and tolerance"—a spirit that governs their relationship within their family. But above all, they are typical of that new generation now in the driver's seat.

Its era really began when Helmut Schmidt became chancellor in May 1974. His was the first West German administration whose members, for the most part, no longer had roots in the ill-fated Weimar era. Of the fifteen members in fifty-six-year-old Schmidt's cabinet, only one, Egon Franke, 62, the minister of intra-German relations, is older than the chancellor himself. No less than ten are under fifty, and the two youngest—Apel and Friderichs—were literally still in diapers when the Weimar system collapsed and Hitler came to power, and barely on the threshold of puberty on May 8, 1945. In Germany, where hoariness had so often been equated with political wisdom, this marked a significant departure from tradition. The days of the father figures, who had either tried to make amends or shared responsibility for the mistakes of Germany's past, were over at last.

The first postwar chancellor, Konrad Adenauer, had been born in 1876—the year of Custer's last stand—and was seventy-three when he was sworn in. As mayor of Cologne from 1917 until the Nazis deposed him in 1933, he was already a powerful political figure when the kaiser was still on the throne. During the turbulent fourteen years of the Weimar Republic he was twice under serious consideration for the chancellorship.

Adenauer used to consider his successor, Ludwig Erhard, "a young upstart." But Erhard himself was sixty-seven when he became chancellor in 1963 and campaign managers unabashedly ascribed his vote-getting success in part to his "grandfatherly image." Although he had not been in politics during the Weimar era, he grew to maturity under its traumatic impact.

Kurt Georg Kiesinger, sixty-two when he succeeded Erhard in 1966, was not only a product of the Weimar years but was so unfavorably impressed by them that he had joined the Nazi party in 1933, serving it faithfully and with considerable enthusiasm in influential government propaganda positions until 1945.

Even Willy Brandt, though only fifty-six when elected chancellor in 1969, was an intellectual outgrowth of the Weimar era, for he started in politics as a teenager and was only nineteen when he had to flee to Norway after Hitler came to power.

But Helmut Schmidt, despite having served in the Wehrmacht and as an officer at that, marked a generational milestone. The years separating him from the German past were never more apparent than in the government declaration he addressed to parliament. Only a man of his generation, or younger, could have said almost nonchalantly that "our inflation rate is merely 7.1 percent and the lowest among the world's top twenty-four industrial nations." For any German just a few years older than Helmut Schmidt, "inflation" remains an awesome, frightening word that conjures chilling memories of 1923 when a loaf of bread cost 32 billion marks and Adolf Hitler staged his abortive beerhall putsch in Munich. "You have no idea what that word means to us," an elderly left-wing intellectual once remarked to me. "For people my age 1923 is a memory indelibly etched on our psyche." But in 1923 when Hitler putsched in Munich, Helmut Schmidt was not quite five years old.

The youthfulness of his administration provided it with an entirely new accent that became apparent within the first few months of his having taken office. The business of government, it was soon obvious, was being conducted largely by men whose political consciousness had been formed in the years since World War Two. The majority of his cabinet members have been in federal politics for only a decade or less. They are pragmatists—technicians rather than theoreticians of politics—who like Schmidt himself care little for slogans and last hurrahs, but for getting a job done.

A strikingly similar generation of politicians has come to power in East Germany since Ulbricht's fall in 1971, more specifically, since his death in 1973. Like Adenauer, Ulbricht was born a subject of the kaiser. He served as a soldier in World War One and became a leading figure in the German Communist party during the Weimar era; and from 1929 until Hitler came to power, he was one of the party's front-benchers in the Reichstag. It followed only logically that when he returned to Germany in 1945 after many years in exile, most of them spent in Moscow, and began building up the apparatus of his Socialist Unity party, a fusion between Communists and Social Democrats, he would draw on the men he knew and trusted, men of his generation and experience. And like the leaders in West Germany, the GDR's often gave the impression of being primarily preoccupied with the political battles of the past rather than the present and future. The legacy of Weimar and the Third Reich ran deep in their veins.

Erich Honecker, who succeeded Ulbricht as party chief, is a man of Willy Brandt's generation. Indeed, he is but one year older and, like Brandt, he was a teenage political activist on whom the last few years before Hitler came to power certainly left their mark. And while Brandt militated against the Nazis from Scandinavian exile, Honecker was an underground Communist resistance fighter, finally arrested in 1935 and sentenced to ten years in Brandenburg penitentiary, from which he was not released until Soviet troops freed him in the spring of 1945. But despite the generational parallel between Brandt and Honecker, there is a striking difference between the two which makes Honecker more a politician of the Schmidt than Brandt genre. For the first ten years in East Germany, Honecker was the leader of the Freie Deutsche Jugend (FDJ), the party's Free German Youth organization. And while hardly of an age himself that could still be called youthful, he surrounded himself with young men and women in their late teens and early twenties who subsequently became his political power base and have since then followed him to the apex of leadership. Like Schmidt's team, they are men in their forties who regard themselves as technicians rather than theoreticians of politics. The Third Reich—that was their childhood; the Weimar and kaiser eras—those are already ancient history.

The nature of Communist politics being what it is, the change since Ulbricht's demise has been slower and more subtle than in West Germany: a promotion from candidate status to full voting membership in the politburo here, a demotion from the party secretariat to a first vice-premiership there. Of the sixteen full members of the SED's politburo, twelve are veterans of the Ulbricht era, including eighty-one-year-old Friedrich Ebert, Jr., the son of Weimar Germany's first president. But Honecker's men are on the move. Those who are not yet full members of the politburo are candidates and central committee secretaries. They have been made the party leaders of East Germany's fifteen administrative districts—political baronries as powerful in the East German scheme of things as the nominally autonomous constituent republics of the Soviet Union. And, they have been inserted in key positions of the governmental administration under Prime Minister Horst Sindermann, sixty, a Honecker appointee.

They are men like Werner Lamberz, forty-six; Werner Krolikowski, forty-seven, and Werner Jarowinski, forty-eight—all three central committee secretaries, with Lamberz in charge of agitation, Krolikowski responsible for the economy, and Jarowinski the party's watchdog for foreign trade and supply. The younger of the "three Werners,"—Lamberz and Krolikowski—have been promoted to full politburo membership since Ulbricht's fall. Jarowinski is still in a candidate's slot, but no one expects him to remain there long. One of Honecker's ploys since 1971 has been to pack the politburo with candidate members while he waits for chairs to empty for them in the inner sanctum itself. Thus, he has brought in Werner Felfe, forty-six, his appointee as party boss of Halle and his former deputy in the Free German Youth; Joachim Herrmann, forty-six, the editor-in-chief of the party daily, *Neues Deutschland*, a veteran journalist who started his career as a copyboy in rubble-strewn East Berlin in 1946 and who, from 1952 to 1962 edited *Junge Welt*, official organ of Honecker's Free German Youth movement; Inge Lange, forty-eight, central committee secretary for women's affairs and, like the others, a veteran youth movement functionary under Honecker; Konrad Naumann, forty-five, party boss of the district of Berlin, and in the late 1940s and early 1950s, one of Honecker's closest aides in the FDJ; Harry Tisch, forty-eight, party chief of Rostock district.

The only party secretary who is not yet either a full or candidate member of the politburo is Horst Dohlus, fifty, in charge of cadres and party organization and also a longtime Honecker protégé. In addition, Honecker has also filled the leadership positions in the districts of Leipzig, Frankfurt-on-the-Oder, and Dresden with his men. All of them are in their mid-forties, and won their political spurs in the FDJ when Honecker was its chief.

Most of these men and the sole woman, whom Honecker has appointed and promoted are, as Joachim Hermann once described himself, members of that generation "which grew up in the air raid shelters." A few may just be old enough to have been drafted as teenaged antiaircraft gunners or *Volkssturm* fighters in the last weeks of the war. But they have spent their entire adult lives under East German-style communism and owe their careers to it. Unlike the older generation, which Honecker will eventually ease out of the seats of power—Communist and Socialist veterans such as Ebert, Erich Mueckenberger, Albert Norden, Herbert Warnke, Kurt Hager, and Alfred Neumann—they know and care little about the ideological debates or the tempestuous and fratricidal battles that shook the party in the 1920s, the 1930s, and even the 1940s. The Spanish civil war, exile in Moscow, imprisonment by the Gestapo, the Stalinist

purges, street-fighting with the Nazis, the Comintern, and even something as recent as the Tito–Stalin split—these are mostly legends for these
men who will be the leaders of East Germany tomorrow, the successors
to Honecker, Sindermann, and Willi Stoph. There is no question of their
loyalty to the system or of their total dedication to the aim of making it
work.

West Germany's political system being infinitely more democratic,
more transparent to public scrutiny, and more susceptible to the favors of
the electorate, safe predictions for the future are of course harder to make.
A decade ago when I profiled Friderichs, Apel, Genscher, and Ravens, I
did so only because they were representative of the members of the
younger generation then certain to enter parliament. But I would not
have predicted a future for them as cabinet members, since the prospects
of the SPD ever forming a government seemed slim and with a
pronounced trend toward a two-party system, the future of the FDP,
Germany's counterpart to Britain's Liberal party, did not seem too
promising. Nor would I want to venture onto the thin ice of political
crystal-gazing now.

Unquestionably, both Genscher and Friderichs will be members of
cabinets through the end of this decade and probably well into the next.
As leaders of the third party, their political future seems assured, for the
FDP regards itself as open to both sides. It was Adenauer's coalition
partner for fourteen years, from 1949 to 1963; Erhard's, from 1963 until
it broke with him in 1966, bringing his government to fall; and then it
was out of power only during the period of the "grand coalition" between
the two big parties, reentering the administration as the SPD's junior
partner following the 1969 election. Although the mood among the
FDP's younger members and supporters is to keep the marriage with the
Social Democrats going indefinitely, members of the party's more
conservative wing, especially its chairman, Genscher, and vice-chairman,
Friderichs, have intimated that they do not rule out another partnership
with the CDU/CSU after the 1976 election. Since 1949 the FDP has
been the little tail that has wagged the dog, and barring an absolute
majority by either of the two major parties, it is likely to have that role in
the future. Genscher and Friderichs will be the two principal benefici-
aries. Both are what Germans call *vollblut politiker*—thoroughbred
politicians who have made politics their career.

The son of a lawyer and a lawyer himself, Hans Dietrich Genscher is a native of Halle in East Germany and still speaks with the pronounced dialect of his native Saxony. A draftee soldier during the last year of the war, he joined the Liberal Democratic party, East Germany's version of the FDP, in 1946 while a student in his hometown's university. Increasing Soviet and Communist pressure on the party, and difficulties in pursuing his studies because of his nonproletarian, bourgeois background, persuaded him to flee in 1952 to West Germany, where he immediately joined the FDP. After getting his law degree in Hamburg, he was hired as an administrative assistant for the FDP's Bundestag faction, eventually rising within the professional party apparatus to become the FDP's national executive director, a job he kept until his election to parliament in 1965. Four years later, when the SPD–FDP coalition was formed, he entered Brandt's first cabinet as interior minister, a position he held until May 1969 when Vice-Chancellor and Foreign Minister Walter Scheel was elected president of the Federal Republic and resigned his cabinet post as well as the leadership of the FDP. Genscher, long his heir apparent, inherited both positions. That his ascendancy to the foreign ministry, vice-chancellorship, and chairmanship of the FDP happened to coincide with Helmut Schmidt's assumption of the chancellorship, was an accident of timing and had nothing to do with Willy Brandt's resignation during that same week. Had Brandt not resigned, Genscher would have become his foreign minister and vice-chancellor instead of Schmidt's, for Scheel's election to the presidency was assured, and as president he had to relinquish both his government and party positions.

Physically, Genscher contradicts the image of the stylish, immaculately tailored, urbane, and widely traveled "new" German. He looks like the embodiment of sauerkraut, boiled potatoes, and beer. A huge, hulking figure given to blubberiness, he complains loudly but resignedly when image-makers force him to pose for publicity pictures on an exercycle or home-rowing machine. His baggy suits usually look as if they were off the rack and had hung there several fashion seasons too long.

Notwithstanding his own pragmatic and sometimes elbowing approach to government, Genscher is totally committed to liberalism and democracy and admits frankly that he still prefers being a member of parliament to being a minister in the cabinet. Following the SPD–FDP victory in 1969, he insisted that "we should speak not of a transfer of power but of functions and duties."

As Brandt's interior minister, however, he exercised and held more power than anyone in the cabinet with the exception of Brandt himself. He was the nominal chief of Germany's entire federal civil service, commanded the armed border troops that guard the frontier with East Germany, and was responsible for internal security.

It was Genscher who took credit for smashing the Baader–Meinhof anarchist gang. But it was also Genscher who was in command of police operations during the Arab terrorist attack at the 1972 Olympic Games in Munich. And to his embarrassment, he was politically responsible for the lax security that enabled East Germany's superspy, Guenther Guillaume, to penetrate right into Brandt's chancellory. Genscher's knowledge of world affairs was limited when he became foreign minister, and on the smooth diplomatic parquet he did not cut the elegant figure of his predecessor and political mentor, Walter Scheel. But after more than six months on the job, the rough edges began to wear off. Moreover, what he may have lacked in diplomatic finesse, Genscher soon made up for with the cagey negotiating skill of the professional politician.

Through it all, he has remained more a parliamentarian. He prefers to drive his own official limousine, rather than be chauffeured, and to this day still lives in the modest Bonn row-house, which he bought years ago, with his second wife and their small daughter.

Hans Friderichs is a politician of an entirely different cut. Tall, handsome, slightly balding, slightly graying, and obviously on to one of the best tailors in Bonn, he cuts a dashing figure and bears a remarkable resemblance to equally dashing French President Valéry Giscard d'Estaing. He is in many respects a total product of the Adenauer and Erhard age of German history—those two postwar decades of the "economic miracle" when prosperity was all that counted and it looked as if it would go on forever.

Born in 1931, the son of a Catholic country doctor, Friderichs is a native of the border region of Luxembourg and France—the Moselle highlands near Trier, the erstwhile Rome of the North and, ironically, also the birthplace of Karl Marx. A "bright boy," he studied law, got his doctorate at age twenty-eight and his first job as an official of the Rhine-Hesse chamber of commerce in 1959, remaining there for four years. As a student he had never shown any particular interest in politics and might never have become a politician had he not gotten involved in a school strike in the Rhine-Hesse area in 1963. The issue in the strike—division of schools along denominational lines—persuaded him to join the FDP's youth movement.

In a subsequent local election he became a county councillor in Bingen on the Rhine and was also elected deputy county chairman of the FDP. It was there that he first caught the eye of Genscher, who asked him to come to Bonn as his deputy in the professional management of the party. Both entered parliament in 1965, and when Genscher became FDP whip in the Bundestag, Friderichs replaced him as the party's salaried executive director.

Although Friderichs planned the FDP campaign in 1969, he gave his own party few chances, and just a few weeks before the election accepted a post as the senior civil servant in the ministry of agriculture and wine-growing in his native Rhineland Palatinate under State Prime Minister Helmut Kohl, now the national chairman of the CDU. Politically, that was a mistake, for, of course, the FDP and SPD won that election and formed a coalition government. Friderichs was on the outs with the FDP while in the service of Kohl, the opposition CDU's candidate for chancellor. But the price he had to pay was minimal. Three years later, over the vehement objections of party cronies, who still refuse to forgive him his brief defection, and the skepticism of the SPD which regarded him as too conservative, Friderichs was back in Bonn as a member of Brandt's cabinet and minister of economics. One smoke-filled-room debate over his appointment is said to have lasted twelve hours.

It was certainly a sensational advance and comeback, and Friderichs wasted no time in trying to prove to his cabinet colleagues that he deserved it. A man who seems to thrive on trouble, he has, thus far, done a better job of coming to grips with stagflation, recession, and the international energy crisis than any economics minister in the Western world.

Following Genscher's promotion from the vice-chairmanship to the leadership of the FDP in 1974, Friderichs was named to succeed him in the party's Number Two spot in a hotly contested battle at a special FDP convention. His political future is virtually assured, regardless of who wins in 1976. For if Helmut Kohl and the CDU should win a plurality, Friderichs is as likely to enter Kohl's cabinet as he would the next one of Helmut Schmidt.

Of all the Social Democrats in Schmidt's current cabinet, one has excellent prospects of becoming chancellor himself one day: Hans Apel. His political future depends on his party's fortunes at the polls and on when Helmut Schmidt decides to relinquish the reins to him. His chance could come as early as 1980, when he will be forty-eight and Schmidt sixty-two, but no later, it would seem, than 1984. By then he will be the most accomplished politician in Western Europe—an accolade almost due him today.

His rise has been nothing short of meteoric and totally deserved, for Hans Apel is a political Wunderkind par excellence. Ten years ago when he first entered parliament he was almost totally unknown. Today, as minister of finance, he holds the national purse strings, determines the federal budget, and, as money manager of the world's second richest country, is clearly one of the most powerful men on the globe.

Born in Barmek, one of Hamburg's poorest districts, he worked his way through university, getting degrees in economics and a doctorate in political science. After graduation, and totally fluent in English and French, he went to Luxembourg as a salaried staffer of the Socialist faction in the Parliament of Europe, remaining there until his election to the Bundestag on the SPD ticket as deputy for Hamburg-North in 1965. To this day, when asked what his profession really is, Apel replies: "I am a European Common Market civil servant on indefinite leave of absence." But he has also been a stevedore, a metal and steel worker, and continues to be a prolific writer of public affairs books, the most successful to date having been *Diary of a Bundestag Deputy*, an outspoken critique of the back-bencher's role in parliament, written during the frustrating years of his first term in the house. By 1972 he had moved from the back to the very front benches and was named deputy minister of foreign affairs for European questions. In 1974 when Helmut Schmidt relinquished the finance ministry to become chancellor, Apel was named his successor.

He is bluntly outspoken, with a tongue as sharp as his mind. But being a poor boy who can still talk the language of his proletarian constituency, he is also a highly popular vote-getter who carried his district with a resounding 57 percent against two other opponents during the last election. Somewhat baby-faced, totally self-confident, and a man who does his homework thoroughly, he was once described by *Die Zeit* as "a 100 percent professional politician in a sailor suit." Asked whether such clichés bother him, Apel replied: "I don't have time to think about them." He is too busy working toward his future.

The man who could dim Apel's future is Helmut Kohl, the prime minister of the Rhineland-Palatinate and since early 1973, national chairman of the CDU. In June 1975, following a protracted power play within the party, Kohl was also formally chosen as the CDU's candidate for chancellor in the 1976 election.

Kohl, the son of a senior civil servant, was born in 1930 in Ludwigshafen on the Rhine, a chemical manufacturing center. He became active in CDU politics as a teenager, and continued to mix political activities with education while a history and political science major at the universities of Frankfurt and Heidelberg in the 1950s. With a doctorate to his credit, he went to work as an advisor to the Chemical Industries Association in his hometown and campaigned successfully first for a seat in the Ludwigshafen city council, later in the Rhineland-Palatinate state legislature. By 1966, at age thirty-six, he became the CDU's state chairman.

He made his mark during the 1967 state election campaign which he ran with totally American methods, including such unprecedented and un-German tactics as door-to-door canvassing. This resulted in a 52 percent majority for the CDU, only 42 percent for the SPD, and 6 percent for the FDP. Kohl's reputation as a spectacular vote-getter was established and his selection as the party's national leader, while retaining the Rhineland-Palatinate state premiership, seemed preordained. The dual role presents political problems, however, for Kohl cannot project from the provincial backwater of his state capital in Mainz the image of a national figure that his party needs. He has tried, nonetheless, making frequent pronouncements on network television and going on fact-finding junkets abroad—including trips to East Germany, the Soviet Union, and the Republic of China—to create the impression that he is as well-founded in world affairs as he is in the parochial politics of West Germany's fourth smallest state.

He is a Christian Democratic politician of a new type. Tall, easy-going, pipe-smoking, and popular, he is regarded as a liberal in a party that tilts to the right, and seems totally free of the strident, militant, self-righteous antileftism that was the CDU's ideological trademark and campaign slogan for two decades. Unlike his primary rival in the party, Franz-Josef Strauss, and the rest of the CDU/CSU's old guard which won its political spurs in the cold war, Kohl does not oppose the SPD-FDP *Ostpolitik*, does not hunt for Communists under his bed, and is a firm advocate of social justice and social welfare. He is keenly aware of the generational change that has been taking place in West German politics during the past decade. He once called it "more than just a rejuvenation of politics, but a transformation of political thinking." In 1969 he declared with a firmness that raised eyebrows among other CDU leaders: "I already represent changes in policy which will probably not become the CDU's platform until 1975." That may have sounded arrogant, but it was a remarkably accurate prognosis. For Kohl it is a goal. The only man who could thwart its realization and turn the political clock backwards is Franz-Josef Strauss.

Strauss is, and has been for decades, one of the most powerful and enigmatic figures in Christian Democratic politics. Now sixty, he has been on the political scene since 1949 when he was elected from Bavaria to the Bundestag, of which he has been a member without interruption for twenty-six years. As minister of atomic science, defense, and finance, he served in a number of cabinets under Adenauer and Kiesinger. He is clearly the most controversial politician in West Germany today and in many respects the most threatening and ominous, for his personal ambitions seem boundless and his powers, as leader of a cohesive bloc without which the CDU is helpless, immense.

That bloc is the CSU, the Bavarian Christian Social Union, of which Strauss is chairman. It has won and lost national elections in total symbiosis and tandem with its bigger "northern sister," the CDU, since the Federal Republic's founding. But it is not merely the CDU's Bavarian "wing" or "state organization." It is a full-fledged independent party in its own right, founded after World War Two under specifically Bavarian conditions.

Unlike the other German states, Bavaria has a thousand-year history of virtually unbroken territorial integrity and a deep sense of autonomy, conceived during the Thirty Years War and nurtured in opposition to Prussia's hegemonical strivings for centralism in the nineteenth century. It was Bavaria's uniqueness which gave rise to the CSU as a distinctly Bavarian party, based on Christian social ethics.

No other political party in West Germany, however, not even the CDU under Konrad Adenauer, came to be so totally centered on its leader as the CSU on Strauss. With but few exceptions, the party presidium, executive committee, and professional staff became his personal instruments. Bavaria's fourth-term CSU prime minister, Alfons Goppel, is largely a benign figurehead. The party weekly, *Bayernkurier*, is for all practical purposes Strauss' personal mouthpiece and he is its publisher.

The CSU's uniqueness caused no problems in the Adenauer era and for some time after. Adenauer's shrewd politicking and strong personality held the two together. His policy for postwar Germany also dovetailed with Bavaria's and Strauss' own concept of a Christian bulwark against Communist encroachment on Europe. Moreover, following his forced resignation from the defense ministry in 1962 for having lied to parliament about his personal involvement in the police raid on the editorial offices of the *Spiegel* magazine that year, Strauss was temporarily offstage.

In 1966 he returned to Bonn as finance minister and more powerful than ever. But then the CDU began changing. Since losing the 1969 election it has tried to appeal to a broader spectrum of "half-left and half-right" voters and become more flexible in East-West affairs, leaving the Bavarian CSU as the sole custodian of conservatism and the holy grail of German national destiny.

Although Strauss paved the way for Kohl's ascendency to the chairmanship of the CDU, the evidence is persuasive that he did so only to manipulate Kohl as a puppet long enough to clear the decks for his own nomination as the chancellor candidate of both parties. For a while in the fall of 1974 and spring of 1975 it looked as if that ploy might succeed. In a state election in Bavaria, Strauss' CSU won a record-setting 61 percent of the votes. And whenever he spoke up north, where his shirt-sleeved, beer-drinking, and rostrum-pounding antics were expected to turn voters off, he filled auditoriums to the rafters.

But several events killed his chances in the party, the most notable among them being a secret strategy speech to Bavarian politicians in November 1974 during which he called for all-out confrontational tactics against Schmidt's government, even if it meant sacrificing the national welfare and letting inflation and unemployment run rampant, so that the voters would blame the SPD/FDP coalition. Moreover, a series of state elections in the spring of 1975, during which Strauss had campaigned actively, left little doubt that although he could fill auditoriums, most people came to see and hear the burly Bavarian out of curiosity rather than conviction. In CDU councils the feeling was strong that Strauss had hurt more than he had helped. The nomination for the chancellorship went to Helmut Kohl.

That left Strauss with three choices. He could bow to the will of the CDU and accept whatever post Kohl might offer him in the shadow cabinet—probably vice-chancellor and foreign minister. He could resign himself to leaving the national scene and becoming Bavaria's prime minister when Goppel retires in 1978. Or he could expand the CSU beyond the borders of Bavaria, ally it with a number of ultraconservative and superpatriotic splinter groups, such as the League for a Free Germany (BFD) which polled 3.4 percent of the vote on its first try in the West Berlin city-state election in March 1975, and launch a nationwide fourth party appealing to the far right.

At the time of this writing he had not yet made up his mind.

If he takes the plunge, it will obviously damage the CDU irreparably, for one-fourth of the votes it has always gotten nationwide were those CSU votes from Bavaria. But there are many in the CDU who would view Strauss' and the CSU's secession as a blessing. These are the new, moderate, pragmatic, middle-of-the-road Christian Democrats—men and women in their thirties and forties—who have gently nudged Konrad Adenauer's old party to the left.

One of them is Bernhard Vogel, who has succeeded Helmut Kohl as state leader in Rhineland-Palatinate and will eventually take his place as the state's prime minister too. Another is Kurt Biedenkopf, the CDU's executive manager and general secretary. Biedenkopf, forty-five, and, like Kohl, a native of Ludwigshafen, gave up a brilliant academic career to become the CDU's full-time manager in Bonn. An exchange student in the United States in 1949 and 1950, he has a doctorate in law and at the age of thirty-eight became the youngest vice-chancellor of a West German university. Dapper—in 1973 the necktie manufacturing industry proclaimed him "tie man of the year"—he is the incarnation of the modern German. He detests ideological double-talk in politics and empty slogans, displays a sporting freshness in debate, and flatly refuses to engage in Strauss-like mud-slinging or to bring personalities into an argument. A tenured professor, he is surrounded by an intellectual aura but is also a self-made man and a man of action. Despite his academic background, he has also worked as a mechanic and electrician and has built a whole fleet of battery-driven model boats. His experience in the United States left an indelible impression on him. The CDU he has been trying to create since entering parliament in 1972 and becoming the party's secretary general a year later, would be committed to the basic values and pragmatic genuine democracy which, Biedenkopf says, "I learned during my stay in America."

One of the youngest CDU politicians is twenty-five-year-old Matthias Wissmann, a law student and national leader of the party's youth organization, the *Junge Union*. Since becoming the organization's chairman in October 1973, Wissmann has tried to reshape it from the political career-building freshman team, which it was for many years, into an active youth-oriented movement that is as critical of party policy as the Young Socialists and Young Democrats are of the SPD and FDP. Wissmann is attempting to move the Young Union into political left field and has already proven so successful that Biedenkopf has admiringly called him a "tough but fair opponent in party caucuses."

Though Wissmann is not yet a member of the Bundestag, his generation is already well represented there. The youngest deputy of all—Andreas von Schoeler, a Free Democrat—is now twenty-eight and was only twenty-five when he entered parliament for the first time in November 1972. Helmut Sauer, a CDU representative, is, at thirty, the next youngest; he was twenty-seven when elected. Juergen Moellemann, another Free Democrat, is five months older than Sauer; and Dr. Uwe Holtz, the youngest SPD deputy, was twenty-eight when elected in 1972. Holtz, in fact, pulled off the political miracle of defeating one of the grand old veterans of postwar West German politics, Gerhard Schroeder, the former minister of interior, foreign affairs, and defense, by sixteen thousand votes in Duesseldorf-Mettmann, a district which Schroeder had carried with comfortable majorities uninterruptedly since 1949. One of the youngest second-term deputies is Volker Hauff, thirty-five, who was elected to his first term at age twenty-nine in 1969 and named deputy minister of research and technology in 1972, following his election to his second term from a district in Baden-Wuerttemberg that traditionally had been a safe CDU constituency.

Indeed, of the Bundestag's 496 members (excluding the 22 appointees from West Berlin), nearly one-fourth were born after Hitler came to power and of these, 39 were not yet of school age when the war ended on May 8, 1945.

The men and women in their thirties and early forties are also staking out their claims in the state governments. The governing mayor of the city-state of Hamburg, a position equal to that of a state prime minister, is thirty-eight-year-old Hans Ulrich Klose, of whom even SPD veterans say: "He's just a little smarter and better than everyone else. His analysis of any situation is always more to the point and more accurate than anyone else's, and his physical resilience is greater. And while the rest of us are still talking about a problem, he just goes out to solve it."

A thirty-four-year-old Social Democrat, Klauss Matthiesen, is his party's floor leader in the Schleswig-Holstein state legislature and almost led it to victory in the state election in April 1975.

At thirty-five, Rita Waschbuesch, mother of four and the Saarland's minister of health and welfare, is the youngest full cabinet member of any state or the federal government. And while she insists that her ambitions do not extend beyond power in Saarbruecken, a national victory by the CDU, of which she is a member, could easily lead to her quick promotion to the cabinet in Bonn.

Although he is now forty-nine, Klaus Schuetz, Willy Brandt's successor as governing mayor of West Berlin, continues to rank as one of the leaders of the younger generation of SPD politicians. Schuetz, for nearly two decades one of Brandt's closest aides and stanchest supporters, managed both the successful 1965 and 1969 campaigns, and during the grand coalition government when Brandt was foreign minister, served as his deputy. Although he says frankly that he misses being in the foreign office, he has given assurances that he has "no ambitions of taking over a new post outside this city." And in his present post, of course, he heads a government which the Soviet Union and the GDR would like to treat as the "third Germany."

While Schuetz will probably remain in Berlin, one of his fastest rising protégés, thirty-five-year-old Guenter Struve, still has his sights set on Bonn. Struve, who is currently the Berlin cabinet's official press spokesman, was one of the key figures in the SPD's 1965 and 1969 campaigns, serving as Brandt's chief speechwriter. Riding on the campaign train on several occasions, I had ample opportunity to watch Struve in operation. What made the greatest impression on me then and has remained indelible ever since, was the dog-eared copy of Theodore White's *The Making of the President 1960* that young Struve clutched in his hands wherever he went and referred to as a Bible. Patterning Brandt's campaigns after those of John F. Kennedy struck me, then as now, as symbolic of the changes in Germany.

How safe is West Germany's democracy in the hands of these new, younger leaders? Very safe, it seemes to me. Much has been said and written in the Federal Republic about the dangers to it in the past year or two. And it would be both illusory and naive to deny that it is being challenged, sometimes even threatened. While there is no danger of a neo-Nazi or right-wing extremist group at present—the National Democratic Party having been relegated to the political fringes—two ultraconservative parties just a breath away from NPD ideology did form themselves in 1974. One, the *Bund Freies Deutschland* (League for a Free Germany), based in West Berlin, is a party with a single-plank platform: reversing Ostpolitik and renewing the cold war era. Its leaders—ultranationalist and far-right journalists and politicians—are for the most part men in their fifties and sixties who sound the slogans and ideologies of yesteryear. The other party, which established itself just a few days after the BFD was founded in November 1974, calls itself the Deutsche Soziale Union. No less conservative than the League of a Free Germany, it has a more broadly based platform and has made no attempt to hide its ambition of joining forces with Strauss' Bavarian Christian Social Union to form a viable fourth party with Strauss as leader.

Both the new BFD and DSU represent one aspect of a German political scene which since the early 1970s has been moving from consensus to polarization. The other pole is represented by the increasingly militant leftists: those within the SPD's youth organization; two Peking-oriented Communist parties; the extremist student groups who would like to keep the universities in chaos; and last but not least, the anarchists who eschew neither terrorist bombings nor political kidnapping and assassination in the pursuit of their goals.

All these groups, left and right, are miniscule, and their importance has been vastly overstated. But what they lack in membership and support, they make up for in the militancy of their slogans and the violence of their action. In a country where political polarization to extremes resulted in chaos once, no one can be blamed for observing them with alarm. And since their machinations occur at a time of economic recession and growing unemployment, the compound that once before led to catastrophe in Germany, the alarm is even more understandable. But it is also the alarm of a people who sometimes seem too close to the trees to see the forest, who are not aware themselves of how far they have already travelled from their own past. In the many interviews with public leaders which I conducted for the express purpose of this book, I was struck by a mood endemic to all of them. In their assessment of German democracy today and in their prognoses for its future, they were all more or less pessimistic. From the vantage point of an outsider looking in over a period of two decades, it is a pessimism I cannot share.

Not only does democracy seem safe, but the Germany that practices it has finally come of age.

Index